THE
POLITICS
AT GOD'S
FUNERAL

ALSO BY MICHAEL HARRINGTON

The Other America

The Retail Clerks

The Accidental Century

Toward a Democratic Left

Socialism

Fragments of the Century

Twilight of Capitalism

The Vast Majority

Decade of Decision

The Next America

THE
POLITICS
AT GOD'S
FUNERAL

*The Spiritual Crisis
of Western Civilization*

MICHAEL
HARRINGTON

**HOLT, RINEHART and WINSTON
NEW YORK**

Library of Congress Cataloging in Publication Data
Harrington, Michael.
The politics at God's funeral.
Bibliography: p.
Includes index.
1. God. 2. Religion and politics. 3. Religion and culture.
I. Title.
BT102.H347 1983   291.1′77   83-73
ISBN: 0-03-062152-6

First Edition

Designer: Christine Aulicino

Printed in the United States of America
1   3   5   7   9   10   8   6   4   2

ISBN 0-03-062152-6

CONTENTS

ACKNOWLEDGMENTS

A FELLOWSHIP from the John Simon Guggenheim Memorial Fund and a sabbatical leave from Queens College helped greatly in the final stages of work on this book.

I am also deeply indebted to Queens College for having broken the rules and made a Master in English Literature a Professor of Political Science; to the Klapper Library at Queens and the Library of the Graduate Center of the City University of New York; to the students at Queens in my seminars on Hegel and on Politics and Religion who followed me down some of the twisting intellectual paths which led to this book; and to the Monday lunch group (and sometimes dinner group) at the Grove, which gave me the experience of academic community.

Selma Lenihan, a warm and courageous woman, helped me organize the preposterous details of my working life while I was writing this book—and made a major contribution to our shared politics at the same time.

Stephanie Gervis Harrington not only had to put up with the absentminded author but also helped him resolve the conflict between the roles of scholar and agitator. So did Richard Seaver, my editor at Holt.

Irving Howe, surely one of the most decent, thoughtful and committed men of our generation, read some of this manuscript in draft and was most helpful. My intellectual and political debts to him are enormous.

Finally, this book is for:

Stephanie, Alexander and Ted

THE
POLITICS
AT GOD'S
FUNERAL

1
A BOOK
CRYING WOLF

GOD, ONE OF THE MOST IMPORTANT political figures in Western history, is dying.

The event, then, is not simply theological. With a few lapses into liberalism, or even radicalism, God has been a leading conservative in Judeo-Christian society. His death not only means empty churches and bereft individuals but also marks the rending of the social fabric.* This insight is corroborated, not contradicted, by the recent revival of a fundamentalism whose desperate orthodoxy tries to will the departing deity back into existence.

Ironically, it was a deeply Christian man who was the first to realize that God was dying. "The eternal silences of the infinite frighten me," Pascal wrote in fragment 206 of the *Pensées*. That was not, as it might first appear, a reference to the awesome infinity intuited by religion. Rather, as Lucien Goldmann pointed out, "it related to the most important scientific conquest of the age, the discovery of infinite geometric space, and counterposes the silence of God to it. God does

---

*I will refer to God throughout this book as masculine. I find it bizarre to picture the Almighty as of one—or any—gender. In part, his maleness is a result of the anthropomorphic description of the suprahuman; in part it is a consequence of the specifically Judeo-Christian conception of God, which was, and is, patriarchal. To be sure, there was another vision of the deity within Judeo-Christianity, much more widespread than many suspect, which worshipped either a goddess or the female aspect of divinity. Theodor Reik, the Freudian, pointed that out as early as 1923 and more recently, under the impact of the woman's movement, feminist theologians like Rosemary Ruether have reinforced the point. That "alternate" God(dess) was not, and is not, the political God of the West but one of his opponents. Since this book is about certain aspects of that dominant Western God, I will follow the historic usage of referring to him as being male.

1

not speak any more in the space of rational science, because in order to elaborate that space, man had to renounce every ethical norm."*

So it was a pious scientific genius who first announced the conflict between faith and science. To be sure, modern science was itself based on the medieval sense of order in God's universe (as well as on the Greek concept of fate). And it is, of course, true that there çan be no scientific refutation—or proof—of the existence of a nonempirical being. But science did substitute secular interpretations of natural events for religious interpretations of them, and if it did not thereby disprove God it certainly restricted his realm. A famous anecdote has it that Napoleon asked an astronomer where God figured in his model of the heavens. "Sir," the scientist replied, "I have no need of that hypothesis in my work."

The young Hegel was one of the first thinkers to grasp the enormity of Pascal's insight. An "infinite sadness" had entered into human life, he wrote in 1802. It was the result of the feeling that "God himself is dead. Pascal only expressed that in empirical terms when he said, 'nature is such that everywhere it marks a lost God, both within and outside of man.' " The Enlightenment, he said a few years later in *The Phenomenology of Spirit,* had replaced the heavens with an "empty beyond," an "absolute without qualities." Perhaps, the mature Hegel speculated, Christianity had become as decadent as the Roman religion it displaced.

The irrepressible Heinrich Heine took these Pascalian and Hegelian insights and turned them into an image which haunted Nietzsche— and still haunts the West: "Do you hear the little bell ringing? They are bringing the sacraments to a dying God." But if this is the case, what are the politics at God's funeral?

It has long been known that God is political. In the ancient West, that was almost all that he was. The Romans insisted upon that fact, and were appalled when the universal deity of the Jews and Christians seemed to become a stateless person. In modern times it was, of course, Nietzsche who defined the link between politics and religion in the most dramatic way. He prophesied that the death of God would lead

---

*The main text of this book is intended for the general reader. Its quotations, intellectual debts and facts are documented, and all of the references for each chapter will be found in the Notes. In addition, where more scholarly comments are in order— material which is not essential to the central argument but important for placing it in a deeper context—there will be appendixes, signaled by footnotes in the text.

to wars and upheavals on a scale never known before. Hasn't the twentieth century been a turbulent confirmation of that prediction? How do we now deal with what Isaiah Berlin has called "the central question of politics—the question of obedience and coercion. 'Why should I obey anyone else?' " If society no longer provides a plausible answer because its most prominent spokesperson in this area, God, is dying, isn't that precisely one of the factors making for the fragmentation, bewilderment and anxiety which can be observed in every Western society today?

Yes and no. No, because reality is not at all as simple as the apocalyptic little sketch of it which I have made. Indeed, the theory just presented has been the stuff of sermons for about three hundred years. There are always those who hark back to some golden and pious past—except that the people who lived in it often regarded it as a decadence and mourned the passing of the golden age that came before them. Mircea Eliade has documented the *reductio ad absurdum* of this phenomenon: the "noble savages" discovered by Western travelers between the sixteenth and eighteenth centuries thought of themselves as the fallen and corrupted descendants of the noble savages who had been their ancestors.

In the United States in 1798, the General Assembly of the Presbyterian Church saw a "general dereliction of religious principles amoung our fellow citizens, a visible and prevailing impiety and contempt for the laws and institutions of religion." The next half century witnessed an enormous surge of religious belief. Yet in 1838 Ralph Waldo Emerson said that there was a "famine of the churches" and argued that no one could avoid the fact that "what hold the public worship had on men is gone or going." Moreover, the relationship between faith and conduct—between religion and society—is extremely complex. In periods of "unshakeable faith and of a deeply religious culture," Huizinga wrote, there is often "an extreme familiarity with things holy, as well as the insolent mingling of pleasure with religion." So it was that in the late Middle Ages prostitutes plied their trade at mass and pilgrimages were often occasions for debauchery.

It is also true that God dies slowly. His shadow, as Nietzsche has said, will linger on for centuries after he has gone. And the political consequences of his going are anything but one-to-one, a fact that is not merely conceded here but insisted upon, analyzed, documented. Yet, the shocking fact is that the tired old cliché about God's death is becoming true. Or, to be much more precise, the Judeo-Christian political God is dying. This book makes no judgment about any other God or gods, or about the future of other kinds of (non–Judeo-Christian) religion. An endless amount of confusion can be avoided if this limitation is kept carefully in mind.

There is an influential modern tradition which defines religion in such a way that it is a constituent of human nature and cannot disappear as long as humanity survives. In this perspective—which has had a considerable vogue among serious social scientists in recent years— what this book might *seem* to be saying is absurd. One historic form of religion, one vision of God or the gods, may indeed vanish; but religion itself cannot. Therefore the political problems posed here, based on the assumption of the death of God, do not, and cannot, exist. God is dead—long live God! Religion, Mircea Eliade has written in this spirit, *"is an element in the structure of consciousness*, not a stage in the history of consciousness" (emphasis added).

I disagree, but that disagreement is not essential to my argument. I am writing about "only" the political consequences of the effective disappearance of the Judeo-Christian God. Perhaps it can be said that religion is not disappearing but only "relocating." But the new religions that the social scientists are so fond of are, almost without exception, personal rather than social. They are part of what Daniel Bell has called a "retreat to the private world where religions have authority only over their followers and not over any other section of the polity or society." That is the definition of the abyss which lies between religion as the expression of the values of a community and religion as a matter of private belief. The latter may well be profound and even holy, but it is not the organizing principle of a civilization. That is what Judeo-Christianity was for several millennia. That is why it is so sorely missed now.

I write, then, about the death of the Judeo-Christian God and its political consequences in the West (defined simply as Europe and the countries of European settlement). This is not because I have some Euro-centric prejudice which sees my own cultural tradition as the only one. It is precisely because I have such a strong sense of the differences between the Judeo-Christian West and the rest of the world, and such a respect for the complexity and richness of the non-Western faiths, that I want to define the limits of my analysis. I make this restriction out of a necessary humility rather than an unthinking arrogance.

The necessity of that humility can be seen at a glance in the Western relation to China. In the seventeenth century, the Catholic Church turned its back upon the possibility of winning over Chinese civilization—by converting its elite—because it insisted upon imposing its own theological terms upon a Chinese culture that could not understand them. The Holy Spirit was transliterated into Chinese as the "Supiritsu Santo" and the Holy Office officially declared that the ancient Chinese were idolators; the moderns, atheists. Voltaire agreed with Rome on that last point and in the process committed its error under the guise of sympathy and tolerance. He congratulated the Chinese on being so much like himself.

The problem is, as Frederick Mote points out, that the West has long assumed that all cultures "have regarded the cosmos and man as products of a creation external to them." But the Chinese, "among all peoples, ancient and recent, primitive and modern, are apparently unique in having no creation myths. . . . that is, they have regarded the world and man as uncreated, as constituting the central features of a spontaneously self-generating cosmos having no creator, god or ultimate cause external to itself." Mote even suggests that this Chinese attitude toward the world is more in keeping with post-Newtonian science than that of the Western tradition.

These philosophic and theological distinctions between cultures may seem arcane. Yet, the conception of God is, as both Hegel and Max Weber so well understood, the effect and, to a certain degree, the cause of society's vision of itself. The Western God is "out there," personal, in communication, even confrontation, with humans. Michelangelo's grandfather of a deity giving life to Adam broods over a civilization. He has left the safety of eternity and become a part of history, he has sacralized the secular and secularized the sacral.* Such a divinity is more deeply and significantly involved in everyday life, including everyday politics, than the more diffuse, impalpable, cosmic divinity of the East who does not establish his own kingdom to come, or speak to men through burning bushes.

Moreover, it is not just the Western God who is different from the Eastern; so is Western religion. Westerners regard it as normal

*See Appendix A.

that there is an independent church, with its own priesthood, separate from the political and social order. Actually that "institutional specialization" of faith is unique. And Americans, living in the Western nation in which this trend has been pushed to its extreme, are accustomed to a great number of institutionally specialized churches coexisting with one another. Our concepts of God and religion and, a critical dimension for this book, of the theory and practice of the relation between religion and society, are deeply influenced by this very particular Western history.

That history also explains why, despite centuries of Christian persecution of Jews within the West, it is still legitimate to talk about a "Judeo-Christian" tradition. No doubt, as John Murray Cuddihy has suggested, the notion of "Judeo-Christianity" can be used as a device to assimilate an authentic Judaism to an arrogant Christianity which asserts its superiority as it condescends to recognize a precursor of the full Christian truth in the Old Testament. But to understand that the God of Judeo-Christianity (and of Islam) is radically different from the God and gods of the East hardly requires one to participate in such attitudes.

Nevertheless, the link between Judeo-Christianity and the West should not be taken to imply that religion "determines" society—or that society "determines" religion. The complex truth is that religion and society are cause and effect of each other. As the contemporary Marxist Karel Kosik vividly puts it, "a medieval cathedral is not only an expression or image of the feudal world; it is at the same time an element of the constitution of this world. *It does not only reproduce medieval reality; it also produces it*" (emphasis added). Kosik likens the relationship of society and culture to that of the God of Deist philosophy "who gives the first impulse, but, as soon as the work is created, transforms himself into a spectator who only observes the autonomous development of his work without influencing its further destiny."

So this book will assume that religion cannot be understood apart from the society which defines, in the broadest sense, the limits within which it functions. But within the range of religious possibility opened up by a given society—and of the social possibilities implicit in a given religion—the actual religious institutions have to be interpreted within the framework of their own structures, their individual geniuses and their historic accidents. The spiritual crisis of the late twentieth century is, in this reading, not simply derivative, a projection, of the contradictions of late capitalism, but it cannot be understood apart from those contradictions.

Another important qualification has just been stated: that the funeral of God described in these pages takes place in late capitalist society. The underdeveloped West—mainly Latin America—did not go through the same political, cultural and religious experience as the imperial West. In many cases, that meant that the poor and dependent countries were subjected to an ossified Catholicism representing the worst of the Counter-Reformation and Anti-Enlightenment. But when the colonial fabric began to rip and tear after World War II, the disintegration of those imposed clerical structures was an emancipation rather than a loss. "Communities of the base" appeared among the laity; "Liberation Theology" emerged among the younger priests and even in the hierarchy. That is a subject in itself, which is why it cannot be treated in an analysis which focuses upon the dialectic of religion and advanced economic-social development. Thus Liberation Theology will be seen here primarily as it influenced some of the most creative religious thinkers of the late capitalist West, not as a topic in its own, very important, right.

Finally, I assume that it is clear by now that I am not concerned here with the existence of God himself but, rather, with his social and political existence. A deeply religious person could agree with everything in this book and so could those who are, like its author, atheists. I do not write, then, about the God of Abraham, Isaac and Jacob, about God the Father, the Son and the Holy Spirit. This book is about the dying of the societal God of the Judeo-Christian West, and his attributes are not omniscience, omnipotence, fatherliness and all the rest. They are political. The God of this book is

- the legitimization of established power and sometimes of revolt against it;
- the transcendent symbol of the common consciousness of an existing community;
- the foundation of all other values;
- the organizing principle of a system of the authoritative allocation of social roles (the God of Western feudalism) or the mo-

tivating and ethical principle of a system of individual mobility (the God of Western capitalism);
• the guarantor of personal, ethnic and national identity;
• a philosopher for the non-philosophers, including the illiterate.

What are the political consequences of the death of *this* God? The answer is implicit in the societal definition just made of that divinity. Some of the effects are directly political; others are more broadly social; still others affect the private self and impinge upon the public life through it. Moreover, all of these factors are interrelated, blurred at the edges, dissolving into one another. Some of the most important among them are:

• a crisis of legitimacy in the late capitalist society, as one of the prime motives for noncoerced obedience and acquiescence in the social order begins to disappear;
• the economic consequences of the shift from the "Protestant ethic" to the compulsory hedonism of unplanned and irresponsible economic growth, and the consequent bewilderment in times of political-economic contradiction and confusion;
• the appeal of totalitarian movements as substitutes for religious solidarity, particularly under conditions of overt economic and social crisis;
• the loss of the philosophic and "common sense" basis for responsibility before the law as various determinisms occupy the territory once held by religious doctrines of free will and/or moral responsibility;
• the dangers of proclaiming men and women as the lords and ladies of the universe as they are manifested in a purely technological and instrumental attitude toward nature;
• the decline in the sense of duty toward unborn generations;
• the loss of one of the most important constituent elements in both group and personal identity;
• the relativization of all moral values and a resultant crisis of individual conscience;
• the weakening of the "superego," which religion did so much to form—for good and very often for bad—and the emergence of the cult of the self;
• the thinness and superficiality of the substitute religions of sex and drugs.

The West has been responding to, as well as creating, this crisis for more than three centuries. So there is a rich history, not simply of events, but of intellectual and aesthetic reactions to them. In developing my theme, I will explore the concepts and images in which this history becomes conscious of itself. There will be a basic narrative progression which moves, for instance, from the Enlightenment to the French Revolution. But once a particular subject has been raised, it will be followed down to the present: the Enlightenment's political analysis of religion will be carried forward to contemporary discussions of the crisis of legitimacy in late capitalist society. I proceed thus in order to emphasize that I am interested in the past not just as past but in terms of its relevance to the contemporary plight and to the future

THE IMMEDIATE POSTWAR YEARS all but chiseled in stone an idea taken from a misreading of Max Weber: that social thought had to be "value-free," objective, impartial. In fact, that was a way of disguising biases from oneself as well as from the public. Every account of society involves a vantage point, a choice of the relevant data, definitions which are given and not taken. And where it is a case of dealing with such emotionally charged areas of life as religion and politics, that is doubly, triply true.

I have tried to be scrupulously honest in this book, and there are some of my conclusions that I do not even like. But I will not pretend for a moment that I began my work with a mind like a blank page. I was, and am, a democratic Marxist. The very existence of such an intellectual category is a shocking surprise to all but a handful of Americans. I will not explain here what it means—I have done that in other books—but, rather, show what it means in nine chapters of very specific analysis. I will note only that a democratic-Marxist account of the death of God—which sees the spiritual crisis of the late twentieth century as an essential part of the societal crisis and which ends with a call for a united front of believers and atheists in defense of moral values—might disturb a stereotype or two.

I have religious, as well as political, preconceptions. Since they will clearly affect my theory of religion, a brief detour into autobiography is important at this point.

I grew up in the pre–John XXIII Catholic Church in St. Louis, Missouri. Thus my original ideas about religion were formed by a hierarchical, rationalistic, parochial version of Catholicism. It owed, I learned later on, more to the systematizing of the eighteenth-century German philosopher Christian Wolff than to Thomas Aquinas, who was supposedly our mentor. This *Weltanschauung* was an exaggerated model of the Western notion of an objective God, "out there," which is criticized by social scientists today, who find it extremely rigid in comparison with Eastern concepts of divinity.

I left the Catholic Church almost thirty years ago. It is relevant to my present attitudes that even though I rejected the Church, it provided me with my original idea of what religion is. And I clearly remain a "cultural Catholic," much as an atheist Jew is culturally Jewish. At the same time, there is a sense in which an apostate's view of religion is "frozen" at the moment of apostasy. The Church I left no longer exists—but it is still the Church I left. For that matter, I sometimes took a rather orthodox attitude toward changes in Catholicism after I turned away from it. "You want us to keep the mausoleum exactly as it was when you left," one Catholic friend told me.

To complicate matters further, I consider myself to be—in Max Weber's phrase—"religiously musical" even though I do not believe in God. In *Civilization and Its Discontents*, Freud tells of a friend who described to him "a sensation of 'eternity,' a feeling as of something limitless, unbounded, something 'oceanic,' " and then admits that he himself never knew that experience. I feel sorry for Freud. In saying that, I do not merely mean that I respond to the sacred music and liturgy of the Judeo-Christian West. More than that, I resonate to the significant reality which those rites and theologies articulate. Only I do not regard that reality as pointing to a being, or even a sphere, located on the far side of humanity. To the tragically finite degree that the communion of the universe can become objective, it is the work of men and women. I am, then, what Georg Simmel called a "religious nature without religion," a pious man of deep faith, but not in the supernatural.

And, to move now from the autobiographical to the political, I think that in the late twentieth century serious atheists and serious believers have more in common with one another than with mindless, *de facto* atheists (who often affirm some vague and sentimental God) and routine churchgoers. Both have looked into the same void at the center of this incredible age. So it is, for instance, that the contemporary Catholic theologian Jürgen Moltmann concedes, even as he affirms the existence of a nontraditional God, that the tragedies of contemporary history corroborate the atheist argument from disorder, rather than the theistic argument from design. More to my point, the committed believers and unbelievers now have the same enemy: the humdrum nihilism of everyday life in much of Western society.

This book, then, cries wolf, like the boy in the fable. God's death has been announced in every generation for about three hundred years, and it was true and not true. But now, when many have become weary of these seemingly endless obituaries for the Almighty, it is more true than false. And truer every day. The boy in the fable, it will be remembered, ultimately told the truth. So, I think, do I: the God of the Judeo-Christian West is in his death agony and that is one of the most significant political events of this incredible age.

2
THE CRISIS OF FAITH AND REASON

IN THE ENLIGHTENMENT, geniuses deeply convinced of the political necessity of religion undermined the very foundations of faith by revealing the atheist implications of the discoveries made by pious scientists.

These are not paradoxes from a dead history, for they stalk the present day. The Enlightenment began the task of destroying the theological basis of despotism and helped create the consciousness which exploded in the French Revolution. But its rationalist substitute for faith turned out to be simplistic and unworkable, which is one of the reasons for the void in contemporary culture. Moreover, at the same time that the Enlightenment put humans in God's traditional place at the center of the universe, it defined that universe as amoral.

If, as Robert Oppenheimer thought during the first atomic-bomb test, remembering a verse from the *Bhagavad Gita*, "I am become Death, the shatterer of worlds," by what values do we exercise that godlike (demoniac) power? Men and women have begun to rewrite the genetic code, to replace natural selection by human selection. They have already blundered into reshaping the ecosystem, with consequences still not fully known. In a relativist, technological society, where is there a social ethic that can save us from our own brilliance?

The Enlightenment was the first Western movement to face up to some of these questions posed by the death of the traditional God.

——— I ———

The conditions of human existence were transformed between the sixteenth and nineteenth centuries. The population of the world and the energy available to it, Carlo Cipolla has shown, was relatively stable from the Neolithic revolution (between the tenth and seventh millennia before the Christian Era) through the eighteenth century. Then came the take-off: in the century and a half after the year 1800, global population grew four times; by comparison with 1300, it had increased by ten times.

This momentous transition was not simply or, until much later on, even primarily technological. The Industrial Revolution is usually dated around 1780, but the break with ten thousand years of the past had already been accomplished by then. That is because the capitalist revolution was first social (the emergence of a class of "free" laborers and of a bourgeoisie), cultural (the Enlightenment and the scientific revolution of which it was a part), economic in a nontechnological sense (the social organization of a traditional technology) and only finally technological (the Industrial Revolution).

The Enlightenment, then, was not an epiphenomenon, a mere cultural by-product of a more serious material revolution. It was one cause of that revolution half a century before the steam engine was invented. And it was also a decisive moment in the development of the *Western* world. Between the sixteenth and nineteenth centuries, Europe (and the lands of European settlement) took over the planet. There was not simply a basic change in the human condition but a change carried out under the leadership of a small, and in some ways backward, part of the globe. In 1500, Europe knew less about science than Archimedes did in 212 B.C.E. For that matter, Aristarchus of Samos, who was born in 310 B.C.E., developed a rigorously heliocentric theory of the universe which was not rediscovered until the sixteenth century. And while the West thus retrogressed for more than a thousand years, China made steady, gradual progress.

Christian geniuses giving glory to God helped overcome that European backwardness and unwittingly created the greatest challenge religion has ever known. The scientific revolutionaries of the sixteenth and seventeenth centuries—Bacon, Harvey, Kepler, Galileo, Descartes, Pascal, Huyghens, Boyle, Newton, Leibniz—were for the most part pious men. Newton, the quintessential architect of the age, might even be described as a religious crank. There was, Robert Merton has documented, such a close link between religious ideas and science that one can properly speak of a " 'holy alliance between science and religion.' " For even if particular theologians—and the Roman Church as a whole—denigrated the new discoveries, the men who made them agreed with Robert Boyle that their work gave witness "to the Glory of the Great Author of Nature."

A century after this scientific revolution, Immanuel Kant generalized its findings in theories which resonate to this day and which seem, at first glance, to be preposterous. "Previously one assumed that all of our experience must base itself upon objects," Kant wrote in a famous passage in the Foreword to the second edition of the *Critique of Pure Reason*. He continued:

> now we must consider whether it would not be better to assume that objects must be based upon our knowledge. . . . That is as it was in the case of Copernicus, who, after he realized that the explanation of the movement of the heavens did not work very well when he assumed that the stars turned around the observer, sought to find out whether it would not be better to assume that it was the observer who turned and the stars which were at rest.

On the face of it, this is absurd: the real world depends upon our knowledge of it rather than our knowledge depending on the real world. Fichte, as a youthful disciple of Kant bent on perfecting the theories of the master, went further. He divided all of reality into the "I" and the "Not-I" and then declared that everything that is "Not-I" is the product of the "I." Such a statement sounds like just one more exercise in the other-worldliness of German metaphysics.

Yet revolutions echo in the most abstruse of these formulations. The "I," Fichte wrote, is defined by striving, feeling; it is driven and comes into being by overcoming opposition. This metaphysical proposition is political, as the young Fichte, a defender of the French Revolution, knew full well. "No man," he wrote, "can be bound except by himself. And no law can be given to any man except by himself. If he let himself be bound by an alien will, he would sacrifice his humanity and turn himself into an animal." And Kant's "Copernican revolution," his insistence that reality turns about our knowledge of it rather than the other way around, is part of the same turbulent process. Humans were now creating reality for themselves instead of accepting it as a given from God, and the laws within the mind were being imposed upon the external world, not simply describing it. It was, in short, a gigantic economic and social and political fact, not a cloudy thesis in metaphysics, that the "I" was shaping the "Not-I."

It was a paradox that the supreme intellectual generalization of this revolution came from the least revolutionary country, Germany. To which it can be added that the greatest of the intellectual revolutionaries was the very model of a cloistered, ineffectual academic. Heine put it succinctly: "The history of Kant's life is difficult to portray, for he had neither life nor history." He lived in only one city, teaching, taking his daily walk and being perfectly submissive to his prince. Yet, Heine also said, Kant was more of a subversive than Robespierre. The Frenchmen only executed a king; the German killed God.

Indeed, Kant might be seen as the culmination of the Christian attack upon Christianity. Like Pascal, he deeply believed in the God whom he did so much to make problematic. Leszek Kolakowski said of him, "There can scarcely be an example of a philosopher going to so much trouble as Kant to invalidate arguments in favor of propositions to the truth of which he was deeply attached." Kant regarded the existence of God as one of the most important truths—political and social as well as philosophical—in the world, and yet he systematically shredded every traditional proof of that existence. For he understood that the scientific revolution was, by its very nature, agonistic, no matter how pious the revolutionaries might have been. There is no God in Newton's universe even if Newton passionately believed there was. At the most, the deity remains as a "cosmic plumber" to keep the Newtonian system in good repair.

Kant was appalled by the political and social consequences of his own insights into these matters and he tried his best to elude them. But he could not. The unintended effects of his brilliance would not permit that, to him—or to us. I take him as a summary figure of the reluctant discovery by Christian geniuses of the conflict between faith and science and the resultant crisis in political morality.

———— I I ————

Kant rigorously and profoundly theorized a commonplace of the modern age: the war between "is" and "ought." On the one hand, he said, there is the realm of science—practical, agnostic about ultimate causes, enormously successful in transforming reality; on the other, the realm of values, now split off from rational proof, problematic and impractical. Not so incidentally, his distinction between "is" and "ought" refracted the position of Germany in Europe (intellectually advanced, economically backward) and of Kant in Germany (a fearless thinker living a routine existence).

Kant, the "idealist," began with the fact of everyday experience. That it exists is undeniable, palpable, but what makes it possible? If there were only sense data, there would be a "rhapsody of perceptions" without that meaning which is part of the simplest experience. So there must be concepts to allow the understanding to sort out and unify the sense data. We see all things in space and time and we interpret them according to categories like cause and effect, yet we cannot demonstrate that these preconditions of human experience are "real." David Hume was right: we can never prove that the effect *necessarily* follows from the cause (necessity is not a fact but a judgment about facts). But basing ourselves on something which is beyond doubt—that we have meaningful experiences—we knew that these experiences are only possible within space and time, understood in terms of cause and effect, and so on.

Because mathematics and the natural sciences accept the limits of our knowledge—because, for instance, physics takes no position on whether the world it describes was made by God or not—they have made enormous progress while metaphysics has turned round and round the same old debates. It is precisely by probing what can be proved, and what cannot, by mapping the "geography" of the human mind, including the frontiers of its various functions, that philosophy becomes systematic. It is the role of pure reason (*Vernunft*) to undertake this task.

Experience within time and space on the basis of categories like causality is the province of the "understanding" (*Verstand*). Understanding is a spontaneous quality of the human mind, the possession of all men and women, operating according to a "hidden art in the very depths of the soul." Reason (*Vernunft*) charts the principles behind the rules which allow the understanding to function. As long as it does this, it is on solid ground (and indeed linked to experience). But the moment that reason looks for ultimate causes of the world, it becomes hair-splitting and contradictory (*Vernunft* becomes *vernünftelnde*).

This was the point of departure for Kant's refutation of the proofs for the existence of a God in whom he deeply believed. One cannot, he said, argue toward the existence of God on the basis of an empirical reality known only by means of categories like cause and effect. Those categories are necessary to the human understanding of reality, but they are not necessarily real (and we can never know whether they are). So one cannot use the subjective preconditions of finite experience to demonstrate the existence of an objective, infinite deity; one cannot employ the categories of time and space which are intrinsic to the mortal mind to show that there is an eternal being beyond time and space. This is why arguments in this area are interminable, for the very same rationality can be unpersuasively invoked by theist and atheist alike.

Not even mathematics, "that pride of human reason," Kant said, can satisfy us that God is in his heaven, the soul immortal and the will free. Then Kant reveals how devastating his own work has been, for he points out that these three questions—God, immortality, freedom—are the very basis of morality in the world. Men and women demand that they be answered, for the mind is "architectonic," seeking a sense of the whole. But reason cannot satisfy that desire so long as it observes its own necessary limits. The success of science and mathematics is predicated, precisely, on their methodological agnosticism, on their refusal to overstep their own borders. Pascal's existential insight that the infinite space of modern science is godless had now been worked out in excruciating detail.

Heine said of the *Critique of Pure Reason:* "This book is the sword with which deism was executed in Germany." But there was also a reprieve, and Heine described it inimitably if somewhat unfairly. Kant took his daily walk with such regularity that the people of Königsberg checked the clocks by his appearance on the "Philosopher's Path." On cloudy days, his servant, Lampe, followed him with an umbrella. Having dispatched God and immortality, Heine wrote, Kant

turned and old Lampe stood there, a mournful spectator, his umbrella under his arm, cold sweat and tears pouring from his face. Then Immanuel Kant relented and showed that he was not simply a great philosopher but also a good man, and he deliberately said, half good-naturedly and half ironically, "Old Lampe must have a God, otherwise the poor fellow can't be happy. But man ought to be happy in this world—practical reason says so—that's certainly all right with me—then let practical reason also guarantee the existence of God."

Heine had perceived a critical moment in the development of modern consciousness, defined by Kant and far from finished today. God and religion no longer exist as a matter of ontological right; they are simply not "there." A century and a half later a Protestant theologian soon to be murdered by the Nazis, Dietrich Bonhoeffer, put the event in Kantian terms: the "religious *a priori*," that pervasive individual and social sense of the existence of God in his heaven, had vanished. But the need for God and the societal need for the God function did not disappear at the same time. "Ought" was still at war with "is." And since the deity had not been disproved but merely marginalized by the dominant scientific ideology, he could be resuscitated. So Kant, having helped to kill the rationalist God, looked for ways to fulfill his social and political functions.

It is here that one first encounters a phenomenon which will appear and reappear throughout this book: the search for a substitute deity to take over the social functions of the dying God of tradition. That has been going on for several centuries now and, even though it is fruitless or worse, it is likely to continue into the foreseeable future. Broadly speaking, Kant gave three answers to the problem created by his own unintended deicide: a new providence, a utopia in the spirit of Adam Smith, another utopia derived from Robespierre. Each of them has its partisans to this day and each is characterized by a dualism which seems to be inevitable in any serious response to the revolutionary experience of modernity.

The world in Kant's time—as in ours—was simultaneously becoming more and more objective and more and more subjective. It was no accident that the Industrial Revolution and the Romantic movement emerged at roughly the same moment in Western history. Technology was, and is, using deterministic laws to transform the environment in the most objective fashion—and it is humans who, in their godlike subjectivity, manipulate those laws. We understand everything, including love and the sacred and what was once called free will, scientifically—and it is our own Faustian will that has forced these secrets from nature. How can we reconcile these opposites of "is" and "ought"? In an age of faith, Dante had said of God, "In his will is our peace."

But where is there peace now when, as that scrupulously honest believer Immanuel Kant knew, the heavens are empty?

Kant's first answer to his question was that a new providence, called history, would take over from God. This was one of his least innovative strategies for dealing with the spiritual crisis he himself did so much to create.

History, Kant wrote in 1794—and the echoes of Adam Smith's *Wealth of Nations* abound—exhibits "a process of uniformity . . . and the way in which an individual acts, which seems to be without any rule, can be seen as a constantly progressive though slow development of the original tendencies in the entire species." Nature accomplishes this surreptitious plan by playing upon the antagonisms in society which, in Hobbesian fashion, force men and women to create a lawful order. Man, Kant held, is pushed into being social by an inherent unsociability; he is an "animal which, when it lives within its own species, needs a master." This is, on the face of it, a bourgeois providence which has replaced God. Kant was not, of course, a paid propagandist of a capitalism which did not even yet exist in his own country. But he, and all of the Enlightenment, uncritically accepted the assumptions of the age, taking the emergent reality of men and women under capitalism as the human essence.

In the process, Kant was one of the first theorists of that most popular of substitute gods, history. A series of important thinkers— Adam Smith, **Kant**, Fichte, Hegel, Marx—sought to secularize the notion of a divine providence. Where God once ruled there is now the invisible hand of the market, the hidden plan of nature, the cunning of reason, the socialist leap from the realm of necessity into the realm of freedom. To be sure, the acolytes of these theories often made them more "religious" than their authors (this is true, above all, in the case of Marx). And they are still one of the most important sources of consolation for the godless world of the last two centuries. They are also the source of one of the social consequences of the death of God which is very much with us to this day: that the very idea of moral responsibility has become problematic.

Why does evil exist? From the Epicureans to Rousseau, philosophers argued about whether it was because of God (who permitted evil in order to allow humans to freely choose the good), the Devil or human nature. Then, Ernst Cassirer has argued persuasively, Rousseau resolved this dilemma by creating "as it were a new subject of responsibility, of 'imputability.' This subject is not individual man, but human society." Rousseau was the man who awakened Kant's social consciousness—it is said that the latter interrupted his daily walks only twice, once when he heard of the fall of the Bastille, once when his copy of *Emile* arrived—and that influence is visible in the Kantian theory of good and evil as the work of a collective subject.

The problem is, there is an obvious truth to the notion that human "free will" is often the plaything of unconscious—psychological, social, economic—forces. But taken to its extreme, that leads to a bleak view in which, as E. P. Thompson puts it, "we are *structured* by social relations, *spoken* by pre-given linguistic structures, *thought* by ideologies, *dreamed* by myths, *gendered* by patriarchal sex norms, *bonded* by affective obligations, *cultured* by mentalities and *acted* by history's script." In short, the new providences and demons may indeed fill up the void left by God's departure, but what, then, is left of our traditional humanity?

Four years after his discussion of universal history, Kant took another tack, one which veered toward both free will and utopia.

The world of freedom, he wrote in the *Critique of Practical Reason*—the book that Heine said he wrote in order to make poor Lampe feel better—is a fact of our experience. We feel moral responsibility. But experience is a part of that world of appearances which humans can only conceptualize through deterministic laws, and these can hardly prove that we are free—that is, that we act independently of external laws. Once again he admits that the scientific analysis of nature proves itself in practice while freedom "is only an idea whose reality is dubious." How, Kant had asked in the *Critique of Pure Reason*, is experience possible? Now he poses the question: how is the freedom we instinctively feel possible? It is a "necessary precondition" of a being with will power, but it cannot be proved. It is a fact of practical—living, acting—reason, not of pure reason. And it is motivated, he intimates, by a political vision, or at least the possibility of one, "that lordly ideal of a universal kingdom of reasonable individuals . . . to which we can only belong if we relate solicitously to one another according to the maxims of freedom *as if* they were laws of nature. . . ."

With this vision, Kant has moved far beyond Hobbes and the idea of unsocial sociability, yet he remains quite bourgeois.* His social goal is to be achieved individualistically; it is the ethical equivalent of the economic outcome in Adam Smith's free market. There are two "maxims of freedom": will, so that what you will can become a universal law; and never treat another human being as a means but only as an end in himself/herself. These propositions express a deep humanism (there were neo-Kantians in the late nineteenth and early twentieth centuries who interpreted the maxim about people as ends as protosocialist). Still, the freedom Kant defines is atomistic. Treating each person as an end rather than a means is "the supreme *limiting condition* of freedom for each man" (emphasis added). I am free insofar as I do not impinge upon your freedom, and vice versa. If everyone follows that rule, then there will be no conflict in society. Thus the sum total of individual choices is, in Kant's morality as in Smith's economy, a social good.

Where is God in all this? His existence, Kant continued to insist, cannot be proved—but if it were a fact it would certainly help motivate people to do their duty. So God is not the basis of morality, for morality rests upon reason, and reason cannot demonstrate that God exists. He is, rather, a *postulate* of morality, a being who gives us cause to act upon the categorical imperatives of the conscience. One acts "as if" God were there. Hans Küng rightly comments: "In the last resort is not such an assumption merely a relic of the old belief in God, of Christian tradition, a product now of civilized custom?" And if, as Fred Hirsch and others have held, that "civilized custom" was the limiting morality which made economic individualism superior to the law of the jungle, what do we do now that it is vanishing?

Kant had one more basic answer to these questions. It was suggested to him by the French Revolution.

His new attitudes, visible in the writings of the 1790s, were not straightforward or unambiguous. In 1798, in *The Conflict of Faculties*, Kant said that the French Revolution was "an event of our age which has proved the moral tendency of the human race." This was written at a time when philosophers like Fichte and Hegel, who had originally welcomed the Revolution, had become horrified by the Terror and turned against the whole enterprise. Yet in that same volume in which

*See Appendix B.

he courageously continues to support the Revolution, there was a
Foreword which capitulated in craven fashion to the royal censors.
And right after the defense of the Revolution he makes it quite clear
that he was against the overthrow of the existing order because the
latter was essentially holy. Still, there was a momentous change, a
move toward a religious utopia located well to the Left of Adam Smith.

In the *Critique of Judgment* there is only one guarded reference,
in a footnote, to the "recently undertaken complete remolding of a
great people in a state," and yet the influence of the French Revolution
is pervasive. This is visible, above all, in one of the most protean
concepts of the period, that of an organism. The late eighteenth and
early nineteenth centuries saw, Cassirer has said, a shift from the
"generic" to the "genetic." That gave new life to one of the most
perennial metaphors of Western political thought, which dates back
to Plato at least: of society as an organic body. It was possible to use
this analogy for conservative purposes, as Plato did. Just as the human
organism is born, grows and dies, so, too, does society. Radicals, who
consciously want to intervene in this natural process, blaspheme against
the laws of nature and risk a terrible retribution (thus the Burke of
the *Reflections on the French Revolution* and the right-wing Hegel
of the *Phenomenology*). But that same analogy can stress that organisms change themselves, that they are capable of self-movement, and
thereby can become an argument for reform or even revolution (thus
Kant in the *Critique of Judgment*, the left-wing Hegel of the *Phenomenology*, and Marx). So it is no accident that Kant's discreet glance at
the French Revolution occurs precisely when he is discussing the organic. Humans, he is saying, can change themselves. That is a shift
from Adam Smith to Robespierre.

But there is an even more remarkable section of this *Critique*. It
does not contain a single reference to the French Revolution, yet it is
unquestionably a refraction of it. Kant first restates the idea—from
the *Universal History*—of the way in which nature utilizes men for
its purposes, which are not necessarily theirs. In a passage which could
have been taken from Hegel, or even Marx, he notes that an increased
division of labor, a necessary inequality and a growing poverty are the
preconditions for this progress. Eventually, these conditions force people to form a civil society, in order to control the antagonisms that
follow from individual freedom, and then—for Kant was, of course,
one of the first internationalists—a civil society of the world made

necessary by the collective antagonisms of nations. The unplanned struggle of men toward this end proceeds by means of unbridled passions, yet perhaps the process conceals the workings of the "supreme wisdom."

So far, there is nothing which goes beyond the limits of the *Universal History*. But then, in a few remarkable pages, a new note is struck. There is, Kant continues, a striving in nature for a higher goal than nature itself contains. Yes, he says, there are evils which accompany the refinement, indeed the over-refinement, of culture, and there are insatiable needs created by its advances. But there is the development of art and science which

> even if they do not make men ethically better, do make them more cultured, conquer the sensual drives *and thereby prepare men for a domination in which reason alone shall have power*. While the evil which afflicts us, in part because of nature and in part because of man's incessant egotism, is still there, at the same time the powers of the soul rise up, increase and become stronger, so as not to be subordinated to those natural drives and to allow us to feel equal to the higher ends which lie hidden within us.

So it would seem there is a purpose in nature. Can it be proved? Kant characteristically answers no; sheer accident and blind necessity are both plausible explanations, and there is no way to choose between them. But if we assume that this purposiveness is the result of an intelligible cause, to what end does it point? To man, the only being in nature that acts according to laws of his/her own making, to men, the only thing-in-itself we can ever know, to man, the moral being. There is in these intricate philosophic analyses the vision of Schiller's "Ode to Joy" and Beethoven's Ninth Symphony. That is Kant's glory— and his limitation.

The limits are obvious in an essay published three years after the last *Critique, Religion Within the Limits of Mere Reason*. It is perhaps the most utopian of his writings. Reason now must, "in addition to the laws which it decrees for each individual, also raise a standard of virtue as a rallying point for all those who love the good. . . ." This will lead to an "ethical community," to "the people of God under ethical laws." Reading such passages, one can understand why the Marxist Lucien Goldmann could interpret Kant as a socialist John the Baptist—and also why the theologian Karl Barth could see him as a great Protestant.

That last interpretation is made ironical by the fact that *Religion Within the Limits of Mere Reason* contains a savage attack on organized religion—church faith—in the name of real religious faith.

There is the rub. The real religious faith which Kant urges is . . . the Kantian ethic. When humans fulfill their duties toward one another, following those maxims of freedom, then, and only then, they serve God. Kant realized that the people would not take to this idea. They would prefer, he wrote (and notice the mocking attitude toward church religion), "a great Lord with a need to be honored, to be praised by means of relationships of subordination." Reason, Kant and the Enlightenment held, was the ultimate substitute for God.

Indeed, at times Kant came quite close to saying that religion was only rational ethics in a symbolic disguise. Writing of the conflict between the theologians and the ethicists in 1796, he said, "The veiled goddess before whom we both bend the knee is the moral law within us . . . but we are in doubt, as we hearken, whether it proceeds from man, from the perfection of the power of his reason, or whether it comes from some other being, unknown to him, and which speaks to man through this reason of his." If, however, that is the case, then God is no longer *necessary*, not simply in the astronomer's model of the universe, but in deciding questions of right and wrong as well. But if the bedrock is Kant's rational morality, can that complex attitude become the principle of society?

Even when Kant was at his most lyrical he rightly had doubts about the answer to that question. In the celebrated conclusion to the *Critique of Practical Reason*, he says that "the starry skies above me and the moral law within me" fill the spirit with awe and reverence. But the former, the scientific explication of the universe, could be resolved into its constituent elements and expressed mathematically. The latter, he acknowledged, had to be worked out by philosophers behind the backs of the people and then handed down to them. That last bit of realism makes the entire vision problematic.

Kant had been the first to think through some of the basic responses to the death of God: the substitution of a secular providence for the Almighty; the affirmation of God as an ethical, rather than an ontological, necessity; an individualistic, bourgeois utopia and then a solidaristic, not so bourgeois, utopia to fill the void in the empty heavens; a religion based on reason. History was not going to be kind to his decency or, for that matter, to Schiller's "Ode to Joy." And it was going to subvert the manipulative cynicism of his predecessors in the Enlightenment as well.

IV

Religion, Kant's Enlightenment predecessors said, was a despicable means of duping the mob into accepting irrational tyrannies, and a necessary means of keeping the people content under rational, benevolent authority. That half-truth will help illuminate the problems of political legitimacy under the conditions of late-twentieth-century life.

It was Napoleon, a political heir of the Enlightenment, who stated the underlying thesis most candidly. Speaking of the "mystery of religion," he commented:

> This mystery is not that of the Incarnation. . . . I see in religion the whole mystery of society. I hold . . . that apart from the precepts and doctrines of the Gospel there is no society that can flourish, nor any real civilization. What is it that makes the poor man take it for granted that ten chimneys smoke in my palace while he dies of cold—that I have ten changes of raiment in my wardrobe while he is naked—that on my table at any meal there is enough to sustain a family for a week? It is religion which says to him that in another life I shall be his equal, indeed that he has a better chance of being happy than I.

The really difficult question in history, Barrington Moore has suggested, is not: why do men revolt? There are thousands of reasons for that. Why do they *not* revolt, given the fact that most of humanity has lived nasty, brutish and short lives and paid dearly for the luxuries of the few? The Enlightenment and Napoleon had an answer: it is religion that makes tolerable the intolerable.

That is hardly a new idea. In the *Laws*, a spokesperson for Plato complains of the atheists—and how modern it sounds—that "the first thing these people say about the gods is that they are artificial constructs corresponding to nothing in nature; they are legal fictions which moreover vary widely according to the different conventions people agree on when they produce a legal code." And he goes on, "This is why we experience outbeaks of impiety among the young, who assume that the kind of gods the law tells them to believe in do not exist; this is why we get treasonable efforts to convert people to the 'natural' life. . . ." Plato's response is clear enough. Three propositions—that the gods exist, that they are concerned for us and that they are absolutely above being corrupted into flouting justice—are to be made compulsory, and those who deny them are to be imprisoned.

You can find cities without walls and without languages, Plutarch said, "but a city without temples and gods . . . —no one has ever seen such a city and never will." "It is convenient that there should be gods," Ovid wrote, "and since it is convenient, let us think they exist." Juvenal had talked of the need for "bread and circuses" to keep the masses happy, and the Enlightenment, in its rediscovery of classical antiquity, agreed. For Montesquieu, the Romans "made a religion for the state while others had made the state for religion."

Perhaps the most famous statement of this theme was formulated by Edward Gibbon: "The various modes of worship which prevailed in the Roman world were all considered by the people as equally true; by the philosophers as equally false; and by the magistrates as equally useful." Those magistrates, he said, believed that "in every country, the form of superstition which had received the sanction of time and experience was the best adapted to its climate and inhabitants." There were many reasons why this cynical, relativist view appealed to the Enlightenment, but one of them was certainly its contempt for the credulity of ordinary people.

And yet, there were moments in which the *philosophes* understood that their analogy to ancient Rome did not actually relate to the Christian West. Before the rise of Jewish, and then Christian, monotheism, the religions of the Roman Empire had, as Peter Gay remarks, "no theology, required not beliefs but ritual acts and were not evangelical." On that very count, David Hume thought that monotheism was inherently intolerant and polytheism tolerant. And Rousseau, of course, regarded "Roman Christianity" as antisocial and subversive, breaking up the unity of society by proposing two sources of authority (state and church) instead of one. Moreover, the Christians, Rousseau said, turned people away from public duty and oriented them toward purely private salvations.

In short, something momentous has happened with the historic development of Judeo-Christianity, as the Enlightenment's great critic,

Hegel, pointed out in the *Phenomenology*. It represented a new innerness, spirituality and freedom; it shattered precisely that unity of the personal and the public, the moral and the civic, that Aristotle had celebrated. That fact was obscured for about a millennium (from Constantine to Luther) because the Roman Church created an orthodoxy which integrated religion and politics. But Rousseau was right: a new, and subversive, principle had been introduced into the body politic. And Hegel was right: this process was not the result of a conspiracy on the part of some princes who needed to gull the people, but the response of a major social movement to the cultural crisis of the ancient world.

The Enlightenment, then, had articulated an important half-truth about the politics of religion. It had rightly understood, citing the Romans as precedent, that faith often serves to rationalize power, that religion is regularly part of the ideology of a ruling class (and indeed, as Marx emphasized, was *the* ideology of feudalism). This was an important accomplishment in demythologizing the gods. But the model of the Roman Empire, a society in which rites were explicitly designed to express political identity, and particularly of the Roman Empire in the period of its decline, does not provide a universally valid example of the relation between religion and politics. On the contrary, that particular case overstates the cynicism of the rulers and the credulity of the masses. It was the error of the Enlightenment not to realize this fact.

The error was not an accident. That cynical Roman upper-class contempt for the plebs was shared by the *philosophes* themselves. Voltaire, for instance, wrote in 1760 to Diderot, "I commend *l'inf* [*l'infame*, the infamous thing, Voltaire's word for the Catholic Church] to you; it must be destroyed among respectable people and left to the *canaille* [the rabble] large and small, for whom it was made." Hume wrote of the doctrine of transubstantiation, "In a future age, it will probably become difficult to persuade some nations that any human two-legged creation could ever embrace such principles. And it is a thousand to one, but these nations themselves shall have something fully as absurd in their own creed to which they will give a most implicit and religious assent." And, in grand Roman fashion, he told a young friend to stay in holy orders since "It is putting too great a respect on the vulgar, and on their superstitions, to pique oneself with regard to them."

Perhaps the summary illustration of this attitude is to be found in an anecdote about Voltaire (which may be apocryphal but certainly tells a truth). At dinner one night, it is said, the guests were talking freely of atheism. Voltaire dismissed the servants and then admonished his friends not to talk that way in front of them. "Do you want your throat cut tonight?" he asked. Similarly, Gibbon talked of "the danger of exposing an old superstition to the contempt of the blind and fanatic multitude." Here, as in the case of Kant, there is no point in blaming the *philosophes* for failing to have a socialist view of the people which only emerged in the nineteenth century. What is to be stressed are the historic limitations, not the failure of individual conscience and consciousness. It was, I am suggesting, their own *manipulative* attitude toward the people that caused them to think that the Roman cynicism was the point of view of all ruling classes. As a result they did not understand the deeper truth developed later on by Marx: that the rulers, as well as the ruled, believe in the ideologies of their society.

The problem was, and is, that the substitute religion which they defined to take the place of the faith their criticism had destroyed was Deism—which could not possibly perform that function. Once, when he witnessed a magnificent sunrise, Voltaire cried out, " 'I believe! I believe in you! Powerful God, I believe.' Then he rose and added dryly, 'As for Monsieur the Son and Madame his Mother, that's a different story.' " But such a rationalist creed could not win the people, who, Voltaire's contempt notwithstanding, often preferred outright atheism to desiccated Christianity.

That last irony has been documented by Gabriel Le Bras. In the nineteenth century, many a French bourgeois, the descendant of the new elite which had read Voltaire so avidly, became religiously pious, while "it was among workers that Voltaire found his readers, and the theorists of free thought developed a popular literature which provided the people with a rational foundation for their lack of religious observance."

So the Enlightenment was overly arrogant, treating a half-truth as if it defined all of reality. And yet there is real substance to its theory about the political importance of religious faith, a theory that helps explain the present crisis of legitimacy in the late-twentieth-century West.

———— **V** ————

Capitalism is now late capitalism. It is no longer a system guided by the invisible hand of free markets but is increasingly run by the visible hand of the state. At the same time, the entrepreneur has ceased to be the dominant personality and the giant, anonymous corporation is in control. The corporation, Joseph Schumpeter wrote just after World War II, "socializes the bourgeois mind; it relentlessly narrows the scope of capitalist motivation; not only that, it will eventually kill its roots." That same process, Schumpeter continued, destroys the bourgeois family and produces a stratum of intellectuals who are hostile to capitalism. The system begins to lose its authority.

The neoconservative intellectuals of the seventies and eighties have been aware of this problem. The liberal and socialistic "new class" of the post–World War II years—the college-educated activists who were the core of the environmental, antiwar and feminist movements— is seen by the neoconservatives as the source of many social woes. For Irving Kristol, they were motivated both by a hypocritical desire to conquer power for themselves in the name of the poor and the oppressed and by a rejection of a bourgeois society which, without God, seemed purposeless. On both the Left and the Right, wrote George Gilder, the economic philosopher of the Reagan administration, there are those who "assume that capitalism is an edifice without an inherent foundation in morality and religion, and that therefore it engenders a shallow and dubious order of human life." And Peter Drucker, a resolute theorist of pro-corporate sympathies, argued that management would have to put workers on the board of directors in order to restore its own legitimacy.

So capitalism desperately needed legitimization of the kind that religion had traditionally provided—at the same time that religion was declining as a social force. There emerged what one analyst called a "symbolic poverty," a society without social sacraments, without outward signs of its inward grace. One response, as we have seen, was the religion of technology, of production for production's sake, with the experts playing the role of priests. That, however, became problematic in the seventies, when there was a decade of economic failure and uncertainty. Another response was the one Drucker proposed: to provide a democratic legitimacy for the authoritarian management of the economy. But, particularly in view of the chronic economic crisis of the seventies and eighties, that was, and is, a dubious tactic.

Has this crisis of capitalist legitimacy been a victory for the anti-capitalists? Not quite, for they were heirs of the Enlightenment, too.

The Enlightenment was, like the French Revolution it inspired, a contradiction in terms, a genuine appeal to universal values but committed to a particular, class-dominated social order. It was utopian in that it sincerely believed in reason and humanity's ability to create a just society; it was apologetic, ideological, because it also despised the mob and looked for consoling myths with which to keep it quiet. The hopes that the masses could thus be gulled were disappointed in the nineteenth century, for the people turned out to be much more intelligent than Voltaire had ever suspected. This led to the crisis of the legitimacy of established authority. Then the hope that rational men and women could cooperatively control their own lives became problematic in the twentieth century. And this led to a crisis of the legitimacy of the disestablished opposition.

There is an unforgettable literary image of this development in Thomas Mann's *Doctor Faustus*. In the light of the savagery and destruction of World War II, the great but insane composer Adrian Leverkuhn wants to "take back" Beethoven's Ninth Symphony, for its harmonies and exaltation have now been revealed as a cruel hoax. Max Horkheimer and T. W. Adorno, colleagues of Mann and writing at the time when *Doctor Faustus* was written, tried, in the name of the Left, to "take back" Kant and the Enlightenment for much the same reason.

Kant, they charged, had, with the best of intentions, equated truth and science. Worse, precisely because he, and the Enlightenment, had defined knowledge in terms of humanity's ability to remake the world, they had in effect said that one could only understand that which one could dominate. The truth thereby had become instrumental, merely practical, without any values. Horkheimer and Adorno wrote in the time of Stalinism and Nazism. The tremendous creative powers of modern science were being used, not simply for the control of external nature, but for the total manipulation of human beings as well.

Horkheimer and Adorno did not say that all of this happened because of some eighteenth-century philosophers. They were neo-Marxists—some would say, Left Hegelians—and they insisted that this process also grew out of the evolution of capitalism. Still, the emancipatory potential of science, which had been central to

Marx as well as the Enlightenment, was not very much in evidence during the thirties. One of Goya's *Caprichos* etchings had been titled, "The Dream of Reason Produces Monsters." To Horkheimer, Adorno and many others this seemed to epitomize an indictment of the Enlightenment.

That idea was, so to speak, in the air. In a brilliant, heterodox book, *History and Class Consciousness*, Georg Lukacs joined together the revolutionary optimism of Marx and the conservative pessimism of Max Weber. Alienation, he said, was everywhere, afflicting the bourgeoisie and its crisis-ridden power as well as the proletariat and its crisis-ridden powerlessness. There was a ubiquitous "rationalization" and bureaucratization of life. Once the socialist revolution took place, Lukacs still affirmed, the workers would smash these dehumanizing structures. But when Stalinism crushed all that was authentically revolutionary in the Bolshevik seizure of power and made revolution itself problematic, this militant indictment of the bourgeois order could be turned into an argument for the hopeless, resigned contemplation of a totally manipulated world.

Then, after World War II, there was another cause for pessimism. The welfare state of the West, it seemed to some on the Left, had "pacified" the class struggle as the masses were persuaded, not by a Deist God but by a hedonist economy, to accept a society which was still basically unjust. The dream of reason, these thinkers said, now produced trivialities. At the same time, it also posed the possibility of human annihilation with the appearance of thermonuclear weapons.

What were the moral limits upon this fearful scientific power? Did not the "dialectic of the Enlightenment" now threaten to blow up the planet earth? Then, in the fifties, scientists "broke" the genetic code. By the eighties, corporations have begun utilizing that knowledge to create new forms of life in the search for profit. "Bio-technology becomes a gold rush," the London *Economist* headlined a special feature. And in a story on new technologies, including genetic "technologies," *Business Week* told of the possibility of the manufacture of "artificial intelligences" which could lead "to the construction of super-intelligences able to explore significant mathematical, scientific or engineering alternatives at a rate far exceeding human ability." It would be absurd to take a Luddite attitude toward scientific advances which might make possible the conquest of cancer and hunger—and equally absurd not to recognize that the scientific genie is creating moral problems faster than men and women can define them, much less resolve them.

One result of all this has been a strange inversion of the traditional Leftist attitude toward science and religion.

From the Enlightenment to the 1930s, most Leftists saw science as a means for creating the just society. Established religion (but not disestablished religion) was regarded as superstition in the service of exploitation. But at least some on the Left, like Horkheimer and Adorno, began to think that the scientific-technological domination of the environment was the model for the totalitarian-technological domination of people. The myth of Eden had been reinterpreted and, Horkheimer and Adorno said, the angel with the fiery sword had condemned humanity, not to labor by the sweat of its brow, but to pursue technological progress

That was, and is, an exaggeration. Communist totalitarianism was not as seamlessly monolithic as these theorists suggested. The Communist regimes in Poland, Czechoslovakia and Hungary, for instance, survived, not because the omnipotent state manipulated the popular consciousness to its own purposes, but because of the very old-fashioned fact that the Soviet Army had greater firepower than the massive internal resistance movements. In the West, the seventies saw the end of the postwar boom and a decline in real living standards rather than "pacification." There is, then, reason to doubt that people are as malleable as these analysts think. And there is also reason to heed their warning. If they overgeneralized the totalitarian evidence of the thirties and the welfare-state evidence of the postwar years, the trend they identified did indeed exist.

Where did that leave religion?

Perhaps the most radical response came from Herbert Marcuse in *Eros and Civilization*. He did not simply conclude that religion and science were both enemies, both subservient to the new structures of power. That would have been a significant revision of the classic Leftist attitude, but Marcuse went far beyond it. Under certain circumstances, he argued, religion was now *superior* to science. He wrote, "Where religion still preserves the uncompromised aspirations for peace and happiness, its 'illusions' still have a higher truth value than science which works for their elimination."

Marcuse was, briefly, a guru of the New Left movement which arose throughout the West in the 1960s. One doubts that too many of the activists followed his complex readings of the German classical philosophy, his intricate Marxist rationale for the revival of a religious consciousness. But they did respond to his conclusions. There was a new stratum of the relatively affluent young, beneficiaries of the mass higher-education system required by late capitalism, freed from the day-to-day exigencies of the production process. They regarded the established parties and unions of the Left, including the Communists in Europe, as one more cog in the machine of power. And they romanticized those—the blacks and the poor, the people of the Third World—who had been excluded from the discipline of capitalist rationality, who had not, they said, been corrupted by either the time clock or semi-affluence.

There was much that was merely trendy in these movements. Marcuse's own notion that the West had become "one dimensional," and that the workers had been totally integrated into the status quo, was not true—even at the high point of postwar prosperity—and has been utterly discredited by the rising unemployment of the late seventies and early eighties. Some of the religious aspects of the protest movements were superficial, with the cult of the self decked out in communal costumes, a fad rather than a significant cultural alternative. Indeed, the hated establishment proceeded in most instances to co-opt and commercialize aspects of this new "spirituality."

And yet, there *was* a profound yearning, and not all of its manifestations were trivial or voguish. The environmental movement of the last two decades expressed a sense of the sacredness of the basic constituents of human existence—of earth, air and water—much as preliterate peoples did. And it has already achieved significant judicial and legislative modifications of that "instrumental reason" which Horkheimer and Adorno thought would sweep away everything in its path. It represents an important road to the future: a new form of communal morality and consciousness, one which is not borrowed from the past or the East, but evolves out of a genuine encounter with the Western present.

That is only a beginning. Still, it is of some moment that within the past two decades religious-political movements have arisen on the Left as well as on the fundamentalist Right. That strange symmetry testifies to the fact that both traditional faith and Enlightenment rationalism are in trouble, that at God's funeral there is a crisis of the legitimacy of both "is" and "ought," of the status quo and its opposition as well. We will not resolve this antinomy, Kant said toward the end of his life, unless the Hobbesian tendencies of humanity are offset by reciprocal love and respect among reasonable beings. "But should these two great ethical powers go down," he continued, " 'so then would nothingness (immorality) swallow with open mouth the whole kingdom of (moral) being like a drop of water.' . . ."

3
"TO KILL GOD AND BUILD A CHURCH"

THE NINETEENTH CENTURY was a time of new faiths, of invented Gods and reverential atheisms. Where the Enlightenment had only imagined substitute religions, men and women now tried to create substitute churches.

The fabrication of creeds continues to the present moment and is one of the signs of the death of the traditional God. "A rain of Gods," Leszek Kolakowski writes, "is falling from the sky on the funeral rites of the one God who has outlived himself." And Albert Camus devoted an entire book to the theme, "To kill God and to build a church—this is the constant and contradictory movement of revolt." Camus limited his analysis to the totalitarian dogmas which resulted from the perversion of revolutionary messianism. He thereby missed the incredible range and diversity of a development in which renascent Christianities prepared the way for atheist liturgies. The West has raised up an entire pantheon to blot out the emptiness of its heavens.

A God cannot, however, be conjured into life just because he is desperately needed. An isolated *philosophe* can dream a faith that should be, but only masses of people, responding to something very real within their own experience, can make a church. And the experience of the last two centuries is a witness to how difficult that is. Some of these new churches lasted for only a few years, and only one of them, the cult of the nation, has lasted throughout the entire period. And yet, it turned out that the "mob" responded to God's death more creatively, more complexly, than the contemptuous *philosophes*.

————— I —————

The French Revolution consciously, but ineffectively, sought to establish Enlightenment Deism as a state church and unconsciously created the most powerful substitute religion of the modern world. Understanding its unwitting success and unintended failure can yield insight into the contemporary problem of willing faith into existence.

One begins with that protean figure, Jean-Jacques Rousseau. His notion of "civil religion" has been blamed for everything from Stalinism to bland, Middle American piety. Yet what he actually said is not what many of his critics think he said. He believed that religion is defined by politics: "From the simple fact that God was placed at the head of each political society [in primitive theocracies] it followed that there were as many gods as peoples." Therefore "the provinces of the gods were marked off, so to speak, by the boundaries of the nations." That was good, he argued, because it united politics and religion—and it was bad in that it encouraged people to kill in the name of God. Christianity, and more particularly Roman Catholicism, is, however, unambiguously negative. It separates church and state, thus creating two loyalties and constantly threatening the subversion of government in the name of Christ. The question must then arise: isn't Rousseau's proposal for the reunification of faith and politics, for a civil religion, a forerunner of the totalitarian churches of the twentieth century?

Not quite. The truly good religion, Rousseau continued, is "without temples, altars or rites [and is] limited to purely inward reverence for the Supreme God and the eternal duties of morality." He is talking of something very much like Kant's "religion within the limits of mere reason." Moreover, he stressed that this public faith was not to replace religion in general but only religion insofar as it is explicitly political. It provides a basis for morality and duty toward others and society, no more. "Aside from that, everyone may have whatever opinions he chooses, and the sovereign has no right to know what they are." The essentials are few in number: "The existence of a powerful, intelligent, benevolent, foreseeing and provident Divinity, the life to come, the happiness of the righteous, the punishment of the wicked, the sanctity of the social contract and the positive law." Rousseau, in short, wanted to tolerate all religions which did not claim a loyalty superior to that owed to the state. That is profoundly flawed from a democratic point of view, yet it is not Stalinism (which has an official position on the ultimate constituents of the material world, sports, sex and everything else).

Robespierre tried to legislate Rousseau's religion into existence. He failed.

As is so often the case, Heine's irreverent insight has been confirmed by more sober scholarship. "Maximilien Robespierre," he wrote,

> the great bourgeois of the Rue Saint Honoré, did indeed have his attacks of destructive rage when it was a question of monarchy and his convulsions were frightful enough in his regicidal epilepsy, but as soon as there was any mention of the Supreme Being, he washed the white froth from his mouth and the blood from his hands, put on his blue Sunday coat with the shiny buttons, and what's more, stuck a nosegay in the front of his broad vest.

The standard interpretation of what Robespierre did has been much influenced by Emile Durkheim and his famous thesis that ultimately religion is always the worship of society by society. Durkheim said that the Revolution had transformed fatherland, liberty and reason into sacred things, creating a new religion with dogmas, altars and feasts. But then he had to admit a fatal flaw in his thesis: that this religion endured only as long as patriotic enthusiasm flourished. A contemporary Catholic historian, Bernard Plongeron, reinforces that point, showing that "de-Christianization" only lasted from the fall of 1783 to the spring of 1794.

This history confirms, and deepens, a point made in the last chapter: that the cosmic clockmaker of the Deists is hardly a God for the masses. The middle-class religion which tried to build upon that concept, called Théophilanthropie, did appeal to some among the cultured elite (including Tom Paine) but in 1801 it vanished from its quite modest place in history when Napoleon deprived this Voltairean church of its right to use public buildings. In fairness it should be noted that another substitute religion was more substantial than Théophilanthropie and, for that matter, gave rise to a word which is still in use today: ideology. The "ideologues" were the wise men placed in charge of the Institut de France by the Convention in 1795. This was, George Lichtheim wrote, one of the first manifestations of "political atheism," a creed that held that schools would take the place of churches.

Napoleon, who in 1798 had signed his proclamations to the Army as *"Général en chef, Membre de L'Institut,"* came to understand the limitations of the "ideologues." They tried, he said in 1812, "to base legislation for the people on first principles instead of taking the laws from a knowledge of the human heart and the lessons of history. . . ." And yet, the heart of the people was not as naïve and passive as assumed by Napoleon and the historians who focus on the Cult of Reason. There was a third faith which emerged from the upheaval in France, and although it might be mistaken for Robespierre's civil religion, it was in fact quite different. That is one reason why it still exists.

The scholars who concentrate on the middle-class rites of reason, Albert Saboul shows, ignore the spontaneous cults of the masses. These effectively canonized revolutionary heroes like Marat, Lepeletier and Chalet and did so, not by adopting a rationalist faith, but by giving a new, political content to the traditional forms of Catholicism (the Catholic historian Plongeron tells much the same story). And this is not simply a moment in French history; it is a process which can be found around the globe. In Mexico, for instance, the place where our Lady of Guadalupe—Mary as Indian virgin—appeared is the hill which had been previously dedicated to Tonantzin, the Aztec goddess of fertility. And one of the most persistent working-class strategies of the nineteenth century was to create proletarian versions, and sometimes even atheist versions, of Christianity.

So it was that the new faith, which survived the French Revolution and lasts until this day, was not Deism but nationalism. The experience of the people gave rise to a new interpretation of the world which men and women could die for, a creed which inspired Napoleon's armies and eventually spread to its enemies. The "Marseillaise" was the most successful hymn of the nineteenth century, the tricolor its most powerful icon. It was not middle-class rationalism which captured the imagination of the masses but a new variant of what Paul Tillich has called "the myth of origin." The ties of birth, blood and language, those bonds which had held tribes together, were now writ large in a national consciousness.

These fervent nationalisms were, in James Billington's words, heralds "of the age of political revolution," of that uniquely modern "total belief in secular salvation." Their great competitor was a socialist internationalism whose rise Friedrich Engels analogized to the emergence of Christianity among the dispossessed of the ancient world. Ultimately—but only briefly—it created an atheist church. Ironically, the prelude to that development was what might be called a second resurrection of Jesus Christ among the workers of Europe and a rebirth of Judaism as well.

Even in countries where the workers eventually became atheists or agnostics, this process was not simple or immediate. It is quite wrong to say, as Alasdair MacIntyre does, "that the industrial working class in Western Europe did not leave the churches at any point because it never entered them." That is to simplify the social history of the death of God in the European proletariat. Engels wrote in *The New Moral World* in 1843—and the title of that journal is a sign of the times— that "the French communists, though a part of a nation celebrated for its unbelief, are themselves Christians. One of their beloved axioms goes: Christianity *is* communism."

Why were the workers as a class so deeply implicated in the religious crisis of the early nineteenth century? Why did they produce both a new Christianity and a new atheism? In considerable measure because they went through the trauma of industrialization and urbanization in a more wrenching way than any other stratum. Peasant life had the Church as its spiritual center; the city, with its huge numbers and its impersonality, neither did nor could. Among the country people who came to Paris to become workers, Gabriel Le Bras has suggested, 90 percent ceased to be practicing Catholics when they arrived. The sidewalk of the Gare de Montparnasse, the port of entry to Paris for some of those peasants, is, Le Bras said, "one of the thresholds of . . . modern disbelief." There are some significant exceptions to this rule: a very large portion of the workers in the Ruhr, the most industrialized part of Germany, remained Catholic until World War I, and the dissenting chapels played a major role in English socialism. There were even peasant atheists in Italy and Spain, and Le Bras himself has charted the complex religious geography of rural France.

But the massive fact is that the traditional God did not fare well among the workers in the new cities of the capitalist era. So they first reinvented that God and then, in many countries, denied him altogether. The proletarian Christ of that phase was usually a Leftist but in one significant case he was a conservative. In Henri de Saint-Simon's version, he was of both the Left and the Right.

Saint-Simon was so seminal a figure that one can only briefly evoke his life and influence. He inspired the capitalists who built the French banking system and the workers who created the labor and anarcho-syndicalist movements. He was a visionary who recognized the possibilities of both the Suez and the Panama canals as well as a premature advocate of "feminism, pacifism, philo-Semitism, Europeanism and Christian socialism." He was the architect of what has been called a "church of the engineers," yet his disciples talked of the "heredity of misery" which existed in the "class of proletarians" and wrote, in lines that anticipated the *Communist Manifesto*, that the "exploitation of man by man," which had counterposed "masters and slaves, patricians and plebeians, seigneurs and serfs," now pitted owners against workers.

Indeed, it can be said fairly that Saint-Simon was simultaneously a man of the Left and the Right, a fact that should not be too surprising since the aristocrats and the workers both hated the new capitalist system—for utterly different reasons—and even made a united front in England in the struggle to limit the working day. Indeed, it was Saint-Simon's Left-Right synthesis which was a key to his concept of a new Christianity. For him—and this puts him light-years away from the Enlightenment and its horror of the "dark ages"—there were two constructive epochs in Western history, Greco-Roman civilization and medieval Christendom. The latter, in particular, he saw as an advance over the military organization of the ancient world. The Reformation and the *philosophes* constituted a necessary critique of an order which had resisted the coming of science, but Saint-Simon yearned to return to a unified social system which would integrate morality, religion, science and industrialism.

His first proposal for a new religion was not Christian but Deist. There would be a "Council of Newton" to represent God on earth. In each of the geographically based subdivisions of the world, the Council would be headed by the mathematician who received the highest vote and would build a mausoleum in honor of Newton. There would be rites in which "all the distinguished services rendered to humanity, all the actions which have been greatly useful to the propagation of the faith, will be honored." It was in this period that Saint-Simon found support among industrialists and bankers and tried to win the backing, first of Napoleon and then of Louis XVIII. However, as his writings became more pointed, the establishment grew worried. In 1820 he suggested that France not only could get along without the Church but could dispense with the nobility and state bureaucracy as well.

It was at this point that Saint-Simon adopted a revealing tactic: to advocate his ideas under the name of "Christianity." The new Christianities of the nineteenth century were not simply the means whereby devout people responded creatively to an unprecedented social upheaval; they were sometimes a pious disguise for atheistic humanism.

"The Catholic system," Saint-Simon wrote to a friend, "was in contradiction with the system of science and modern industry. Hence its collapse was inevitable. It is happening, and this collapse is the signal for a new belief which, by its enthusiasm, will fill the spiritual void left by criticism; a belief that will draw its strength from all that is lacking in the old belief as well as from all that belongs to it." So he appealed to the "new spiritual power" in Europe—the Academies of Science—to subordinate politics to "the fundamental principle of Christian morality."

This new "Christianity" bore a considerable resemblance to Kant's "religion within the mere limits of reason." It had one basic principle: "Men should treat one another as brothers." The Christian clergy, the Pope and the cardinals as well as the Protestants, were all "heretics" but in spite of them Christianity would become universal and the "true doctrine" prevail. All of this was "Leftist" and "Rightist," a blending of positivism (Auguste Comte, Saint-Simon's secretary, obviously borrowed much from him) and traditional conservative nostalgia for medieval Catholicism. Indeed, one of Saint-Simon's chief disciples, the organizer of the Saint-Simonian Church after his death, praised the counterrevolutionary theorists de Maistre and Bonald and was a supporter of Metternich—even as he was giving a socialist interpretation of the master's doctrine!

That Saint-Simonian religion—feminist, philo-Semitic, in favor of erotic freedom and in search of a woman messiah—made politics fervid. George Lichtheim described its impact:

> The originality of the Saint-Simonian movement lay in the fact that it combined the Romantic yearning for harmony with a prophetic vision transcending the quarrel between bourgeois liberals and Catholic conservatives. Saint-Simon's *Nouveau Christianisme* had affected the orig-

inal fusion and by 1830 the Saint-Simonian "religion" . . . released an emotional torrent that swept thousands of men and women off their feet. Here, all of a sudden, was a new vision of man, no longer dull and rationalistic but sentimental and passionate. . . . Socialism was a *faith*— that was the great discovery the Saint-Simonians had made. It was the "new Christianity" and it would emancipate those whom the old religion had left in chains—above all woman and the proletariat.

There is an unforgettable image of that new faith in one of the most famous works in Western literature: Goethe's *Faust*. Goethe was deeply influenced by Parisian ideas during the 1820s, when he was writing the Second Part of *Faust*. He even felt it was providential that he had delayed so long in taking up that work again, since this had given him the opportunity to make contact with Saint-Simonian (and Fourierist) ideas. It was in this period, too, that he thought that "the human race is involved in a religious crisis." At the conclusion of the Second Part of *Faust* these concerns were fused. Faust had been engaged in a gigantic project to reclaim land from the swamp—not unlike the Saint-Simonian proposals for the Suez and Panama canals, which fascinated Goethe—and in the process he has not only driven the workers brutally but also unwittingly been associated with the killing of an innocent, aging couple who stood in the way of "progress."

That elderly couple are a part of the complexity which Goethe stresses even at his most utopian. One of them, Baucis, tells how the night is filled with the sounds of pickaxes and spades and the anguished cries of the driven workers—and then, in the morning, there is a dam or a canal. Baucis cries out

> Godless is he who lusts after
> Our hut, our grove.

From the vantage point of tradition, such progress is indeed blasphemy. And even Mephistopheles complains, after Faust is dead, that he needs help in claiming the soul he had bargained for since

> Traditional customs, ancient rights,
> One can't trust in anything anymore.

But Faust is consumed of a vision, an epic version of what Saint-Simon and his followers had dreamed. He had reclaimed swamp from the sea and "opened up space for many millions." Yet in this "para-disical land," all is not perfect for

> Freedom, like life, is only won
> When it is conquered each day anew.

Still, even recognizing these "Faustian" complications, Faust ends—he willingly seals his own fate—with a utopian statement which is justly famous in world literature. There could be, he admits, a moment of contentment

> If I could see a throng stand
> Free among a free people,
> Then I would dare say to the moment:
> Stay, you are so fair.

With Goethe, Ernst Bloch said, utopia leaves the sky and comes to earth, as science and engineering are married to a dream. And it is clear, as Marshall Berman argued in his insightful reading of *Faust*, that Goethe translated that Saint-Simonian faith into dramatic poetry.

Goethe was not a Christian (he was either an atheistic pantheist or a pantheistic atheist). And one can speculate about Saint-Simon, whose "Christianity" may have been only a tactic. But then the workers made their own interpretation of Saint-Simon and it was even more daring than that of the bankers and engineers. They ignored all of the technocratic values, seized upon the Saint-Simonian concept of "association" and turned it into the watchword for the French working-class commitment to a decentralized, semi-anarchist socialism. The late-medieval revolutionaries, Ernst Bloch once wrote, "productively misunderstood" Plato's *Republic*, turning an aristocratic utopia into a call for plebeian revolt. The French workers had a similar productive misunderstanding of Saint-Simon, democratizing and socializing his doctrine until they all but turned it into its opposite. And they listened, as workers all over Europe did, to Hugues-Félicité-Robert de Lamennais, the author of a tremendously popular book, *Paroles d'un croyant* (*Sayings of a Believer*).

Lamennais began as a conservative Catholic theologian, a champion of papal authority and a sworn foe of liberalism. In 1830 he made a total reversal and came out for democracy and liberty of religious belief, and against monarchy, earning a papal condemnation in 1832. Two years later he published the *Paroles d'un croyant,* a passionate book, more poem than anything else, which identified Christ with the cause of the exploited and oppressed. Like Saint-Simon, Lamennais admired the Middle Ages but saw that the medieval church's hostility to science had been part of its undoing. He, too, wanted to unite religion and science in the service of the people. As Alec Vidler puts it, ". . . instead of trying to exorcise the Revolution, he decided to baptize it."

There was a new·Judaism at about the same time as these new Christianities. It was the inspiration of the man whom Friedrich Engels once called the first communist in Germany. His name was Moses Hess and he was also one of the first Zionists in the world.

In the seventeenth and eighteenth centuries there were privileged "court Jews" in Central Europe while the Jewish masses lived a medieval existence in the ghettos and *shtetls* of Eastern Europe. By the end of the eighteenth century, the educated Jews in Prussia, like Moses Mendelssohn, were lionized, Lessing's play *Nathan the Wise* was seen as a plea for tolerance and Shakespeare's *Merchant of Venice* could not be performed in Berlin unless it was preceded by an apology to any Jews who might be in the audience. With the emancipation of the Jews, beginning with the French Revolution, the lives of the poor Jews were changed, too. They moved to the great cities—and to America— and all Jews were faced with a crisis of identity as a result of the secularization of society.

Until emancipation, a Jew was a member of a religious community, officially discriminated against by Christian societies, unable to hold public office. Now Jews gradually gained access to the universities, the professions, even public service. Between 1815 and 1914, Shlomo Avineri has written, Jews went from the margin of European life to its center, making this "the most revolutionary century in history" for them since the destruction of the Temple in Jerusalem in 70 A.D. But what, then, was Jewishness? A religious commitment which could be abandoned by a simple act of apostasy? A nationality—and, if so, then an alien nationality in the new nationalist states of Europe? Some, like Karl Marx's father, responded to the new situation by becoming Christians. Moses Hess's family, though a part of the upper stratum, remained true to the old faith, and Hess himself received a Jewish education.

In part, he broke with the tradition and came under the influence of radical ideas. And yet, even then, in his first book, *The Holy History of Humanity*, he portrayed his utopia as a new Jerusalem.

The Jews, he said, would disappear, but only because their prophetic vision had been realized by socialism. It was at this time that he first met Marx and Engels, who, though they recognized his contribution to the movement, thought him "vague and mystical." In the 1850s and '60s he was an activist, working with another Jew, Ferdinand Lassalle, in the nascent German labor movement. But then in the 1860s there came a dramatic turn. He continued to identify Jewishness with socialism, but now he argued that the Jews must have their own homeland. He was against the pietism of the Orthodox—and against what he saw as the Reform Jews' tendency to reduce their religion to a few Enlightenment banalities. Hess's ideas did not have the immediate impact of those of a Lamennais, yet they were to have a profound influence upon masses of Jews in the twentieth century.

So there was a Jewish working-class and socialist religiosity and, of greater influence in the nineteenth century, a messianic atheism of those whom Isaac Deutscher called the "non-Jewish Jews." It is clear, for instance, that the prophetic vision of a Karl Marx cannot be understood apart from the Judaism he himself never practiced. That form of political Jewishness did penetrate the impoverished Jewish masses of Eastern Europe. Indeed, they were the ones who brought Marxism to the East—and to Russia.

In short, quite contrary to Alasdair MacIntyre's theory, religion, both Christian and Jewish, was in complex fashion a vital factor in the early working-class and radical movements. The sectarian, mainly Christian, interpretation of socialism was so widespread in the 1840s that Marx and Engels made it a precondition of their membership in the Communist League that all churchly rituals be eliminated from the statutes. The English utopian John Goodwyn Barmby styled himself the "Pontifarch of the Communist Church" and proposed to fund his future by getting back all the church lands confiscated by Henry VIII; in Paris, the worker-run newspaper *L'Atelier* depicted Liberty and Equality as angels wearing Phrygian caps. Billington writes that "Communism probably would not have attracted such attention without this initial admixture of Christian ideals." At the very same time, however, there was another new Christianity which was creating a pious defense of the emergent capitalist status quo.

Methodism, it has been argued, was a major factor in staving off a "French" revolution in England. John Wesley, the founder of the Methodist Church, was a Tory monarchist, and his sober, abstemious reading of the Bible, with its stress on individual righteousness rather than collective action, had a profound impact, political as well as religious, on workers. After the French Revolution, E. P. Thompson writes, the successive Methodist Annual Conferences "were forever professing their submission and their zeal in combatting the enemies of established order." They promoted "loyalty in the middle ranks as well as subordination in the lower orders of society." The nineteenth century had Christ the capitalist as well as Christ the communist.

One man, Dr. Andrew Ure, clearly understood the conservative function of such a version of Christianity. Ure was immortalized by Marx in *Das Kapital* as the "Pindar of the automatic factory," but he was also a political theologian, devoting a section of one of his books to the "Moral Economy of the Factory System." The factories, Ure said—and in this passage he sounds very much like a Marxist—naturally compress "a vast population within a narrow circuit; they afford every facility for secret cabal . . . ; they communicate intelligence and energy to the vulgar mind; they supply in their liberal wages the pecuniary sinews of contention. . . ." How, then, to discipline such a place? By persuading the workers that their tasks are a *"pure act of virtue*. . . . Whence then shall mankind find this transforming power?—in the cross of Christ."

Is it really clear, however, that Methodism, in contrast to the communist theologies of France and Germany, was a prop of the established order? Not quite. For even if the dissenters after 1789 fulminated against Sin and Tom Paine rather than against Sin and the Pope, their faith sometimes had libertarian consequences. The Chartist hymns—which is to say, the songs of the first mass political movement of the working class in any country—were, as E. P. Thompson points out, both radical and Methodist in inspiration. Here was another "productive misunderstanding."

Finally, there were occasions when the new Christians of both Right and Left agreed as to the problem and differed "only" with regard to its solution. Robert Owen was as appalled by the "idleness and drunkenness" of the working class as Andrew Ure. But Owen, the "kindly Papa of Socialism," "chose neither the psychic terrors of Methodism nor the discipline of the overlooker and of fines to attain his ends." If you treated the workers decently, he thought, they would become, not simply more moral and upright, but more productive as well. Himself a successful industrialist, he hated class war and tried to convince the British upper class—and the American Congress, which he addressed in the 1820s—to become socialist out of enlightened self-interest.

He won a hearing of sorts for these ideas within the establishment until he frightened it with his anti-clericalism. Rebuffed, he turned to the proletariat, which, like the French workers responding to Saint-Simon, reinterpreted his doctrines to fit its needs. The apostle of class peace became an inspiration for class war; the benevolent advocate of top-down philanthropy was used to legitimize worker-owned cooperatives seeking to transform the system from the bottom up; and the atheist became the guiding spirit of a secular religion. Surprisingly enough, given his earlier uprightness, it was a rather erotic movement. It held that "celibacy, in either sex, beyond the period designed by nature, will no longer be considered a virtue" but, rather, a "crime against nature."

So the new religions of the nineteenth-century workers were complex and often shrewder than the doctrines of the intellectuals which were reshaped to meet the needs of those at the bottom. And these churches prepared the way for the cult of No God.

——— I I I ———

There was in the late nineteenth and early twentieth centuries a political atheism which, with careful qualifications, can be called a church of the unbelievers. There is a totalitarian state atheism which uses the same name as that early movement—Marxism—but which is almost its exact opposite. Karl Marx would have disdained the first church named in his honor and abominated the second.

Middle-class atheism (and its shamefaced cousin, Deism) flourished in the eighteenth century but declined in the nineteenth, when heterodoxy became subversive of the new, bourgeois status quo. But then a new phenomenon emerges: the disbelief of the poor. Hostility to religion, the young Marx wrote to Ludwig Feuerbach in 1844, has become a power among the workers. As E. J. Hobsbawm summarizes this trend in the light of contemporary scholarship, "there is little doubt

that from the middle or perhaps late nineteenth century religious practice declined almost everywhere" among the workers. It was in this
period that the Marxist-atheist-social democracy established what was,
in effect, the first proletarian church of No God.

The disaffection of a significant part of the European working class
has not been disputed by religious thinkers. Pope Pius XI spoke of
the "great scandal" of the nineteenth century, the loss of the working
class by the Church, and Hans Küng wrote, "The Communist Manifesto
had been published in 1848 but it was only in 1891 that the first papal
encyclical on the social question—Leo XIII's Rerum Novarum—appeared. 'Forty years too late' as someone said, making use of the title
of the second social encyclical, Pius XI's Quadragesimo Anno (1931)."
But the Protestant churches in Germany began to face the problem at
an even later stage. Had a German worker gone to a Protestant church
in the last century, says a present-day theologian, he probably would
have been told that his or her lot had been ordained by God and that
the Revolution of 1848 was a violation of holy law.

Even so, Karl Marx was against creating any kind of socialist-
atheist "church." If Marx became furious when one of his followers
went to America and adopted a religion of love as a means for social
struggle, he nevertheless did not believe that atheism was a necessary
part of the socialist movement. Tactically he remained committed
throughout his life to the proposition he formulated as a young man:
"We do not assert that the people must transcend their religious limits
in order to transcend the limits of the real world. Rather, we argue
that they will transcend those religious limits as soon as they transcend
the limits of the real world."

The contemporary theologian Helmut Gollwitzer is right to say
that "for Marxism, atheism is not an independent goal and the struggle
against religion cannot be an independent task of socialism." Marx
maintained this not merely during his youth but throughout his
life. In 1871 he wrote contemptuously of Bakunin's making atheism a
compulsory dogma for the members of the International Working
Men's Association. Engels was even more scathing. How could the
socialists in Naples make atheism a precondition for membership
in a city in "which not only God is almighty but where one has to
deal seriously with the holy Januarius"? And the mature Marx wrote,
in his "Critique of the Gotha Program," about the socialist society of
the future, "Everyone must have the right to fulfill his religious as

well as his bodily needs without the police sticking their nose into his affairs."

Anti-Dühring, Engels's polemical volume designed to educate the socialist rank and file, repeats this point. Religion will die when the means of production are communally guided and no longer loom over man like a fate. Dühring, his authoritarian "socialist" foe,

> who cannot wait for religion to die a natural death, proceeds more radically than that. He out-Bismarcks Bismarck by proposing an even stricter May law [Bismarck's anti-Catholic decrees of May 1873], not simply against Catholicism but against all religion. He sets his gendarmes of the future against religion and thereby helps it to martyrdom and a longer life. In this we see the specific characteristics of Prussian socialism.

By the last quarter of the nineteenth century, the German social democracy, the very model of a Marxist party, had declared religion to be a "private matter." Under socialism, said August Bebel, its most authoritative working-class leader, "Religion will not be 'abolished,' one will not 'depose God' or 'rip religion out of the hearts of men' and all the other stupidities which are said in attacks against atheistically disposed social democrats. Such inversions make social democracy into a bourgeois ideology which, in the French Revolution, used such means against religion and went aground." This was a principled position—and good politics. In the Ruhr, that most proletarian of German regions, the Catholic Party outpolled the Socialists by 45 percent to 20 percent in 1898, and fourteen years later the Catholics were still slightly ahead (36 percent against 32 percent). God was dying, but slowly.

However, if the first working-class atheist movement did not call for the suppression of religion, it did organize its own church.

Its theologian was Engels, not Marx. He, along with Karl Kautsky, the Russian Plekhanov and a few others, developed a scientistic version of Marxism in the years after Marx's death in 1883. Engels died in 1895, but his influence in these matters dominated until World War I. Small wonder. The party grew steadily and so did the unions and it seemed that socialism was indeed going to be the result of an inexorable, secular providence. There was a socialist counterculture—and counter-religion. It was possible for an individual to live his or her life almost entirely within the confines of the movement, to be born into it, work for it, vacation within it and be buried with atheist solemnity by it.

The elaboration of this Marxist faith coincided with the heyday of a vision of science which was "simple and coherent . . . not very far distant from common sense," in A. J. Ayer's words. So Engels developed a comprehensive account, not simply of society, but of nature and physics and chemistry, and called it "dialectical materialism." That phrase was never used by Marx and, more to the point, such an attempt at a total "Marxist" explanation of all reality cannot be found in his writings. Nevertheless, at Marx's funeral Engels hailed him as the "Darwin of the social sciences" and thus made the claim that Marxism had discovered a political inevitability as certain as the natural selection of the species. It was no accident that the most popular book among the German socialist movement before World War I was *Moses or Darwin*, a nonsocialist work debunking religious faith.

There was a climactic moment in this Marxist quasi-religion at the special antiwar Congress of the Socialist International in Basel in 1912. Julius Braunthal describes the event: "At two o'clock, the delegates began to march through the streets of Basel toward the cathedral. At their head was a group of white-clothed children bearing a forest of red flags before them. As the procession neared the cathedral, the bells pealed, and as it reached the door the organ intoned Bach's C-Minor Mass." There had been a similar international meeting in this cathedral before: in 1431 an ecumenical council of the Catholic Church had been held there. At the 1912 ecumenical council of working-class atheism, August Bebel gave what turned out to be his last speech.

He talked of the hospitality of the cathedral and of the pealing bells which had greeted the opening session. "Party comrades," he said, "these signs of Christian tolerance are unfortunately rare. . . . I myself am convinced that if the Christian Saviour came down to earth once again and saw these many Christian communities, these hundreds of thousands calling themselves Christian . . . he would stand, not in their ranks, but in ours." There was, the Congress minutes reported, "stormy applause" at that point.

The delegates at Basel were living out the last, lovely moments of an illusion. Quantum theories, relativity, indeterminacy principles were all starting to undermine the serene scientific faith, bourgeois and proletarian. World War I was to shatter all the idylls of automatic progress, capitalist and socialist. The proletariat of Europe marched out, singing patriotic songs to slaughter itself along national lines— just like the Christians of Europe. That gradual, seemingly inevitable progress which had been the basis of Engels's vision of Marxism came to an end. In the ruins of those hopes, however, there came a second "Marxist" religion, utterly unlike the first: the compulsory state church of totalitarian Communist countries.

——— I V ———

"The Catholic priest corrupting young girls (about whom I have just read by chance in the German newspapers)," V. I. Lenin wrote in 1913, "is *much less* dangerous, precisely to 'democracy,' than an ideologically equipped and democratic priest preaching the creation and invention of a god. For it is *easy* to expose, condemn and expel the first priest, while the second *cannot* be expelled so simply; to expose the latter is 1000 times more difficult and not a single 'frail and pitifully wavering' philistine will agree to 'condemn' him."

This is clearly a shift from both Marx and the first generation of German Marxists. For them, religion would collapse of its own weight once social justice subverted the misery which drove people to God(s). But now Lenin is talking about the Marxist party's engaging in a direct confrontation with the Church. Why this change? That question does not merely raise scholarly issues about the past. It points toward what Stalin and all of his Soviet successors did and are still doing: making adherence to the totalitarian state religion of atheism as much a requirement of good citizenship as Roman Catholicism was in the Middle Ages.

Lenin moved in this direction—and he was the unwitting precursor of Stalin on this count (and many others)—for two reasons. Religion played a different role in czarist Russia from the role it played in the Kaiser's Germany; and Lenin himself was the proponent of an integralist brand of Marxism, borrowed in considerable measure from Engels, which was to provide the anti-theology for Stalin's atheist church.

In semi-democratic Germany it was possible to look toward a gradual, evolutionary transformation of society; in Romanov Russia it was not. The classical social democrats in Russia either became proponents of capitalism in the name of Marxism (Struve) or else moderates working for a bourgeois revolution which would then, in proper sequence as defined by a mechanistic Marxism, be followed by a proletarian revolution at an unspecified later date. Lenin was an activist, the organizer of an underground party of committed revolutionaries rather than of a mass electoral party like that of the German socialists. Under such circumstances, the party's ideology had to be an all-consuming faith which would provide the cadres with a reason to risk their freedom and their lives.

Lenin was aware of these national differences. It was all right, he said in 1909, to say that religion was a "private matter" for the party member in Germany. Indeed, he conceded that in such a country "bourgeois anti-clericalism" was often "a means of drawing the attention of the working-class masses away from socialism—this is what preceded the spread of the modern spirit of 'indifference' to the struggle against religion among the Social Democrats in the West." That, we know, is not accurate: Marx and Engels had a principled position which regarded religious issues as of secondary importance for the movement. Still, Lenin was right about the way in which conditions diverged in Germany and Russia. In his own country, he continued, the "party must be the ideological leader in the struggle against all attributes of medievalism, including the old official religion and every attempt to refurbish it or make out a different case for it."

Lenin proceeded to make a supreme virtue out of this alleged necessity—and unintentionally to prepare the way for a state cult of atheism under Stalin which would be every bit as orthodox as the Orthodox Church he wanted to smash.

There is a problem in documenting this analysis. With one exception, Lenin never wrote a single word, even when discussing the most abstruse philosophical question, which was not influenced by political and organizational considerations. When, for instance, he was in a political bloc with a fellow Bolshevik, Bogdanov, who disagreed with him on some basic theoretical issues, he declared that these disagreements were "completely irrelevant to the question of the social revolution." Shortly after, when his tactical coalition with Bogdanov broke up, he devoted the better part of a book to demonstrating that Bogdanov's political heresies were the inevitable consequence of his metaphysical heresies.

The only time Lenin ever considered such matters in a nonpolitical fashion was in 1914–15, when the outbreak of World War I convinced him that he had no political future and allowed him to read Hegel's *Logic* and some other philosophic volumes in a relatively relaxed mood. However, the results of those meditations were not published until

1929, after his death, and played no role in the formation of the "Leninism" described here.*

The book which attacked Bogdanov and other heterodox Marxists was a response to some fascinating developments in the Russia of the first decade of the century. First, there were "God-seekers," non-Bolshevik Marxists who framed their revolutionary socialism in religious terms. Many of them were eventually to become Christians. Then came the emergence of "God-builders" in the ranks of the Bolsheviks themselves, part of a faction opposed to Lenin. Maxim Gorky, the novelist and Bolshevik sympathizer, was one of them; Lunacharski, a Bolshevik intellectual, was another. For Lunacharski, the means of production were the Father, the proletariat the Son and scientific socialism the Holy Ghost. Gorky wrote of a "new religion": "Thou art my God, O sovereign people, and creator of all gods which thou hast formed from the beauties of thy spirit. . . . And the world should have no god but thee, for thou art the only god that works miracles."

All of this, as Leszek Kolakowski points out, was secondhand Feuerbach and without any lasting impact on Russian Marxism. Yet Lenin responded with fury to all such deviations from what he took to be the scientific faith of Marxism. Marxist philosophy, he wrote in *Materialism and Empirio-Criticism*, "is cast from a single piece of steel, you cannot eliminate one basic premise, one essential part, without departing from objective truth, without falling a prey to bourgeois reactionary falsehood." In this view, as the French existentialist Merleau-Ponty wrote, Marx's concept of "history seen as a relation between persons incarnated in things" is replaced by the idea of society as "a 'second nature,' opaque and determined like nature itself."

But Lenin's scientistic determinism was not like that of the social democrats of the West. He was a voluntarist who sought to understand the laws of social development in order to change them, and his insistence on the dialectic—and particularly that dialectical "leap" which occurs when "quantitative change" becomes "qualitative"—was a philosophic way of stating his commitment to revolution. As water turns into steam at the boiling point, so semi-feudal Russia would hurdle the capitalist phase and initiate socialism. The dream became reality—and it was disillusioning. At the end of his life a desperate Lenin recognized that the Russian working class had proved incapable of creating a truly

*See Appendix C.

new society. At times he wrote of escaping this history by means of a "cultural revolution" among the peasants; at times he looked East and saw salvation in the colonial masses. But he died before he could even begin to face up to all the contradictions he had wrought.

Stalin found a way out of the impasse—the bureaucratic and totalitarian collectivization of the society, a "revolution from above," as he himself once called it. But how, then, to justify a workers' and peasants' revolution made over the dead bodies of a good number of workers and peasants? By the Gulag, of course. But also by a new religion: "Leninism," with its mummified, atheist God in Red Square and its theology, "dialectical materialism."

In 1931, when the revolution from above was in full swing, the Bolshevik Central Committee, now led by Stalin, denounced the two major philosophic tendencies which had claimed to represent the authentic Marxism. This was, Gustav Wetter has written, a decisive turning point in Soviet life; now there was a totalitarian political line on all issues, including philosophic and religious questions. Not too long after the shift, Stalin personally supervised the writing of the *History of the Communist Party of the Soviet Union* (*Bolsheviks*), a volume which became the catechism for Communists around the world. In recounting the history of Bolshevism, the Yugoslavian Marxist Branko Horvat has noted, the *History* did not find one single occasion on which the Party had erred.

The Party's infallibility was no longer an opinion; it was a dogma enforced by the secret police. Stalin then proceeded to outline the meaning of "Dialectical and Historical Materialism . . . , the world outlook of the Marxist-Leninist party." It is an authoritarian exegesis of an extremely simplified version of Engels's simplification of Marxism. History comes to be an inexorable progress from primitive society to Communism and the party of the proletariat is seen as "guided by the laws of development of society, and by practical deduction from those laws. Hence Socialism is converted from a dream of a better future for humanity into a science."

There is a world-historical mistranslation here, the rendering of the German word *Wissenschaft* as science in the sense of natural science. In German philosophy, *Wissenschaft* meant "systematic," not natural-scientific, knowledge. Kant, who carefully distinguished metaphysics from natural science, called his *Critique of Pure Reason* a *Wissenschaft*, and Hegel wrote a *Wissenschaft* of *Logic*. Moreover, in a dispute with Bakunin, Marx specifically said that all he intended by the term *wissenschaftlicher Sozialismus* was to counterpose his view to a utopian socialism "which will fasten new phantoms on the people." Bakunin had argued that the claim to "scientific" certitude could provide an ideological rationale for a new technocratic aristocracy ruling over the workers in the name of socialism. Marx in effect conceded the point but denied that he had made any such "scientific" claim. Both Marx and Bakunin were right: under Stalin, Marxist "science" became the irrational theology of a new atheist tyranny.

In Stalinism, Leszek Kolakowski wrote (when he was still a Marxist), "every new ritual and every new truth had to be accepted under threat of irrevocable banishment from the company of the blessed." Herbert Marcuse, also writing as a Marxist, compared this totalitarian faith to primitive magic with its belief in the practical power of incantations. It was Branko Horvat, however, who attempted to theorize this phenomenon in a systematic way. In societies, like Russia and the countries of Eastern Europe, which leapt from a pre-bourgeois to a post-bourgeois world, party members who had gone through the experience of persecution lived in a "semi-religious environment." Once in power, "the state and the party were needed to replace the king and the church," and Stalin's new religion was thus a functional necessity, the "religious consciousness" of such a society.

Bertolt Brecht, who was to become disillusioned later on, idealized this process. In *Die Massnahme* (*The Decision*), a play which glorified Stalin's policies in China in the late twenties and was performed as agitational theater in the Berlin of the early thirties, Brecht has the "Control Chorus"—a Greek chorus in the guise of a communist Control Commission, the supreme disciplinary body for the enforcement of party morality—chant:

> The individual has two eyes.
> The party has a thousand eyes.
> The party sees seven states.
> The individual sees a single city.
> The individual has his moments,
> The party has many moments.
> The individual can be annihilated,
> But the party can never be annihilated,
> For it is the vanguard of the masses
> And leads their struggle

With the methods of the classics, which are created
Out of our knowledge of reality.

In this guise, "Marxism" becomes the knowledge of all things through their final causes, and thus can be subsumed under the same formula which decadent Scholasticism used to misdefine Thomism. And the inexorable stages of history become a secular providence, a substitute for the benevolent God.

Karl Kautsky unknowingly glimpsed a precedent for this development in 1908 (at a time when Lenin still regarded him as one of the pre-eminent Marxists in the world). He wrote of a situation in which "the organization of a proletariat, rebellious communism, became the staunchest support of despotism and exploitation, a source of new despotism and new exploitation." He was referring to the Christian struggle against the Romans. "The crucified Messiah," he concluded, "became the firmest support of that decadent and infamous society which the Messianic community had expected him to destroy down to the ground." Substitute "Marxism-Leninism" for the "crucified Messiah" and the analysis holds for the Soviet Union.

And yet, one must take care not to exaggerate the power of such consciously fabricated gods. Talcott Parsons was wrong, I think, when he equated the Director of the Institute of Philosophy of the Soviet Academy with the "Dean of the Theology Faculty of the Religion of Marxism-Leninism." Within a decade or two "Marxism-Leninism" accomplished a task which had taken Byzantium centuries, moving from a passionate underground faith to an ossified Caesaro-papist cult.

—— V ——

The Central European, Marxist counterculture lasted perhaps half a century (from 1883 to 1914 in its heyday, from 1914 to 1939 in its decline). The "religion" of Stalinism in the West—it still has a potential in the Third World, for the reasons that Horvat outlined—endured as a significant reality from Lenin's funeral in 1924 to Khrushchev's speech at the Twentieth Party Congress, in 1956, and it survives now only as a compulsory state cult. The sects and churches created by the affluent young in the counterculture of the sixties still exist at the margin of the society but without any potential for replacing the dying political God.

That counterculture was many things. The environmental movement grew out of the untraditional spirituality of the 1960s and it is,
as the last chapter indicated, serious and significant, a genuine revival
of the sense of the sacred under modern conditions. But the gurus
with their coteries, the psychoanalytic salvations, the Hare Krishnas
and the Unification Church were something quite different from the
environmental movement. They were the desperate response of the
offspring of affluence—from "conventional and comfortable, often religious childhoods"—to the death of God. They had discovered something quite real: the alienation and emptiness of a meaningless
materialism. But they were only a remnant and they turned inward
in any case.

At times the claims for this movement were messianic: "to proclaim
a new heaven and a new earth so vast, so marvelous that the inordinate
claims of technical expertise must of necessity withdraw in the presence of such splendor to a subordinate and marginal status in the lives
of men," to challenge all the "mainstream assumptions since the Scientific Revolution of the seventeenth century." To be sure, they sometimes echoed more serious innovators. At the Feast of the Supreme
Being in revolutionary Paris in 1794, the people were urged to begin
the day with a "tête-à-tête with a flower" and garlands were everywhere, even decking the guillotine. And there were revolutionaries
who protested against industrial discipline and urban alienation, like
the Carbonari, the Italian "charcoal-burners," and the Society of Swans
in Switzerland. The composer Bernardo Porta favored woodwinds for
ideological reasons. But none of these protests, even the most whim-
sical, was merely individual; rather, all flowed into the great socialist
and communist currents of the nineteenth and twentieth centuries.

These new sects and churches of the 1960s and 1970s were something else. They were part of that rain of new gods upon the funeral
of the old God. And they confirm the truth with which this chapter
began: that deities and churches cannot be invented simply because
there is a need for them. They must grow out of the shared experience
of a people. The effective founders, the messiahs who make a difference, reveal what is already there, they prophesy the present. When
movements try to fabricate a religious experience the result is either
a concocted and ephemeral superficiality or else a new and monstrous
god.

4
THE INVERTED WORLD

WITH THE RISE of capitalism, the traditional society which was both cause and effect of the Judeo-Christian God began to disintegrate. "External insecurity and movement," Karl Marx wrote, "distinguish the bourgeois epoch from all previous periods of history. . . . The holy shudder of pious ecstasy . . . had been drowned in the ice-cold water of egotistical calculation. . . . All fixed and deeply rooted relations, with their train of venerable images and world views, were dissolved." That the greatest anti-capitalist of the modern world would hold such a theory hardly comes as a surprise. That his mentor in these matters, G. W. F. Hegel, the chosen philosopher of the Prussian monarchy, had the same analysis of the spiritual crisis is not so well known.

In *The Phenomenology of Spirit*, Hegel described the transition from feudalism to absolutism to bourgeois society. It was, he argued in his oblique way, a movement from aristocratic service to self-interest and the search for wealth. The result, he continued, is an "inverted world" in which good is evil, evil good, and language is as deranged as that music which " 'mixes thirty arias, French, Italian, tragic, comic. . . .' " Shameless lying becomes, as in *Rameau's Nephew* by Diderot, the greatest truth. As a result, human consciousness is "torn apart" (*das zerrissene Bewusstsein*). To be sure, Marx and Hegel differ profoundly with regard to how to respond to this situation they define in similar ways. They are, however, not counterposed as an "idealist" against a "materialist"—Hegel is often more of a "materialist" than most people calling themselves Marxist. Rather, the one is a contemplative and the other a revolutionary. That is the real, and enormous, difference between them.

Hegel and Marx did not simply understand—and invent—what has become a cliché in social science: that the death of God is implicated in the decline of human community. They developed that concept in rich and concrete interpretations of the social, political and economic history of religion—and the religious history of society, politics and economics. Only when the profundity of that accomplishment is appreciated can one move to their very different solutions to the spiritual crisis they had defined: Hegel's dream of a feudal capitalism, a classical Greece with modern industry; Marx's vision of a technologically advanced *Gemeinschaft*, of the primitive communism of prehistory become the sophisticated communism of post-history.

———— I ————

A philosopher as protean and complex as Hegel can hardly be summarized in a sentence or two. Yet there is an important partial truth that can be stated at the outset: he spent his entire life seeking for ways to cope with the death of God.

His sense of alienation did not derive only, or simply, from the religious crisis which he was one of the first to define. His world was torn apart by other forces, too, which was why wholeness and unity were such central categories for him. He was a German, living in the "anarchy" of a fragmented, largely fictional, empire: he experienced the capitalist division of labor, with its degradation of the work process, vicariously, through economists like Sir James Steuart and Adam Smith, but it made a deep impression on him even in economically backward Germany; and he saw, and feared, the rise of new social strata, a "mob" without a sense of its own proper place and dignity. As a theorist he was to integrate these various religious, political, economic and social factors into the concept of a societal totality; as a man he lived in the vortex of their interaction.

As a young man he was a radical critic of society and religion. He attacked Christ—comparing him unfavorably with Socrates—and Christianity. He saw Luther as a man who had abolished Catholic political authoritarianism only to substitute his own ideological authoritarianism for it. It was during these years that he sought a "people's religion" which would appeal to the heart and not, as with Kant's religion within the limits of mere reason, only to the head. In 1795, he wrote a letter to his friend, the philosopher Schelling, that, George Lichtheim has said, "sketched a scheme of liberation as far reaching as anything envisioned in the *Communist Manifesto*. . . ."

Hegel told Schelling:

> I believe that there is no better sign of the times than the fact that mankind as such is being represented with so much reverence. It is a proof that the halo which has surrounded the heads of the oppressors and gods of the earth has disappeared. The philosophers demonstrate this dignity [of man]; the people will learn to feel it and will not merely demand their rights, which have been trampled in the dust, but will take them and appropriate them for themselves. Religion and politics have played the same game. The former has taught what despotism wanted to teach: contempt for humanity and its incapacity to reach goodness and achieve something through man's own efforts. With the spreading of ideas about how things *should* be, the indifference of the people who always sit tight and take everything which is as eternal will vanish.

Hegel clearly moved away from his youthful enthusiasm. He went from the early rejection of Christianity to a reinterpretation of it as a radical faith and then, by 1800, he seemed utterly to contradict his letter to Schelling, declaring that one must "understand that what is must be, i.e. that it is not arbitrary or accidental. . . ." And yet, he admired the activist Napoleon and when he saw him in Jena in 1806 said that he had witnessed "the world soul ride through town." Even more to the point, Napoleon can be called the "hero" of Hegel's masterpiece, the *Phenomenology*, where he is pictured as the very culmination of history. That attitude—which Hegel maintained as late as 1813—was, it should be noted, subversive, identifying him with a foreign leader against the patriots of his own homeland.

In 1818, when he became a professor at Berlin—and, in effect, the court philosopher of the Prussian monarchy—he repudiated those pro-French sentiments. Even then, however, his *Philosophy of Right* was, in terms of civil liberties and religious tolerance, well to the Left of anything in Prussia. And his method, the Left Hegelians understood, could be used for the relentless criticism of the status quo as well as for its defense.*

In any case, the political analyses of the mature Hegel dealt with

*On Hegel's evolution, see Appendix D.

the same problems defined by the young Hegel: how, under the "torn-apart" conditions of life in the modern world, was it possible to create a sense of community which would unite the people in society and in a faith? From first to last, this theologian and philosopher was also a sociologist and political scientist who knew that life could not be made whole again in one of its aspects while it was fragmented in the others. For him—as for Marx—the religious question was the social, economical and political question as well.

Religion, as Hegel saw it, is philosophy developed in symbols and therefore accessible to the people even when they are illiterate (he anticipated Nietzsche, who called Christianity "Platonism for the masses"). It is precariously perched midway between sense perceptions and abstract thought, sharing some of the qualities of both. Moreover it is political, a fact that the rational religionists, like Kant, ignored. "The popular feasts of the Greeks," the young Hegel wrote (and the mature Hegel did not change on this count), "were all religious feasts to honor either a god or a man who had served the state well and therefore become godly."

Therefore, "Religion is the place where a people defines itself. . . . From this point of view religion is the closest of relationships with the state." In the Orient—and Hegel's analysis here is clearly limited by the scholarship of his time—there is despotism, and God is either the empty heaven of China or the One of India. The lack of subjectivity in the divine is a mirror image of the same lack in the great mass of the people: only one is free (the Emperor) and God is merely the One. In Greece, the gods have become more subjective, more human, and so have the citizenry, yet the latter are still constrained by the mores of the community, and slavery is the precondition of a kind of "democracy": some are free. In Christianity, the religion above all others, God becomes man in the Incarnation and/or man thereby becomes God. In principle, all are free, even though it may take centuries for the principle to assert itself, as in the belated Christian opposition to slavery.

These particular points are, of course, of a piece with a basic Hegelian insight concerning the interrelatedness of all social phenomena. As he put it in his youthful manuscript on a people's religion: "The spirit of a people and its history, its religion, its degree of political freedom, cannot be considered in isolation from one another and their reciprocal influence on one another. They are all woven together in a

unity." This idea was not new. Enlightenment historians like Montesquieu and Voltaire had made much the same point (and Hegel himself
acknowledged his debt to Montesquieu's "immortal work," *The Spirit
of Laws*).

But Hegel was to use that Enlightenment concept in a brilliant
attack on the Enlightenment which further emphasizes how profoundly
social his concept of religion was. The *philosophes*, he wrote in the
Phenomenology, see faith as a mass of superstition imposed on the
people by priests in league with despots. It therefore functions to
ensure the "peaceful domination" of superstitious subjects by their
cynical rulers. That, Hegel argues forcefully, is wrong; a people cannot
be deceived by their religion because religion is the expression *of* the
people, it is a refraction of their common life. The Enlightenment
denounces God as an alien being whom the priests foist off on the
uneducated—but the uneducated see themselves, are certain of themselves, in their religious rites. The problem, Hegel continues, is that
the Enlightenment looked for abstract reason in a sphere that speaks
in symbols. Worse, it derided the stone and wood and bread of religion
as if they were deified stone and wood and bread, and failed utterly
to understand that they were only external expressions of an indwelling
spirit.

Marx and Engels agreed. "A religion that brought the Roman
world empire into subject," Engels wrote of Christianity, "and
dominated by far the larger part of civilized humanity for 1800 years
cannot be disposed of merely by declaring it to be nonsense gleaned together by frauds." But there is a problem here and it is signaled by
the fact that atheists could support the views of a man who spoke in
terms of Christianity. If religion is a "representation" (*Vorstellung*)
of truths which philosophy thinks through abstractly, then isn't
religion less than philosophy? Or, to put it even more strongly, isn't
religion only valid until Hegel reveals the rational truth contained
in its myths? That, I think, is the view of the *Phenomenology*,
but the lectures on religion (which date from Hegel's years at Berlin
as an official philosopher) tend to see philosophy and religion as simply
two ways, each valuable in its own right, of articulating a
single truth.

However, the debate over whether Hegel the manifest Christian
was a latent atheist need not concern us here. For our purposes it is
enough to stress his social and political definition of what religion is.

And that, in turn, points toward his dynamic analysis of how religion changes in history.

For Hegel, above all in the *Phenomenology*, individuals, societies, religions and arts are aspects of a single historic process and go through an interrelated development. Thus, the merely sensuous life of the infant corresponds to primitive society with its nature gods (the sun, totemic animals). It is with the emergence of reason and self-consciousness—"in the vigorous youth of spiritual life," in classical Greece—that the intertwining of Western religion and society begins. Hegel leaves out a great deal of history (most of the Middle Ages) and focuses on three turning points: the rise and fall of Greek and Roman society; the consequent emergence of Christianity out of Judaism and the Greco-Roman crisis; the victorious struggle of Enlightenment reason against religious faith and the void which opens up in Western mankind in the early nineteenth century. In all of this, since religion is seen as social, the crisis of religion is *ipso facto* a crisis of society.

For Hegel, as for almost every artist and thinker of his generation in Germany, ancient Greece (and to a lesser extent, Rome) was a utopia masquerading as a historic place. He saw it as a civilization in which the people were not torn apart, a triumph of harmony over alienation. It produced the religion of beauty, of the glorification of man, and that was the source of its rise as well as of its fall.

In his enormously influential analysis, *On the Aesthetic Education of Men*, Schiller had anticipated much of the Hegelian dialectic. In the modern age, he wrote, the emergence of independent sciences and the complex class structure meant that "the inner bonds of human nature were torn asunder and a ruinous quarrel shatters its harmonious power." But in Greece, people were whole, in unity with nature. Yet they were not primitive, since they brought both art and wisdom to nature, perching, so to speak, midway between the raw simplicity of the early times and the sophisticated alienation of the contemporary world. And once this synthesis was achieved, it was inevitable that it would break down, for that was the precondition for the development of "the manifold talents in humanity."

The young Hegel gave a rather Jacobin interpretation of this standard German theme, writing of the "free republican" of ancient Greece or Rome who is so at one with his society that he gives his life without question. There is no split between freedom and authority, subjective and objective, in this imagined Greece: "What can an Oedipus demand for forgiveness of the guilt of his unguilty grief, since he believes himself in the service of, under obedience to, a fate?" For the Greek, "the idea of his fatherland, of his state, was the invisible and higher value for which he worked, that which drove him, the purpose of the world. . . ." That, not so incidentally, was the exact opposite of the German, living in an empire which was not an empire, a state which was not a state. In short, the Greek religion did not just unify the society; it was the motivating force within every individual psyche.

As he matured and as he became somewhat disillusioned with the French Revolution, Hegel dropped the references to republican virtue, but expanded on almost all of the other elements in his idyllic picture of Greek life. That society was for him the very model of *"Sittlichkeit,"* a term that has to be described rather than translated. Under conditions of *Sittlichkeit*, the individual lives in immediate unity with his community and its "substance." That substance is the unchanging, unquestionable, pre-existing unity of a free people organized by custom and law into social hierarchies in which, however, "the individual is satisfied with the limitations of his existence. . . ." That is not the simple tribal unity of those peoples which worship nature gods (the sun, animals); it is the complex unity of a stratified, but nonantagonistic, society. Its God is therefore not a natural force, but spiritual.

The original Greek gods, Hegel said in his lectures on the philosophy of religion, were simply storms and thunder. But they became spiritual, subjective—and political. This happened—the Marxist Hegel is at hand—when men achieved domination over nature and were no longer the plaything of its elemental powers. "The consciousness of this subjugation of the natural powers by the spiritual powers was expressed by the Greeks [in religious myth] in Zeus's victory over the nature gods, their dethroning, and the establishment of the power of the spiritual gods." There were, to be sure, ancient divinities, like the Furies, which had a spiritual aspect, but it was raw and undeveloped. "On the contrary, Zeus is the political god, the god of *laws*, of domination, but of *known* laws, not the laws of the conscience." That last phrase, contrasting "known laws" to "laws of the conscience," is an attack on the merely subjective morality of Kant and much of the German classical philosophy; it is Hegel's oblique way of saying that the laws of a society must be palpable and objective, not merely the expression of individual subjectivity.

For Hegel this political-religious spiritualization of the gods in

Greece even glimpsed the possibility Christianity was to realize: that God is man and vice versa. The humanization of the heavens proceeds to such a degree that Heracles, who is only human, may succeed Zeus on the throne. But even though that does not come to fruition (until Christ dethrones Zeus), Greek religion keeps changing. At first, Zeus rules as a patriarchal god, the father of the divine house. But then there develops the notion of a higher power, of a fate, a necessity that stands above even the gods. This reaches its height in Sophoclean tragedy: "the fate of the individual is presented as something which cannot be understood in concepts, yet the necessity is not blind but recognized as true justice."

In all of this, a dialectic is at work, and it eventually destroys the utopia from within. The Greeks were more individual than any previous people; their gods were more and more spiritual, expressed in a religion of art, in visions of the divinity of the human. But precisely because of that extraordinary unity, precisely because the laws were objective and not a matter of individual conscience, this magnificent culture lacked the fullness of subjectivity and self-consciousness. Because of this it tolerated slavery: it did not understand the imperishable worth of each and every individual; because of this it was a particular, not a universal, society. It was good and necessary that individuality come to such a civilization—and it was utterly destructive.

The young Hegel, who saw the civic virtue of Greek and Roman society as an anticipation of the French Revolution's spirit, described how this individuality arrived in very concrete terms:

> Fortunate wars, the increase in wealth and familiarity with more of the good things of life produced in Athens and Rome an aristocracy of military distinction and money, with domination and influence over many men. . . . there was a loss of that consciousness which Montesquieu described under the name of virtue and made the principle of republicanism, that readiness of the individual to sacrifice himself for an idea which, for the republican, is realized in the fatherland.

The mature Hegel still had an economic dimension in his analysis of Greek decadence—he saw, for instance, that Athenian democracy was based on a class of excluded slaves—but he shifted that thesis more and more to Roman society.

In Rome, a "spiritless community" emerges based on individual rights but no longer binding people together. Philosophy becomes Stoic—

it retreats into subjectivity—and then Skepticism doubts the very existence of an external world. At the same time, an empire is created—Hegel personifies it as the "lord of the world"—and the abstract unrelatedness of Roman society becomes international. The nations are so many separate entities gathered in an abstract "community" ruled by a foreign power (Hegel is deeply indebted to Montesquieu for this thesis). All this culminates in an unforgettable image (in the *Phenomenology*) of the corruption of *Sittlichkeit* in the ancient world:

> Trust in the eternal laws of the gods is silenced as well as trust in oracles. . . . The temples are only corpses from which the animating soul has fled, the hymns are only words without belief, the tables of the gods are without spiritual food and drink and their games and feasts no longer give a joyful sense of their unity with their essence. The works of the Muse lack the power of the spirit, that certainty of self which came out of the crushing of gods and men.

The "idealist" Hegel thus explains the decline of Greek and Roman society in terms of the shattering of the community which their religion expressed. That breakdown was one of the preconditions for the rise of Christianity. Judaism was another precondition.

Since Hegel is often quite sharp in his characterization of Jewish theology and life, it is important to note at the outset that he was not an anti-Semite. In his *Philosophy of Right* he explicitly attacks political anti-Semitism, at a time when it was very much on the rise in Prussia. Moreover, his most stringent critique of Judaism is found in his (unpublished) essay on "the positivity of the Christian religion" in which he is at least as acid toward the Christians as toward the Jews. Finally, Hegel's view of Judaism is extremely dialectical: it is precisely their unhappy consciousness, itself the product of a world-historical advance in the human concept of God, that prepares the way for Christianity, which, for the mature Hegel, is the highest form of belief.

Hegel saw the Jews as the first people to envision God as a truly spiritual being. In simpler times, he said in his lectures on the philosophy of religion, the gods were seen as friendly, and people lived in unity with them and with nature. But then that unity was shattered, and men and women were torn in two (*Entzweiung*), counterposed to nature. With the loss of that primal innocence and wholeness came alienation. For the young Hegel, the Biblical account of the Flood reflects that loss of confidence in nature. But for the mature Hegel, the tree of the knowledge of good and evil in paradise is a much more profound symbol, "the eternal myth of how man became man."

The Biblical paradise is a poetic representation of that primitive oneness with nature which actually existed. In it, humans (who were not yet really human) did not know of good or evil any more than animals did or do now. And the eating of the apple—which God condemns because it is man's attempt to become godlike—is the new, and sad, knowledge of human alienation, of man's doubleness, of the war between subject and object, freedom and reality, and so on. The Jews dream of an end to the punishment of this original sin—"The snake's head will be trod under"—but for Hegel that will only come with the emergence of Christianity (and in the Catholic iconography, Mary is presented as crushing the head of the Satanic snake).

For Hegel, the Eastern religions also know that humanity has been "torn apart" from nature, yet their conception of God does not really differentiate him from the cosmos. It is in Judaism that the deity first appears as a spiritual being ruling over nature. This makes the Jews the first Westerners. And yet, this sublime definition of the nature of God involves the degradation of man. If God is all, then "the highest worth of man is to know himself as nothing." Jean Hippolyte writes in his commentary on the *Phenomenology:*

> The Jewish people were [for Hegel] the unhappy people in history because they represented the first total projection of consciousness outside of life. While the Greeks remained within life and achieved a harmonious unity of the self and nature, transposing thought into nature and nature into thought, the Hebrews incessantly counterposed themselves to nature and life. By that fact they discovered a more profound subjectivity than the Greeks.

It is this misery which gives the Jews their "world-historical importance," Hegel wrote; they are the first people to see spirit as absolute self-consciousness in God. In the Psalms of David and in the Prophets, this becomes a lovely yearning for God and for justice.

But it is also the basis for a servility in Jewish life in which God is the lord and the Jews merely his passive serfs. Therefore their religion becomes primarily a matter of obedience to positive laws with regard to food and dress. The whole Hebrew nation, the young Hegel said, was like a monastery. Indeed, there was a flagrant contradiction between the universal and monotheistic conception of God—an enor-

mous advance in human consciousness, a victory over the particularism
of all the nature gods—and the assertion that this universal God had
identified with one, and only one, people. Jesus was to attack Jewish
legalism and counterpose his doctrine of love to it.

Both the young and the mature Hegel agreed that Christ's coming
was related to the political defeat of the Jews. Israel was subjected
to a foreign yoke and there were attempts at spiritual renewal, like
that of the Essenes. But the Jews in defeat did not, as the Roman
Stoics had done, simply deny the existence of external evil and retreat
into a passive consciousness. Rather, they purified and spiritualized
their vision of God, and this was to prepare the way for Christ. Twentieth-century social science corroborates Hegel's reading. The Messiah
as an eschatological figure is, Guenter Lewy argues, a late development
in Judaism, appearing

> against the background of the loss of Judean independence in the apoc-
> alyptic writings popular during the days of Roman rule and oppression.
> Confronted with a reality that seemed to contradict Yahweh's promises
> to his people, his people longed for a personal saviour who would restore
> Israel to its former greatness and at the same time inaugurate a new age
> of happiness for the entire human race.

So there are social and political dimensions to Hegel's theory of
Jewish greatness—in being the first people to formulate the historic
break with nature—and Jewish unhappiness—which arises out of the
conception of God himself, and then out of the experience of political
defeat, and prepares the way for Christianity. And Hegel's interpretation of the rise of Christianity further emphasizes his insistence upon
the links between politics and religion: it is where he first developed
his analysis of revolution—an analysis later borrowed by Karl Marx.

The victory of Christianity over the entire pagan world, he wrote
in 1795–96, was simply a ratification of a sea change that had already
taken place. There had been a "quiet, secret revolution in the spirit
of the age" and it is this reality which explains what happened. So the
mature Hegel will see the French Revolution as the overthrow of a
monarchy which had already become unreal and will liken the triumph
of the Enlightenment to the spreading of a scent which permeates the
atmosphere before it is even identified. Revolutions are thus the culmination of evolutions, the *de jure* recognition of a *de facto* transformation.

What was the basis of that "quiet, secret revolution" of Christianity? The intersection of a number of decadences. The Jews were, as we have just seen, defeated, and that led them to spiritualize the idea of the Messiah; the traditional mores (*Sitte*) of Greek society were subverted by the rise of individualism. But it was in Rome that the critical moment occurred. In the Roman world, "men no longer found satisfaction in what had previously satisfied them." Culture lost its capacity to explain nature or ethics and "the world sorrows over its present, and there is doubt and unbelief everywhere. . . ." The very heart of the world, Hegel wrote, was broken and it was "only out of this feeling that it is possible for the free spirit of Christianity, rising above the merely sensuous, to emerge."

As the young Hegel described the moment, "The despotism of the Roman princes had expelled the spirit of man from the surface of the earth, the rape of freedom had forced people to take refuge in the eternal, the absolute, in divinity, the poverty which was spreading forced them to seek and wait for their happiness in heaven. The objectivity of the Godhead vanishes in step with the corruption and slavery of men. . . ." The result is a total collapse of public spirit—a refusal, for example, of military service. Impotence is made a duty and an honor, and when the barbarians menace Rome a Christian saint has the people pray to God for deliverance rather than defend themselves on the city walls.

All of this drives people inward and discredits the "objective" gods. The Stoics and the Skeptics articulate this trend in philosophy, but their inwardness, their discovery of self-consciousness, is only one of the many forms of a change in the very way people think. Under these political, social and cultural circumstances, the young Hegel said, ideas become chimeric and one looks for salvation from an individual—from Christ. And this bears on Hegel's account of the social origins of the doctrine of the evil in human nature derived from original sin.

The early Christians, he wrote, were passive, wishing for an end to their crisis, but incapable of willing it, waiting first for the imminent return of Christ and then postponing the second coming to the end of the world:

In the womb of this corrupted humanity which despised itself morally but still held itself high as the favored of God, the doctrine of the corruption of human nature must be produced and adopted. On the one hand, it coincides with the experience of these people; on the other, it helps their pride by taking their guilt away . . . by making it a sin to believe in power.

The mature Hegel did not dwell on this point but, rather, emphasizes the breakthrough represented by the Christian concept of God. But even here, when he was treating the complex doctrine of the Trinity, he emphasized the social roots of theological subtlety.*

The earliest notions of God had seen him—it—as a force of nature. Then, with the Greeks and Indians, there were more sophisticated theories, and even anticipations of the Trinity in Indian mythology, Pythagorean mysticism and Aristotle. But all of these notions located the deity in the far beyond, outside of the world, and Aristotle, who came closest to the truth, was still quite abstract. Now, however, there was a new force at work, not simply among philosophers, but among the people. "Faith," Hegel points out, is a Christian term: the commitment to an inner conviction apart from tribal or social identity. The Greeks did not talk of their "faith" in Zeus, or the Egyptians in Apis. But the Christians, the children of a time of sorrowing subjectivity, were introspective about their God. And since they were subjective so was their God.

Hegel was, of course, aware that the theology of the Trinity was not developed by simple people and owed much, for instance, to the Jewish neo-Platonist Philo, who was himself a product of this age of decadence. The famous prologue to the Gospel of John is hardly the expression of folk wisdom but, rather, as Peter Berger puts it, "a world-shattering marriage of reason and revelation . . . in which the Greek idea of logos is identified with the Jewish Messiah. . . ." And yet the political and institutional victory of these subtle ideas was only possible because there was a community which had gone through the quiet—and not particularly edifying—revolution occasioned by the decadence of Rome. They had been prepared for a radically subjective vision of God.

God was therefore no longer the distant abstraction of Greek philosophy or even the fearful Lord of Hebrew theology. He was now spirit, three *persons* in one nature. That God the Son becomes man means, for Hegel, that God entered into history, became part of nature

*See Appendix E.

and human life and therefore opened up the possibility that men might rise up to God. All this was, to be sure, expressed in earthly images, of fatherhood and sonhood, but there was a profound truth in them nevertheless. Now there was a universal, nontribal and spiritual God who recognized himself in humanity—and allowed humanity to see itself in him. The particular, the natural, the parochial had been stripped away from the vision of divinity, which was why Hegel regarded Christianity as the highest form of religion, in a sense as the only religion. And this advance in theological consciousness could not be explained apart from the mundane facts of Roman economic, social, political and cultural history.

But how did that community of early Christians turn into the Roman Catholic Church and come to need a Martin Luther to reform it?

The young Hegel gives an answer to that question which is quite close to the famous twentieth-century distinction made by Ernst Troeltsch: the Christian sect became the Catholic Church. It is part of Hegel's theory of religious revolution, itself the prototype of his description of social and political revolution. An established church, he argues, becomes routinized and ceremonial (the Jews before Christ). A reformer appears who attempts to give spirit and life to the dead doctrine (Christ), and he and his followers initially form a sect of the convinced. But if that sect succeeds, it in its turn becomes established, turns into a church and is in need of a new sectarian challenge. When, as was the case with Christianity, the sect-become-church also achieves political power, becoming worldly rather than spiritual, that process is still further accentuated.

For Hegel, the Middle Ages were an unfortunate interlude of a thousand or so years between the rise of Christianity and the Reformation. The power of the spirit (*Geist*) turned into the power of the priests (*Geistlich*) and the Church became a secular force. As a result, Roman Catholicism became a kind of theocracy and this entire historical period was characterized by barbarism, albeit a barbarism of the highest type, perverting the most noble of ideas. Hegel, in short, was in the grip of an Enlightenment view of the medieval period, and his treatment of it is perfunctory and shallow.

Then comes Luther. The young and radical Hegel, we have seen, was quite critical of the German reformer, accusing him of an authoritarianism only slightly less objectionable than the one he attacked. For the mature Hegel Luther represents a turning point in human history even more important than the French Revolution. That dramatic shift in interpretation is, as Georg Lukacs argued, probably linked to Hegel's becoming the "official" Prussian philosopher. Yet Hegel still spoke of 1789 as "a magnificent sunrise" and said that, at the time of the Reformation, "the world was not yet ripe for a political restructuring based on the reform of the Church." This is a delicate way of admitting that Luther made an alliance with Protestant princes against peasant revolutionaries bent on establishing the kingdom of God on earth.

If the Reformation did not lead to revolution, the Enlightenment did. Hegel's analysis of his philosophic predecessors is critical, even biting, but respectful. For him, the Enlightenment was another one of those "quiet revolutions." It spread through the society, invisible and unnoticed, and then—Hegel quoted from *Rameau's Nephew*—" '*on one fine morning* it gives its comrade / the god it has infiltrated / a shove with its elbows and bang! crash! the god lies on the ground.' " So it is that reason is victorious over superstition, over faith. It has derided the priest-ridden masses and sought to save them from their intellectual subjugation.

But—and the question which Hegel asked has not yet been satisfactorily answered—"when all prejudices and superstitions have been banished . . . *what next? What is the truth which the Enlightenment has prepared in place of the one it destroyed?*" In fact, the Enlightenment's alternative was the French Revolution. But for Hegel, even though it marked that "magnificent sunrise," the Revolution was driven, by excessive rationalism, to wipe out those intermediate institutions which buffer the individual from the state, and ultimately to the Terror itself. Thus it was part of that modern trend toward "abstract" politics, toward a society in which all the customary bonds were being shattered. It was, in short, an incarnation of the "torn-apart" consciousness.

So was capitalism. Part of the shift from the young Hegel to the author of the *Phenomenology* occurred because of his readings in economics, first through the influence of Sir James Steuart, then through that of Adam Smith. In *Jenaer Realphilosophie*, a remarkable manuscript of 1805–06 (posthumously published), there are almost Marxist comments on the way in which capitalist wealth creates poverty, misery, the stunting of human life in the factory. Those same ideas are repeated in the *Philosophy of Right* (from Hegel's conservative period). So Enlightenment rationalism, Hegel thought, had corrupted popular faith without providing any new alternative; French Revolutionary rationalism had created an "abstract" society without human mediation; and capitalism was ripping community apart. The result? "As in the time of the Roman Empire, because the general unity of religion had vanished and the gods had been profaned and political life was without wisdom or trust, reason took refuge in private rights . . . and private well-being was turned into an end in itself, *so it is now*." But if the modern age is as torn-apart as ancient Rome, what will the new equivalent of Christianity be?

At first glance the answer seems simple: Hegel substitutes the state for God. He was one of the first modern political idolators. In a remarkably concise statement of his point of view in the lectures on the philosophy of religion he argues that at the beginning of history both absolute truth and man's understanding of it are incomplete. That truth is abstract, not yet real and in the world; and human consciousness has only glimmerings of it, expressed in mythic gods who are merely nature in disguise. But over time, absolute truth and man's knowledge of it—objectivity and subjectivity—move on converging paths. As human subjectivity becomes more rational, absolute truth thereby becomes a worldly force. The culmination of this process is the state. It is the "shining forth of the divine life," the universal as an actually existing community. In such a society, Hegel said in his lectures on the philosophy of history, "the counterposition of freedom and necessity vanishes." The state is based on reason and therefore reasonable individuals find their fullest freedom in obeying it. Subjectivity is objective and vice versa.

Isn't it clear that we are in the presence of a philosopher who is rationalizing the totalitarian state as a replacement for the dead God? Isn't this, as Karl Lowith argued, the new religion of the " 'educated' . . . whose skepticism is not vigorous enough to live entirely without faith"? And the decisive proof of this reading, it is argued, is provided by Hegel himself. In the *Philosophy of Right* he asserts "the state is the march of God through the world." Sidney Hook, and others, cite such statements as evidence for the indictment of Hegel as at least an authoritarian. But did the philosopher actually make that substitution of the state for God?

I think not. The quotation about the march of God was an inter-

polation in a posthumous edition based on lecture notes, and the editor
himself noted that such additions were not to be taken literally or
verbatim. But much more to the point, Hegel was ambiguous in his
actual political attitudes. It is a simplification to say, as generations
of scholars have argued, following the lead of Rudolf Haym, that "the
Hegelian system became the scientific abode of the spirit of the Prussian Restoration." That is true—and not true. Which is to say that
Hegel, like everyone else trying to work out a practical response to
the death of God, is quite confused.

All he wanted to do when he got down to cases was to square a
circle. He was, as Raymond Plant has noted, opposed to the French
Revolution *and* to Enlightened despotism *and* to political democracy,
and yet he regarded the growth of subjectivity, of individual freedom,
as the great triumph of history. He was against the liberal theory of
the state, from Hobbes to Kant, because it accepted atomization of
social life. He was appalled by the self-seeking of the emergent capitalist order for the same reason and terrified of the "mob" which was
produced by a society in which wealth and poverty marched together.
His analysis, as Lucio Colletti rightly insists, parallels Marx's and is
much more profound than Feuerbach's. He was, for instance, the first
philosopher to understand that economics is the basis of the modern
world.

But when he comes to solutions, Hegel was either excessively
pragmatic or excessively utopian. Ultimately, he defined religion in
almost Marxist-Weberian terms as the faith of capitalist society. It is
the glory of Protestantism, as compared with Catholicism, he writes
in the *Encyclopedia*, that it honors marriage rather than celibacy,
work as against charity, rational obedience as against blind obedience.
In this guise, as Colletti says, Hegel has a "bourgeois Christian" ideal.
But, as we have seen, he does not really accept bourgeois society. So
in the *Philosophy of Right* he dreams up a system in which workers
will belong to "corporations," a cross between medieval guilds and the
"syndicates" of corporatist theory: the bureaucracy is a universal class
and the king a necessity.

What Hegel wanted was a modern society as organic as the Greece
of his youthful imagination. But that is a contradiction in terms. And
if this great thinker undeniably left many comments which could be
construed in an authoritarian or totalitarian manner, his real failure

was that his analysis of the loneliness of a social world without God is so much more brilliant than his proposals for coping with it. Here is the thinker who, as Jean-Yves Calvez has remarked, is *the* source of all of the discussions of religion and society in the nineteenth century— and, I would add, of much of the debate in the twentieth. He made an unforgettable study of the social roots and consequences of the death of God but provided no answers to his own questions.

His greatest pupil—a student greater than the teacher—not only deepened his analysis but also tried to come up with practical solutions to the crisis it revealed. I speak, of course, of Karl Marx.

——— I I ———

One sentence by Karl Marx is routinely taken as an accurate summary of his analysis of religion: "Religion is the opium of the people."

As the Catholic theologian Hans Küng shrewdly points out, even those few words are regularly misread. People think that Marx said that religion is opium *for* the people; the actual comment is that it is the opium *of* the people. Opium *for* the people is the Enlightenment theory: that the rulers consciously use faith in order to keep the people politically quiescent. Opium *of* the people is one part of the Marxist thesis: that religion objectively functions to divert attention from human suffering, or even to rationalize it, but that this is the consequence of a structure of society and of history, not the outcome of a ruling-class plot. As a pupil of Hegel in this area Marx inevitably had that second, anti-Enlightenment attitude.

Even more to the point, that famous sentence about religion as opium is preceded by one of the most generous tributes religion has ever received, from an atheist or a believer. ". . . religion is an *inverted consciousness* because the world is an *inverted world*," the young Marx wrote in 1844. He continued:

> Religion is the general theory of this world, its encyclopaedic compen-
> dium, its logic in popular form, its spiritual point of honor, its enthusiasm,
> its moral sanction, its solemn competition, its universal basis of trust and
> justification. It is the *fantastic realization* of the human essence because
> the *human essence* possess no other reality. The struggle against religion
> is also mediately the struggle against *that world* whose spiritual aroma

religion is. Religious poverty is an *expression* of actual poverty on the
one hand and a *protest* against actual poverty on the other. Religion is
the sigh of the oppressed creation, the heart of a heartless world, just
as it is the spirit of a spiritless situation.

Küng is right. For Marx, "religion is not simply the invention of
swindling priests or rulers. Religion is the utterance of suffering humanity in its quest for consolation." Moreover, that phrase "the opium
of the people" was, as a number of scholars have understood, not an
invention of Marx's but an idea that was in the air, not the least, as
the Jesuit Henri de Lubac acknowledged in his study of Proudhon,
because it was quite true.* But if Marx is quite Hegelian on this point—
much more so than Feuerbach, with whom Marx is usually linked—
he also has a perception which is parallel to, but significantly different
from, Hegel's. For Hegel, the modern world was "inverted," upside
down (*Verkehrt*); for Marx, *any* class society is an "inverted" world in
the sense that the real powers of men and women take the form of
alien powers (political, economic and social) which dominate them. If
Marx agreed with Hegel that the contemporary—capitalist—world is
particularly and uniquely topsy-turvy, it is within the framework of a
class analysis of that phenomenon which applies to all history, ancient
Greece included.

But what separated Marx from both Hegel and Feuerbach—and
we now come to the theoretical underpinnings of his political attitude
toward religion as discussed in the last chapter—is, of course, his
revolutionary perspective. This is the Marxist answer to the death of
God and the inverted, torn-apart world in which it takes place. It is
not enough, Marx wrote in his "Theses on Feuerbach," to argue that
the earthly family is the "secret," the basis, of the heavenly family.
That is only the beginning of a process which then requires the revolutionary transformation of family life on earth, the creation of a
society of justice in which there will no longer be a need for religion.
Hegel was the sworn foe of positivism, of accepting the facts as facts
and not placing them in their intellectual (ideal) context. But ultimately, the young Marx held, Hegel is the agent of a "false positivism,"
"an uncritical positivism." At the end of the Hegelian system, nothing
was changed in the world—except that it is not *understood* in terms

*See Appendix F.

of its hidden meaning. "Man, who has learned to recognize that he leads an alienated life in law, politics, etc., leads in that same alienated life his true human life."

The point, Marx shrewdly aruged, is not that Hegel made an "accommodation" with religion and the state. This is, so to speak, the gossip's critique of him, the *ad hominem* attack. What is critical is that this accommodation—this "lie"—is a basic principle of his philosophy. Therefore, if Marx shares Hegel's analysis of religion as a social phenomenon to a degree not normally recognized, he still differs profoundly with him on this count. Indeed, this is *the* difference between the two thinkers: that the one is a revolutionary and the other a thinker who contemplates reality but leaves it unaltered.

Marx, in short, has an answer to the death of God: create a society which will not feel lonely without God, and then God will disappear. He does not look forward to an atheist society, for that implies the need to deny God. He sees the coming of a communism in which the question of God will simply not exist. Therefore, he writes, atheism will no longer make any sense. Marx, as the Jesuit scholar Jean-Yves Calvez realized, is a practical atheist, a proponent of the *fact* of atheism, not the doctrine of atheism, which will become superfluous. That is why a "Marxist" campaign against religion as such is completely un-Marxist.

Marx's answer to the death of God is much more profound than Hegel's. But before examining whether or not it is adequate—and relevant today—we must deepen the account of his analysis of religion. In the process we will understand that, contrary to the seemingly obvious evidence of his writings, Marx did not take up the issue of religion as a young man and then ignore it for the rest of his life. Rather, his perceptions with regard to God are basic to themes which will concern him all of his life. To paraphrase a famous comment of Lenin's, whoever has not grasped Marx's theory of religion cannot understand *Das Kapital*.

Unfortunately, the critical Marxist document in this area is one that fairly invites misunderstanding, the essay *On the Jewish Question*, written in 1843. The second half of that work is filled with references which equate Jewishness with greed, commercialism and the like. They use—and there can be no doubt on this issue—an anti-Semitic vocabulary. Whether they prove that Marx was an anti-Semite—a classic "self-hating Jew"—is another question. I will merely state my conclu-

sion here and annotate it in an appendix: Marx, like practically everyone else of his generation including the first Zionist, Moses Hess, wrote
in a vein which was objectively anti-Semitic but without himself being
an anti-Semite.*

What is important from the point of view of this book is that Marx's
analysis of Judaism—and Christianity—makes these religions para-
digms of economic and social relations. More broadly, the structure of
alienation, which Marx first defined with a religious context, provides
him with an understanding which he then applies to economics and
social structure. This is why religious metaphors and analogies play a
central role throughout Marx's life—why they are key to the compre-
hension of *Das Kapital*.

The Jews, the young Marx wrote, are without political power;
indeed, they are second-class citizens (and, not so incidentally, a major
purpose of this polemic with its anti-Semitic language is to argue the
need for a specific defense of Jewish rights!). But Jewish wealth is
enormously influential. (Hannah Arendt documented this reality in *The
Origins of Totalitarianism*.) "The contradiction between the practical
political power of the Jews," Marx concludes, "and their political rights,
is the contradiction between politics and the power of money in general.
While ideally politics stands above money, in fact politics has become
money's servant."

For Marx it is the essence of bourgeois democracy that the citizens
are, before the law, theoretically equal and, in point of social and
economic fact, basically unequal. The Jews dramatize this basic capitalist contradiction since their economic power more than compensates
for their second-class citizenship. Capitalism is then seen as basically
"Jewish" because it is characterized by the very same asymmetry of
political and economic power that defines upper-class Jewish life in
nineteenth-century Europe. Then Marx used a similar analogy to prove
that the capitalist state, even when it is officially agnostic, is really
Christian.

This paradox was explained in the course of a discussion of one of
the most exceptional political-religious situations in the modern world:
the United States. In the 1840s, when Marx was writing, the United
States was a remarkable example of a nation without an official religion.
In Germany, this period saw the elaboration of Julius von Stahl's official

*See Appendix G.

theology of the Christian state. Therefore, Bruno Bauer, Marx's antagonist on this occasion, held that one should fight, not for the civil liberty to be a Jew, but for the abolition of all religious privileges, Christian as well as Jewish. That, he thought, would lead to genuine human emancipation.

Look at the United States, Marx replied. There is no established religion and yet, as Tocqueville and Beaumont document, it is the most religious country in the world. As Beaumont put it—and Max Weber was later to emphasize—"in the United States they do not believe that a nonreligious man can be an honest man." So, Marx answered Bauer, the state can emancipate itself from religion while the society is still very religious. Why? Because capitalism itself is a secularized version of Christianity. The democratic state, where everyone is theoretically equal, is its heaven; the economy, where there is enormous inequality, is its vale of tears. Where the people once looked to the Church for salvation, they now look to the state. Their psychology, their mindset, remains religious even though the government proclaims itself atheist.

Moses Hess had made the same point in 1845 when he talked of the "atheistic Christians" who had repudiated God but—in the name of some higher value—had retained that basic dualism of the miserable world of reality and the perfect world to come. For Hess—and for Marx—what was required was not a new beyond but the genuine life of people in the here and now. They were, therefore, critics not simply of Christianity, but of the Christian mind-set even when it was totally secularized, of all ideologies which leave social evil unchallenged in the name of some distant kingdom to come.

Marx, then, was the foe of all gods, of atheist and secular deities as well as the supernatural (which makes his present status as the prophet of a state church in the Soviet Union all the more obscene). His ultimate vision throughout his life remained, I think, one in which communism was seen as a "naturalism," as "the *real* dissolution of the contradictions between men and nature and men and men, the real dissolution of the conflict between existence and essence, between objectification and self-assertion [*Selbstbestätigung*], between freedom and necessity, the individual and the species." And any ideology which leaves those basic contradictions intact is, like secular democracy, religious, for it divides life into a heaven to come and an earth that is.

It was Friedrich Engels who most clearly stated how anti-supernaturalist this point of view is. That was an irony, since Engels—who, unlike Marx, went through a protracted religious crisis—in his later years sometimes became a rather mystical materialist, attributing divine and providential qualities to matter itself.* And yet, in the *Dialectics of Nature* (a collection of writings from the years 1873 to 1886), a book which contains more than a little of that mystical materialism, Engels shows himself, as Gustav Mayer puts it, as a "cosmic pessimist" as well as a "dialectical optimist." Communism, he argues, will not solve everything, not the least because eventually the earth itself will be unable to sustain human life.

> Millions of years may come and go, hundreds of thousands of generations may be born and die; but inexorably the time comes when the sun exhausts itself and its warmth is no longer sufficient to melt the ice coming from the poles . . . and finally there is not enough warmth for life itself. Gradually the last traces of life disappear and the earth becomes a dead, frozen globe, like the moon. . . .

Marx and Engels's supreme value, then, is totally of this world. And yet, as Lucien Goldmann pointed out, there is a Marxist "wager," in the Pascalian sense of the word. It is, however, a wager, not on a distant God or a providence, but upon the ability of men and women to create a future whose basic principles will be, not supernatural or outside of history, but supra-individual. Humans would not discover a substitute for God but, rather, in living up to their own potential for the first time in history, they would find out that there was no need for God. That was the truly radical response to the death of the traditional God.

How has it worked? We now judge Marx by hindsight. His basic analysis, we have seen, was shared with Hegel: religion is the expression of community and it is in crisis in the modern world—God is dying—because community is being torn apart by the reality of capitalist society. His alternative, the creation of a new, communist community with no need for God, was distinctively his own.

Marx thought history would execute the dying God. Actually, it has sentenced him to euthanasia.

Marx changed his mind on how "revolutionary"—how abrupt and

*See Appendix H.

sudden—the communist revolution would be. In his youth—indeed, up until 1850, when he was recovering from the disappointment of his hopes for the Revolution of 1848—he thought that socialism was imminent, a matter of years. But in 1850 he realized that capitalism was not in its death throes but its birth pangs, and therefore conceded that its successor might not come for half a century. We now know that he was profoundly wrong on this account, for it is almost a century and a half since he adopted the slower scenario for socialism and the long-awaited moment has yet to come. It was Antonio Gramsci, one of the most brilliant of the Marxists after Marx, who systematized the needed revision and understood that the struggle for Marx's future would take place over an entire historic epoch and—particularly important from my point of view—would involve a battle for socialist "hegemony" in the institutions of culture, most specifically including religion.

But if Marx, and then Gramsci, revised the time schedule for the socialist revolution, neither doubted that, when it came, it would mark a decisive break, not simply in the economic organization of society, but in human consciousness as well. They envisioned, as a present-day Marxist, Antonio Banfi, puts it, a "Copernican man . . . for whom there is no metaphysical outlook, who acts as a part of nature, who completes his own historic work and so achieves the universality of consciousness and the rationality of knowledge. . . ." There would be a *de facto* atheism—or, rather, irrelevance of God—brought about as a by-product of the revolutionary transformation.

There is indeed a *de facto* atheism in the West today, but it did not come about as a result of a heroic struggle to create a new type of human consciousness. God is dying, but without an heir. Or, more precisely, the heir is not the heroic, this-worldly consciousness of Marx's communism but the this-worldly consciousness of a hedonistic capitalism which wallows in an eternal, spiritless present. This is part of the price being paid for the failure of that socialist transformation Marx sought. Whether it is a terminal condition in Western culture or a limited phenomenon in a much more protracted transition to a just society depends on political analyses which go far beyond the scope of this book. Suffice it to say that whatever the future may bring, the century since Marx's death has disappointed his hopes and at least temporarily falsified his theories.

But what if the long-waited change finally does come? I am not talking about some worldly perfection, a utopia in the present, for no serious Marxist can, after the experience of the past century or so, look toward such a development. I speak simply of some rough approximation of Marx's hopes: a modern society which transcends the atomization and alienation of capitalism and Communist totalitarianism and somehow finds community under the conditions of twenty-first-century existence. Would one then reinstate the Marxist prediction?

Not necessarily. Since Marx wrote, it has become plain (to some, if not all, Marxists) that there was a simplification in his analysis of religion and society. That *one* of the sources of alienation and the religious consciousness was, and is, social evil is beyond question. That this has been the *main* source of the religious impulse throughout history up to the present is also a compelling idea. But that it is the *only* basis of that alienation is not at all proved. In some notes, the Italian Marxist Labriola—the first academically trained Marxist philosopher since Marx himself—made a similar point:

> Is religion a permanent fact or simply an invention, an aberration and a deceit? Certainly it is a need. Were the nineteenth century rationalists therefore mistaken? Yes. Is it not true, then, that the last century was an age of science? That is only partially the case. Is it then impossible to suppress religion? The fact that it is sometimes suppressed proves a certain theory but does not define its limits. Is it the case, then, that man can never become master of the natural and historical world by virtue of his own intellect, moral autonomy and aesthetic sensibility? Yes and no.

There were other Marxists who rethought Marx's position in much the same way as Labriola. The Austro-Marxists were explicitly aware that Christianity was one of the two major sources of the socialist movement in their country (bourgeois liberalism was the other). Even more to the present point, Max Adler, the leading Austro-Marxist philosopher, fought against the "dogmatism of unbelief" and, integrating Kantian and Marxist insights, held that religion was a profound form of human consciousness which was non-, but not anti-, scientific.

Indeed, it seems to me that the end of a social misery could give rise to an existential impulse to new forms of religious feeling. The very fact that people begin to die, not because they were born poor, or born in a pre-scientific age which lacked the serum to fight plagues, but because they were born, because humanity is finite even at the very height of its development, could provide the basis for loneliness and alienation and religion. Even the perfection of Marx's imagined communism—which is unlikely in any case—will not transform those fundamental limits of the human condition. There will be, then, space for a Pascalian sensibility in a Marxist world.

If one thus criticizes Marx in a Marxist fashion, an important point emerges: that the atheistic humanist and the committed religious person now have the same enemy, that slack, hedonistic and thoughtless atheism which, often embellished with a sentimental religiosity, is the real faith of contemporary Western society. Those one-time foes, however, will be able to respond to the death of the traditional God only if they understand, with Hegel as well as with Marx, that it is one of the consequences of the death of the traditional society. Any new faith, whether secular or sacral, has to be social.

5
CATASTROPHIC ATHEISM

WITH NIETZSCHE, the mood at God's funeral turns apocalyptic.

The Enlightenment was essentially optimistic about the disappearance of the traditional deity. Reason and reason's God were going to replace Judeo-Christian faith. Hegel thought that a new, philosophical interpretation of Christianity and a judicious compromise between capitalism and feudalism could restore the shattered community that was cause and effect of the spiritual crisis. Marx saw the collapse of the bourgeois system, of its—Protestant and Deist—religious ideology as well as its economy, as the opportunity for creating, not simply a just society, but a social order in which God would no longer be a question, much less an answer.

But Nietzsche believed that the decadence of two thousand years of Christian civilization (and of its Jewish prehistory) was a catastrophe leading to "shatterings, earthquakes, an inversion of mountain and valley such as has never before been dreamed." He was against every political movement of the day yet he announced that "after me there will be, for the first time on earth, *great politics*." The disappearance of the Western God, he argued, would transform the secular constituents of modern life—capitalism, militarism, nationalism—into demoniac forces. He therefore projected a sense of "cultural despair" which, carelessly interpreted by lesser men in a time of social collapse, helped prepare the way for the rise of a fascism which Nietzsche himself most certainly would have detested.

Indeed, Nietzsche may have anticipated the misreading which would be made of his work. "I know my fate," he wrote in 1888, a year before he went mad. "Something monstrous will cling to the memory of my name. . . ." So it has. His reputation, as he prophesied, has indeed been implicated in "a crisis the likes of which the world has never known, the most profound collision of consciences, of a decision conjured up against everything which, until now, had been believed in and sanctified." He went on, in a famous passage:

> I am not a man. I am dynamite.—And yet there is nothing in me of the founder of a religion. Religions are matters for the mob and I have found it necessary to wash my hands after touching religious men. . . . But my truth is *fearful:* it is that in the past we called lies the truth.—*The devaluation of all values* . . . The concept of politics is completely taken up in a war of the spirits, all the structures of power are blown up into the air, for they are all based on the *lie.* There will be wars of a kind that have never happened on earth.

In the same vein, there is his earlier proclamation of the death of God in *The Gay Science* (1882). He wrote:

> Have you not heard of the madman who lit a lamp in the bright morning and went to the marketplace crying ceaselessly, "I seek God! I seek God!" There were many among those standing there who didn't believe in God so he made them laugh. "Is God lost?" one of them said. "Has he gone astray like a child?" said another. "Or is he hiding? Has he gone on board ship and emigrated?" So they laughed and shouted to one another. The man sprang into their midst and looked daggers at them. "Where is God?" he cried. "I will tell you. *We have killed him*—you and I. We are all his killers! But how have we done this? How could we swallow up the sea? Who gave us the sponge to wipe away the horizon? What will we do as the earth is set lose from its sun?"

Is this poetry, no less—and no more? Do "great politics" have any meaning? Or "to wipe away the horizon"? Are these merely images which resonate to the tumults of twentieth-century experience but explain nothing? I think not. These symbols are part of a brilliant analysis of the social and political crisis brought about by the death of God. To understand that analysis, however, it is necessary to realize how utterly paradoxical Nietzsche's thought is. For instance, in the passage just quoted, isn't it clear that he is contemptuous of the cynical agnostics in the marketplace and identifies with the madman who does not simply announce, but is appalled by, the death of God? This most militant atheist of the nineteenth century took religion so seriously that he believed that the emptiness of the heavens would open up an abyss on earth.

——————— **I** ———————

Nietzsche's basic theory about Judeo-Christianity—that it represents a "slave uprising" in morality, an ethics of *ressentiment*—is so well known that it has become a cliché. As a result, most people have missed the fact that it contains its contrary: that religion is a positive, affirmative force. Indeed, if Nietzsche had not had these paradoxical views, he would simply have rejoiced in the disappearance of the traditional faith.

Religion, Nietzsche argued in *Human, All Too Human*, begins as an attempt to control a terrible, mysterious and unknown natural world.* How can humans control the processes upon which life itself depends? People who believe in magic and superstition try to impose their will upon that unruly nature by means of spells and incantations. This, Nietzsche argued, is how religion begins. Even more important for our purposes, the weaker tribes, Nietzsche held, try to get an advantage over the stronger through the same magic. The very origins of faith, then, are to be found in the attempt of the lowly to control forces which are superior to them, whether cosmic or military. The "slave morality," which exalts the inferior, is thus to be found at the very beginning of history.

It is, however, the Jews who theologize this attitude. They accomplished "the deepest and most sublime, ideal-creating transformation of values," Nietzsche wrote in *The Genealogy of Morals*—and they did so out of hate and resentment against those who lorded over them. At first glance, this might seem to be a proof of Nietzsche's alleged anti-Semitism—only he was not an anti-Semite, regarding anti-Semitism as "fake intellectual humbug" (*Schwindel-Geisterei*) derived, in part, from the fact that the Germans indulged in too much beer and Wagnerian music.† What is really involved here is a critical difference

---

*In this chapter I will synthesize materials from various periods of Nietzsche's life into a summary statement of his analysis. In the case of other authors, like Hegel, this would be an impermissible procedure, but not with Nietzsche. He knowingly contradicts himself, as Karl Jaspers has emphasized, but the contradiction occurs within each stage of his life, not so much between them. (See Appendix I.)

†See Appendix J.

between Nietzsche and Hegel, one which reveals some essential aspects of Nietzsche's theory of religion.

For Hegel, political and military defeat led the Jews to spiritualize their vision of God, to turn from a tribal deity to the Lord of the entire universe. In our time Paul Tillich put the same point even more forcefully. The Jews, Tillich wrote, were the only nation of the ancient world who came to worship a God who sometimes, in anger at the faithlessness of his chosen people, sided with their enemies. They broke, Tillich would say, with the parochial, with the cult of mere kinship and blood. Precisely, Nietzsche would reply. That is the decadence of the Jews. In them, "morality is no longer the expression of the conditions of life of a people, but become abstract, opposed to life. . . . The history of Israel," he continued, "is priceless as a typical history of the *denaturing* of natural values.—A God who demands— in the place of a God who helps."

This decadent element in Judaism, the spirituality of defeat, the reactive, resentful universalism of a subject nation, is the bridge to Christianity. Christian love, Nietzsche noted, is often thought of as the antithesis of Jewish sternness. In fact, that love is the very culmination of Jewish rage, for it exalts the lowly, the sick and the sinner, even more than the Jews. "God on the cross," Nietzsche argued, is a formula which "devalues all of the values of the ancient world"; in other words, it marks as great a turning point in human history as the coming of nihilism, which Nietzsche subsumes under the very same formula. The crucified deity, he went on, "is the Orient, the profound Orient, the Oriental slave who in this way vents his rage upon Rome and its aristocratic, frivolous tolerance, its Roman 'catholicism' of unbelief. The slaves did not rise against the faith of their masters but against their freedom from belief."

Then came the essential: "The slave wants the unconditional, he understands only the tyrannical, in morality as well as elsewhere he loves as he hates, without nuance, to the depths, to sorrow, to sickness—and his often *hidden* suffering rises up against that aristocratic taste which seems to deny suffering." The slaves, in short, cannot tolerate the "half stoic and amused indifference [*Unbekümmertheit*] toward the seriousness of faith" which they found in the ruling class.

So Christianity appeals at first to "the lowest strata, the *underworld* of the ancient world." The evangelists lead us "into a world like a Russian novel in which the dregs of society, the psychotics and 'childish' idiots meet together." "The history of Christianity is based upon the necessity that its faith had to be as sick, as lowly, as vulgar as the needs which it satisfied were sick, lowly and vulgar." Even though these quotations are taken from one of Nietzsche's most polemical works, *The Anti-Christ* (or *The Anti-Christian*, both being possible translations from the German), the views which they propound can be found throughout his writings.

But if Christianity is thus the expression of the resentment of the deprived and corrupted poor against agnostic aristocrats, how could Nietzsche also call it "Platonism for the 'people' [*Volk*]"? What does this barbaric faith have in common with the most ethereal of the Athenian conservatives? The answer is found in one of Nietzsche's most fundamental philosophic principles: opposition to any "true" world which is said to exist on the far side of the actual world. In a brief "History of an Error" in *The Twilight of the Idols*, Plato is seen as the first exponent of such a "true" world. In his thinking, only the wise and the virtuous can know it. In Christianity that Platonism is "feminized," to use one of Nietzsche's favorite pejoratives: it is softened with sympathy and made available to the illiterate mob. In fact, Nietzsche asserted in opposition to both Christianity and Platonism, there is only one world.

But Christianity is worse than Platonism, for it links its other world with an enormous increase of guilt in this world. The universalist, monotheist God emerges out of a universal and despotic empire, and the guilt which his devotees feel toward him is so much greater precisely because he is so all-powerful. Christianity, Nietzsche held, dramatized this guilt in the doctrine of original sin and made salvation dependent, not upon the acts of the individual, but upon the forgiveness purchased by the suffering of the very God before whom one was condemned as guilty. At this point in the analysis, Nietzsche became uncharacteristically optimistic: if God was dying, and God was the source of guilt, perhaps the atheism of the nineteenth century would bring about a "second innocence."

That hope was, however, a deviation from a basic rage and contempt toward Christianity. The young Hegel, it will be recalled, had also linked the theology of original sin to the political and social corruption of Rome at the time of the rise of Christianity. But the mature Hegel had recoiled from that harsh theory and had even declared himself—if ambivalently—a Lutheran. Nietzsche, on the other hand, remained fixated upon the depravity which he saw in the origins of the Christian church—so much so that he omitted about fifteen centuries of history. His Christianity was defined in terms of its origins and of the socialist interpretations of it in the nineteenth century. The millennium and a half in between—when Roman Catholicism triumphantly animated medieval civilization—was ignored.

For now, we have summarized the familiar Friedrich Nietzsche and his theory of Judeo-Christianity. The Judaism of the Roman occupation is the first great slave uprising in morality, an impotent feminization of God on the part of a defeated nation, the prelude to the hate-filled love of Christianity. The latter arises out of the decadence of Rome and the protest of the lowly, who hunger for certitude and obedience, against their tolerant, faithless rulers. This rage spreads among the most barbaric peoples of the ancient world and creates a life-denying, servile, guilt-ridden religion of the plebs. Modern socialism is only the secular version of this vicious theology.

At the same time that he believed in all these things, Nietzsche also felt that Christianity had played an important, and even yea-saying, role in human history. That is why he was so frightened of his own announcement of God's impending death.

I do not base this interpretation on Nietzsche's open admiration for Christ. That is well known and perfectly in keeping with his condemnation of Christianity. Christ, Nietzsche said, was a kind of Nietzschean: a "free spirit" without any idea of guilt or punishment or rewards for doing good. "He had no formula, no rite, for communication with God—not even prayer." And he did not die "to 'save men' but to show one how to live." Therefore "the very word 'Christianity' is a misunderstanding. In fact there was only one Christian who died on the cross. The 'Gospel' [*Evangelium*] died on the cross. What from that moment on was called the 'Gospel' was the 'bad news,' an anti-Gospel [*Dysangelium*]." Indeed, Nietzsche saw Christ, like himself, as the "destroyer of morality."

This distinction between Christ and Christianity is the standard fare of many atheists who want to excoriate the Church but admire its founder. What is shocking, and not at all standard, is that Nietzsche had a profound respect for Christianity, not simply Christ. That is clearly said in one of his last books, *The Genealogy of Morals* (1887). Indeed, the point is also made in his first book, *The Birth of Tragedy from the Spirit of Music* (1872). The latter source is particularly im-

portant since it is routinely cited to attribute to Nietzsche views which
contradict those he actually held.

The Birth of Tragedy contains a bitter attack on Socrates, the
founder of that "Platonism" which became a mass phenomenon in Christianity. Socrates is seen as the "tribal progenitor" [*Stammvater*] of an
"Alexandrian culture" which is based on theory and denies the Dionysiac force of life itself which had been central to the pre-Socratic
culture in Greece. Dionysus, Nietzsche had written earlier in this book,
is associated with intoxication, narcotics, spring. Isn't it obvious, then,
that Nietzsche, as both the young scholar and the inspired genius on
the eve of his own madness, was committed to the irrational, the
uncontrollable? Therefore he must have remained profoundly hostile
to Christianity, with its doctrine of original sin and its emnity toward
the body and all of its pleasures.

I am not for a moment suggesting that such reasoning and consequent hostility are absent from Nietzsche (or even from *The Birth
of Tragedy*); it is just that their opposite is also present. This can be
seen in the way Nietzsche distinguishes the Dionysiac in Greek culture
from the same phenomenon in other societies of the ancient world.
"From Rome to Babylon," he wrote, "to the very ends of the
world . . . we can demonstrate the existence of Dionysiac feasts." But
the non-Greek rites of Dionysus relate to the Greek

> as the bearded satyr, who borrows his name and attributes from a goat,
> relates to Dionysus himself. In almost every case the center of these [non-
> Greek] feasts is an over-arching sexual licentiousness whose waves sweep
> over each family and carry away its most honored principles. The wildest
> beasts of nature are unshackled in a loathsome mixture of voluptuousness
> and cruelty that has always seemed to me to be the real "witch's potion."

There is, Nietzsche argued, an "enormous gulf" which separates
the Greek Dionysiacs from the barbarians, and it is defined, precisely,
by the fact that in Greek culture there is a dialectical unity of the
Dionysiac and the Apollonian. This unity—uneasy peace would be a
better way of putting it—means that whereas the Babylonians in their
rites regressed to tigers and apes, the Greeks found illumination and
even salvation. This complexity becomes clearer a little later on in *The
Birth of Tragedy*, when Nietzsche compares Dionysus to . . . Hamlet!
What Shakespeare's hero proved, Nietzsche said, was not that an
excess of reflection makes action impossible. That theory, he noted

contemptuously, can be left to "Hans the dreamer." Hamlet symbol-
izes, rather, one who has looked very deeply into reality, knows that
it cannot be changed—"that it is ridiculous or disgusting to demand
that he set right things which are out of joint"—and will, through that
knowledge, not act.

So the young Nietzsche, who exalted the Dionysiac, also saw a
"lethargic element" in it and recognized the enormous contribution of
Apollo to Greek culture. Indeed, by the standards of twentieth-century
scholarship, Nietzsche's Dionysus is less "Dionysiac" than he actually
was.* And the mature Nietzsche's analysis of Christianity as the enemy
incarnate regarded it as both life-denying *and* life-affirming, which is
rather plainly said in *The Genealogy of Morals*.

Nietzsche's paradox is striking: "these ascetic priests, these seeming enemies of life, these *nay-sayers*—they belong to one of the great
conserving and *yea-creating* forces of life." There are, Nietzsche noted,
priests and ascetics in every culture and they come from every social
class. And they are a contradiction in terms, "using power to stamp
out the very source of power," turning life against life. But precisely
because this phenomenon is so pervasive, "it must be a necessity of
the very first order which makes this species, which is *hostile to life*,
grow and expand—it must be *in the interests of life itself*" that this
happens. So it was that Nietzsche argued that "*the ascetic ideal is the
defensive and healthy* instinct of a degenerated life which tries to
maintain itself by every means and struggles for its very existence."

How can this be so?

> That man is sicker, less secure, more subject to change, more precarious
> than any other animal—of this there can be no doubt. Man is *the* sick
> animal. . . . But certainly he has also dared more, changed more, defied
> more and challenged fate more than all the other animals put together.
> He is the great experimenter with himself, the unsatisfied, insatiable,
> who struggles with animals, nature and the gods for domination. . . . The
> no which man says to life brings, as though by magic, a fullness of delicate
> yeses to life. Even when he wounds himself, this master of destruction,
> of self-destruction—behind that is the wound which forces him *to live*.

But that is only possible if man has a purpose, an ideal. The sick animal
that is man does not suffer from suffering itself but because "there is
no answer to the question 'Why suffer?' . . . The senselessness of suf-

*See Appendix K.

fering, not suffering, was the curse which previously was placed upon humankind—*and the ascetic ideal gives a sense to that suffering.*"

In times past, Nietzsche continued—and note well this qualification—that ascetic sense of life was the only one possible, and:

> any sense of life is better than none; the ascetic ideal was in this perspective the *faute de mieux par excellence* in all of history. Through it, suffering was *interpreted;* the horrible emptiness seemed to be filled; the door closed in the face of all the self-murdering nihilisms. The interpretation—there is no doubt—brought about new suffering, gnawing and poisoning the innermost depths of life; it brought all life under the perspective of *guilt.* . . . But in spite of everything—man was thereby protected . . . the will itself was protected.

This view (which, not so incidentally, is very close to Marx's) is echoed in one of the most celebrated passages in Nietzsche's final masterpiece, *Thus Spake Zarathustra.* In the first book, the prophet refers to the "thousand and one goals," to the varied and contradictory definitions of good and evil which he encountered among the people of the world. "Life," he says, "is not possible for a people until it has first established its values. . . ." There must be a purpose for societies as well as for individuals and for all of mankind. "The creators are first of all a people and only later individuals," Zarathustra asserts. Morality is social, tribal.

If you want to understand the culture, the values, of a society, Nietzsche said in a kind of Marxist interpretation, then you must know "the needs and land and the heaven and the neighbors of a people." The ideal grows out of the life situation of a people and is indispensable to survival. So Nietzsche sees a functional value in faith in general and in Christian faith in the West in particular. If Christianity had been simply evil, he would have greeted its passing with unalloyed jubilation. But he was ambivalent about its decline, a fact which can be most dramatically seen in a youthful work, *Schopenhauer as Educator*, but which reverberates throughout all of his writings.

In the Europe of his day, Nietzsche wrote, there were

> certain powers, monstrous powers, wild, primitive and completely pitiless. . . . We live in the period of the atom, of atomistic chaos. The hostile forces were kept in a rough equilibrium by the Church of the Middle Ages; they were more or less assimilated to one another because of the

Church's power. As this equilibrium shatters, that power falters and the hostile forces rise up against one another. The Reformation declared many things to be a matter of indifference to religion, as spheres which were not ruled by religious ideas. This was the price it paid to live just as early Christianity paid a similar price to maintain itself against . . . ancient society. From the Reformation on, the superation of the spheres grew and grew. Now everything on earth is determined by the grossest and most evil powers, through the egotism of the acquisitive and of the military. The state in the hands of the latter seeks, just like the egotism of the acquisitive, to organize everything anew, to be the repressive force, the unity of the hostile powers. That is, the state wants to be able to drive men into that same idolatry the Church forced them to practice.

With what effect? We will yet experience it. In any case, we now find ourselves in the ice-driven torrent of the Middle Ages. The ice has melted and become a mighty, devastating current. Ice floe piles upon ice floe, the shores are flooded and in danger.

So that comment in *Ecce Homo*, toward the end of Nietzsche's active (sane) career—that "the concept of politics is completely taken up in a war of the spirits"—has a quite specific meaning. As religion declines, militarism, capitalist greed, nationalism and class war are all "spiritualized." To translate this into the terms of *The Birth of Tragedy:* the raw, Dionysiac forces are no longer subject to Apollonian constraints. Therefore the decadence of the despised church is a catastrophe. There will now be "social wars" waged over "philosophic principles."

In this apocalypse, the state becomes more powerful as it takes over the functions of religion. It can even be used by the old faith in an attempt to restore itself, or by irreligious leaders wanting to put an end to the sectarian bickering of the churches. The new, sentimental Christianity based on feelings is a philistine and foolish attempt to confront this crisis, and so is the substitution of science for religion. In fact, Nietzsche argued, science rests upon the same trusting assumptions in the meaningfulness of the world as religion. "Hasn't the self-belittling of men, their will to self-belittlement, grown mightly since Copernicus?" he asked. Or, as he said on another occasion, "Since Copernicus, man has rolled out of the center into X."

None of this should be understood to imply that Nietzsche was a metaphysical fortuneteller whose vague apocalypses could apply to any possible twentieth century. The contrary can be seen in an area which can only be mentioned here: Nietzsche's extraordinary accomplishments as a philosopher's philosopher. He anticipated Wittgenstein and analytic philosophy as well as world wars. The structure of language, he said, derives from a primitive, fetishistic psychology in which all that happens is purposive, the effect of causes, the act of an actor. But what if—as Nietzsche believed—there are no purposes in reality? What if happenings simply happen, if the lightning and its light are not subject (lightning) and predicate (light) but simply lightning? Thus, if one wants to be truly finished with God one must drive him out of grammar, where he hides as an unnoticed assumption.

And yet, the inherent teleology of language, exactly like the asceticism of the priest, is the means by which the European spirit has achieved "strength, ruthless curiosity, dynamism." Theorizing everything that happens "according to a Christian schema and discovering God in every accident," this "tyranny, this arbitrariness, this stern and grandiose stupidity, educated the spirit." If, as Kolakowski remarked, Kant was at enormous pains to destroy the proofs for the existence of a God in whom he devoutly believed, Nietzsche was just as energetic in insisting upon the value of the religion he despised. In the process, he opened up the way to some of the most important philosophic discussions of the twentieth century. He painted on a large canvas, yet the detail is exquisite.

It is only when one realizes how profoundly Nietzsche respected the social and political function of the Judeo-Christian religion he excoriated that it becomes clear why, in *Ecce Homo* (one of the final works), he makes this extraordinary statement: "The *disclosing* [of the concealed reality] of Christian morality is an event beyond compare, a veritable catastrophe. Who illuminates this phenomenon is a *force majeure*, a destiny—he breaks the history of humankind in two. One lives *before* him, one lives *after* him." Nietzsche is saying, rather plainly, that his own work is a prelude to disaster. Like Marx, he was convinced that the Christian falsehoods were no longer believable; and unlike Marx, he saw no alternative to them in the immediate future. Therefore he proclaimed himself a "destiny."

But how can one base a politics on the prediction of an apocalypse?

——— I I ———

In *Ecce Homo*, Nietzsche described himself as "the last *anti-political* German." That makes obvious sense when one considers that he was opposed not only to the masses but also to the capitalists and capitalism and socialists and socialism. And yet, there is such a thing as an anti-politics, and under certain conditions it can have enormous political impact, turning into what Fritz Stern has called "the politics of cultural despair," one more consequence of the death of God.

But before getting into the unintended—fascist—consequences of Nietzsche's anti-politics, it is important to define that phenomenon itself. In the process it will be discovered that the reactionary geniuses can have privileged insights *because* they are reactionary. That, Marx thought, was the case with Sir James Steuart, who understood capitalist individualism because he was a member of the declining aristocracy, and with Honoré de Balzac, whose monarchist Catholicism provided him with an unparalleled sense of bourgeois reality. And it is the case with Friedrich Nietzsche.

First, there is Nietzsche's contempt for the "mob."

"Life," Zarathustra declared, "is a fountain of delight. But where the mob also drinks, all the fountains are poisoned." That sentiment was a commonplace of the age, and not just among its conservatives. The Enlightenment, as we have seen, feared what the *canaille* would do when it learned that there was no Judeo-Christian God; Hegel was concerned about the *Pöbel*, the identityless rabble which he saw as a product of the new industrial system. Even Nietzsche's emphasis upon the role of the city in creating a mass society was not unique. He wrote of the physiological decline of the race which went along with the corruptions of urban civilization: "The peasants eaten up by the huge cities; an unnatural overstimulation of the mind and senses." That sentiment can be found in Baudelaire and Dickens, to name just two of the many people who responded to the change in human life wrought by capitalist urbanization.

But where Nietzsche was quite original was in his insistence that mass culture was, in considerable measure, the fault of the *upper* classes. "One complains of the indiscipline of the masses," one of the posthumously published notes commented. "Were this proved, the judgment would then turn back upon the cultured; the mass is precisely as good or evil as the cultured." Another of the notes said:

> The general symptoms of the *dying* of a culture, of complete rot. Haste, the waters of religion flowing away, the struggles between nations, a science that splits up and dissolves everything, the contemptible money

and luxury economy of the educated strata, its lack of love and greatness. That the educated strata are part of this movement is becoming more and more clear to me. . . . The great flood of barbarism is outside the door.

The phenomenon of massification, of the mob, then, affects the entire society and not just the masses themselves. "The great mob and slave uprising: small people who no longer believe in the holy and great virtues (Luther, Christ, etc.); the bourgeois who no longer believes in the higher type of ruling caste (consequently revolution); the scientist who no longer believes in a philosophy; the women who no longer believe in the higher type of men."

Nietzsche blames capitalism for this development. He wrote in another of the posthumously published notes: "The merchant spirit has the great task of planting a passion in men who are incapable of elevating themselves, of giving them a broader purpose and a rational use of their time. But this is done in such a way as to level all individuals and it defends itself against the spiritual as if the spiritual were a debauchery." In a comment on the American spirit, the link between the rise of capitalism and the decline of religion is even more obvious:

There is an Indian-like primitiveness indigenous to Indian blood, in the way that the Americans seek after gold. Their breathless haste in work— the characteristic vice of the New World—already begins to infect Old Europe, to make it savage, to create a remarkable spiritual vacuum. One is ashamed now of quiet. Long meditations make for remorse. One thinks only of the hour at hand as one eats at noon, the eye fastened on the news from the stock market. . . . There is no longer time and desire for ceremony, for the civility of the roundabout, for the spirit of amusement and, above all, for leisure.

In *Beyond Good and Evil*, this critique is used to deepen the analysis of the decline of religion. The religious life, Nietzsche held, requires leisure. Therefore the frenzied work ethic of the capitalist world leaves people with no sense of the uses of religion and they are astonished that it survives at all. Not that they are foes of the churches, Nietzsche shrewdly observed in anticipation of the *de facto* atheism and *pro forma* religiosity which so often rule today. If the government requires that people participate in religious ceremonies, they do so as a matter of course. They are not so much hostile to religion as distant from it. Those indifferent agnostics jeering at the news of the death of God are here explained sociologically.

It is capitalism, then, which levels people, subverts the aristocratic virtues and creates a passionless mass atheism. Socialism is worse— in most, but not all of Nietzsche's writings—for it is the culmination, the *reductio ad absurdum*, of these capitalist tendencies.

The belittling of men—literally, the "making small" of men—is rooted in the capitalist factory system, in which the individual is reduced to a part in a machine. Zarathustra even speaks of modern people as "inverse cripples," huge ears on a tiny stalk, as a result of the division of labor. The impersonal machine deprives the individual of any pride in craftsmanship and creates the anonymous slaves of the working class. "The press, the machine, the railroad and the telegraph," Nietzsche wrote, "are the premises whose thousand-year conclusion no one but me has yet dared to draw." And the socialists are contemptible because they speak for the degraded mass of this new slave society, preaching to it envy and rage, appealing to the cowardliness, the mob instinct of the repressed.

Dogmatic Christianity is at an end, Nietzsche argues—but "latent Christianity" is at hand in the form of socialism. The socialists are the new Jesuits of a godless world, seeing the people as means to an end. Like the early Christians, the socialists laud inferiority and seek the "tyranny of the least and the dumbest," the "herd morality." This is just one more slave uprising, like those of the Jews and the Christians and the French Revolution, but now it takes place in the capitalist machine society with its mass men and women.

At times—deviating from his central theme—Nietzsche seemed to think that liberal democracy would defeat socialism. The socialist egalitarian vision, he wrote in 1879, might turn out to be "a sickness that had been survived and forgotten." This would happen when the people used democracy to introduce progressive taxation and thereby create a new middle class which would be inoculated against socialist ideas. He returned to that thought in the notes made near the end of his life, hoping that the socialists would triumph somewhere and thereby give a *"demonstratio ad absurdum"* of their doctrine. In any case, he continued, there "will always be too many people owning something and socialism will therefore never be more than an attack of a sickness."

That reformist—even liberal-democratic—anti-socialism departs from the main thrust of Nietzsche's thought. But, then, Nietzsche's vision of the future literally swarmed with contradictory possibilities, not the least because he never systematically worked out his attitude about what would come after God died. Still, all of his futuristic tangents were responses to a single question: how can one build a society without God?

Socialism, Nietzsche said, was one answer. Most of the time he thought that it would, in part for religious (or irreligious) reasons, lead to terrorism. Since religion is no longer believable and the state can't cloak itself in the aura of sacred legitimacy—and, indeed, because socialism strives to eliminate religion—the socialists would have to rely upon terror to rule. They would use the word "justice" to disenfranchise the half-educated masses in whose name they spoke; they would bring statism at its worst. Now everyone would be forced to join the contemptible masses. Excellence would be denigrated, and even those geniuses who refused to sing hymns to the rabble would be forced to become, or at least to appear to be, mediocrities. Socialism is the cultural and psychological triumph of the middling, the inferior, the ordinary, as well as the political victory of the masses.

There were other possible futures after the death of God, only they are found in Nietzsche's *obiter dicta*, not in his theories. A Europe united as a union of peoples could rule the globe; there would be world wars as the petty politics of merely national rivalries gave way to planetary conflict; the Russians and the Germans could exercise a condominium; and so on. (Karl Jaspers has very usefully sorted out, and documented, these futures in his *Nietzsche*.) But one strange feature of the possibility that is relevant here is that in it Nietzsche agreed in some important details—while disagreeing on everything basic—with Karl Marx (whom he never read). The great nay-sayer was a utopian—but a reactionary utopian—in at least one of his personae.

Nietzsche had a remarkable sense of the way in which technology might transform culture and consciousness. "Air travel," he remarked on one occasion, "would subvert all of our cultural concepts. . . ." Indeed, the possibility of the *Übermensch*, like that of Marx's vision of communism, only emerged because of technological revolution. Man, Nietzsche said, has *"powers* in excess at his service." Therefore he has the possibility "to make of himself something newer, higher." A number of virtues "that are now the *conditions of existence* will become outmoded." He returned to that argument about the progressive role of the priests and the religions: "they were means to *make possible* a tremendous self-discipline on the part of man through the emotional impact of a great fear." Now, however, technology had obviated the need for that religiously motivated discipline.

Indeed, this same process also held out the possibility of changing the very nature of work. Wage labor, Nietzsche said, was *"the slavery in the present:* a barbarism." The workers, he went on, should be paid "an honorarium, a salary, not a wage! No relation between pay and performance! But each individual should be so placed that, *according to his nature,* he performs the most that he can of what is possible in his sphere." All of this has the most remarkable similarity to the Marxist vision. Marx, too, believed that religion had once been necessary to make class society functional but that technology had now rendered it, and so many other "virtues," obsolete. He, too, looked to a time in which there would be "no relation between pay and performance," when the rule would be: From each according to his ability, to each according to his need. There, however, the Marx-Nietzsche likeness ends.

At his most progressive—perhaps, it would be better to say, at his least monstrous—Nietzsche dreamed of a reactionary utopia, an "active nihilism," a "new Buddhism." The beliefs which had been rendered necessary by the "pressure of the conditions of existence" would become irrelevant. A new and manly ruling class would emerge precisely because of the catastrophic times. At the same time, democracy has made the masses more manipulable and more intelligent, and the new rulers would have superior but still subordinate human material at their disposal. Here, of course, is the total and complete contrast between Nietzsche and Marx. If they agreed on the decadence of the religious function and on revolutionary possibilities for new forms of social existence, Marx saw that potential in the end of all ruling classes and the autonomy and self-determination of the people, whereas Nietzsche made it the precondition of a new, more sophisticated—but atheist—form of class society.

Or, rather, Nietzsche at his most liberal argued in that way. At times he simply retrogressed to Enlightenment cynicism. "We good Europeans," he said, ". . . are atheists and immoralists but we support the religions and moralities of the herd instincts. Through them a type of man is being created that, once he falls into our hands, must *crave* our hands." Perhaps the most sustained statement of this monstrous politics is to be found in *The Gay Science*, a work of his mature middle period (1881–82).

"We children of the future," Nietzsche proclaimed in that book, " 'conserve' nothing, we don't want to go back to the past. We are not at all 'liberal,' we don't work for progress, we don't have to plug up our ears against the siren songs about the future of the market. Those who sing of 'equal rights,' 'free society,' 'no more lords and no more serfs,' do not entice us." This is the quintessential statement of Nietzsche's anti-politics: it rejects conservatism, liberalism (in the European sense of the term) and socialism.

"We rejoice," this reactionary manifesto continued, "in all who, like us, love danger, war, adventure . . . we think upon the necessity of a new order, of new slavery—isn't that so?" And a little later there is a characteristic assault on religion: "The 'religion of sympathy' which one thinks might persuade us—oh, we know the hysterical little fellows and women who make this religion their ornament and veil! We are not humanists, we would never dare allow ourselves to speak of our 'love for humanity.' " Then there comes a remarkable admission: "Why do we do these things? Because of our disbelief? Because of every kind of disbelief? No, you know better than that, my friend! The hidden Yes in you is stronger than all the Noes and the Maybes which make you sick with this age. And you must go forth on the sea, you wanderers, what drives you there is . . . a faith!"

That last comment about faith is not a literary flourish, for Nietzsche makes much the same point in the final book of *Zarathustra*. The prophet meets the last Pope, who is now out of work since God is dead. The Pope tells Zarathustra that the deity has died, sitting wearily in the corner by an oven, choking on his own excessive sympathy. Zarathustra replies that the reason God had to be done away with was that he did not speak clearly, that he was a potter who had not learned his trade and who blamed his pots for his own faults. God, he concludes, lacked good taste in his piety and therefore, "Away with *such* a God! Better no God, better make one's destiny with one's own fist, better to be a fool, better to be God himself!"

And the last Pope tells Zarathustra, "you are more pious than you believe, with such an unbelief. . . ." That is, I suspect, Nietzsche's self-portrait. His work, as Manfred Kaempfert has documented, is pervaded by religious references; *Zarathustra* itself is Biblical in tone and structure. Ultimately, even though Nietzsche said that he would "raise up no new idols," he could not tolerate that godless, totally immanent world he sometimes celebrated. So he sought a new faith. His vision of it was sometimes monstrous and always vague. What was solid and substantial were the insights into capitalism, mass society and the negative potential of socialism (if not into socialism itself, which he never understood) which his reactionary utopianism facilitated. But precisely because he was so dialectical, so seemingly equivocal, a *"Doppelgänger"* with two faces as he himself said, he lost control of his own heritage—much as he said Christ did. That raises the question of Nietzsche in the twentieth century—and of Nietzsche right now.

——— I I I ———

God has died many deaths in the twentieth century. That is, the impact of his going has varied according to the social classes that missed him and the historic circumstances under which they did. This can be seen in the way contemporary history has misread Nietzsche and in the limited utility of the thesis that he was among the first to enunciate: that a world without God would become terrorist and totalitarian.

There has been a considerable reaction to the notion that Nietzsche was a premature Nazi—and sometimes an overreaction. Arthur Danto cites a typical error as he reacts to the "fascist" Nietzsche. In *The Genealogy of Morals*, Nietzsche described the "superior races." In each of them, he wrote, there is "the beast of prey, the splendid, blond beast, roaming, greedy for booty and victory." Isn't that a clear, if unwitting, anticipation of the Nazi "blond beast," the Aryan fascist? That reading loses its plausibility, however, when one looks at the "superior races" Nietzsche enumerates: "The Roman, Arabic, German, Japanese knights, the Homeric heroes, the Scandinavian Vikings." In fact, as Danto noted, the most sensible interpretation is that when Nietzsche spoke of the "blond beast" he was thinking of the lion (an animal that was always an important symbol for him).

However, there is also overreaction in defending Nietzsche against the caricatures which have been made of him. Walter Kaufmann's *Nietzsche* is an excellent study which retrieves the philosopher from some of his friends and enemies. Kaufmann wrote:

> Nietzsche is perhaps best known as the prophet of great wars and power politics and as an opponent of political liberalism and democracy. That is

the idol of the "tough Nietzschians" and the whipping boy of many a critic. The "tender Nietzschians," on the other hand, insist—quite rightly—that Nietzsche scorned totalitarianism, denounced the state as "The New Idol" . . . and was himself a kindly and charitable person; but some of them falsely infer that he must therefore have been a liberal and a democrat or a socialist.

So far so good. But then Kaufmann continued: "We have tried to show that Nietzsche opposed both the ideology of the state and political liberalism because he was basically '*anti-political*' and, moreover, loathed the very idea of belonging to any 'party' whatever." That is to miss a basic fact of twentieth-century life: that an anti-politics can, under certain circumstances, be dangerously political.

In *Die Zerstörung der Vernunft* (*The Destruction of Reason*), Georg Lukacs fundamentally misrepresents Nietzsche—and shrewdly grasps the nature of his influence upon a certain stratum in late-nineteenth- and early-twentieth-century Germany. Lukacs's book is flawed, Stalinist, filled with Cold War exaggerations. It links Nazism with the irrationalist trend in German thought represented by Schopenhauer and his disciple Nietzsche. There was, Lukacs argued, a basic shift in bourgeois culture, a pessimism engendered by the fear of socialism on the part of the capitalists and their tributary classes after the Revolution of 1848. That is unfair to Nietzsche, who regarded the German cult of feelings and its related hostility to the Enlightenment and reason as a great danger (which he wrongly thought had been worked through). And at times the Lukacs thesis becomes simply silly, as when he compares the reactionary Catholic cardinal of New York in the fifties, an earnest and simplistic Cold Warrior, to Nietzsche.

And yet, if Lukacs was wrong to see Nietzsche *simply* as an anti-socialist, he was right to stress that Nietzsche was one of the first and greatest of the anti-socialists. Moreover, this perception helps in the understanding of the political consequences of Nietzsche's analysis of religion. The Enlightenment, Lukacs wrote, fought religion as the fading ideology of feudal absolutism—but Nietzsche was against religion not because it rationalized despotism but because he thought (wrongly) that it preached compassion for the poor and was a latent form of socialism. There is indeed a shift in cultural mood. And it reached out, in particular, to a disillusioned educated class at the turn of the century. This was Nietzsche's first audience.

Nietzsche provided that class, Lukacs held, with a "religious atheism." It was not the natural scientific atheism, which rejected God on optimistic grounds, but a moralizing and disenchanted atheism. George Lichtheim, who thought *The Destruction of Reason* to be worthless, agreed with Lukacs on this point. Lichtheim wrote

> of the fin de siècle attitude of the 1890s . . . prevalent throughout Europe among a section of the educated bourgeoisie. There was a middle class which had lost its faith in Enlightenment, no longer took political liberalism really seriously, saw Socialism as a more or less dangerous enemy and satisfied its metaphysical cravings by variations on a theme which Nietzsche had given it; the coming redemption of man by the Superman.

The younger Thomas Mann described that pessimistic mood in *Buddenbrooks* and some of his short stories (although he saw Schopenhauer, not Nietzsche, as its key philosopher). Mann was at that point, as I wrote some time ago,

> a particularly brilliant representative of a sensitive, selfish minority that was stranded by the twentieth century. The children of capitalist individualism, they were overwhelmed by the triumph of the capitalist corporation. They sought to disaffiliate from the technological and economic revolution their fathers had unwittingly begun. And since they were victimized by a success rather than by a failure, they gave a most paradoxical definition of Western decline. They protested against a dynamic decadence.

To be sure, this was a pampered despair of the middle classes. What Lukacs said of Schopenhauer could be applied to these "Nietzschians": they lived "in a lovely, modern hotel with all conveniences on the edge of the abyss, of nothingness, of meaninglessness." World War I and German defeat changed all that. Suddenly, there was upheaval and uncertainty everywhere and despair was a political fact rather than a philosophic pretense.

At this point, a book by the "poor man's Nietzsche," Oswald Spengler, had an enormous impact. *The Decline of the West* had been finished in 1917 but, fortunately for Spengler, publication was delayed until 1918, when its melancholy fatalism seemed to offer an explanation of what the "half-educated" public was feeling about the German defeat. Spengler made much of one of the most persistent metaphors of the nineteenth and twentieth centuries: the contrast between culture (organic, spontaneous, good, creative) and civilization (rootless, mechanical, urban). Fritz Stern argues that this distinction goes all the way back to Kant, but it is most familiar in the terms defined by Comte (organic and critical epochs), Tonnies (*Gemeinschaft* and *Gesellschaft*) and Durkheim (mechanical and organic solidarity).

The city, Spengler argued, produces "spiritual nomads," and it is intrinsically irreligious. Democracy is the instrument of the dictatorship of money because all of the parties are bought and paid for. In *Prussianism and Socialism*, Spengler proposed to deal with this crisis by means of a "genuine" socialism, the socialism of Hegel rather than of Marx (the latter was seen as culturally English and not at all German). There are obvious Nietzschian themes in all of this—and Spengler was quick to acknowledge his debt—yet the work was intellectually vulgar and second-rate and, as Walter Kaufmann has pointed out, its fatalism was the direct opposite of Nietzsche's implacable rejection of any theory of purposiveness in human history and his insistence upon heroic action.

And yet, if Spengler was a vulgarizer, he was also a political force, a self-fulfilling prophet. A second-rate intellectual with a pretentious theory, he nevertheless intuited the trend that was moving toward Nazism. The people, Spengler said, were rootless, without their "household gods." The rule of "money"—not of capitalist property relations, which can be the subject of a complex analysis, but of "money," a populist curse-word which can be shouted on the Right as well as the Left—was destroying democracy. The chief instrument of this destruction was the press, which now reached to the four corners of the globe and shaped the masses to do the bidding of the moneyed rulers. The "democratic" people were as subordinate and oppressed as the serfs of old. Spengler, T. W. Adorno has commented, anticipated Dr. Goebbels and the Nazi manipulation of the press.

All these things, Spengler argued, would bring forth a counter-movement: "Caesarism." "The word triumphs over money, the will to domination [*Herrenwille*] once again vanquishes the drive for greed. We call the power of money capitalism; and socialism is the will to call into life a system which rises above all class interests. . . ." That is, of course, Spengler's own "Prussian" socialism or, in historic fact, a precursor of Adolf Hitler's national "socialism" (even though Spengler eventually opposed the Nazis). But Spengler did not simply predict these events. As Adorno put it: "Behind the Spenglerian proclamation of the decline of culture, the wish was father to the thought."

For his theories—and others in a similar vein—spoke to a real need, one which permeated the Weimar Republic of the twenties and prepared the way for the Nazism of the thirties. There was, Peter Gay wrote in his study of Weimar, a "hunger for wholeness," for roots and community. This yearning was "awash with hate"—hatred against "the dehumanizing machine, capitalist materialism, godless rationalism, cosmopolitan Jews and the great, all devouring monster, the city." Nietzsche's anticipation of that spiritual crisis had been subtle and dialectical, reactionary yet insightful. He would have been appalled by Spengler's crude use of his themes and even more so by their further degradation at the hands of militant political simplifiers. And yet, his anti-politics played a significant role in preparing the German middle classes to accept a monster like Hitler.

There is an incredible irony here. Nietzsche had said that working-class socialism would lead to the terrorist and total state. When that state did come to Germany, it arrived by means of the terrorist suppression of the working class and it acknowledged Nietzsche as an honored predecessor. At a 1934 conference, Alfred Rosenberg told Hitler: "You, *mein Führer*, have rescued from oblivion the works of Nietzsche, Wagner, Lagarde and Dühring—works which foretold the doom of the old culture." Rosenberg was wrong: Nietzsche would have despised Hitler. Rosenberg was right: Nietzsche's enraged anti-politics prepared the way for a new ruling class—only it was composed, not of aristocratic *Übermenschen*, but of the refuse of the mass at the head of the masses.

There was, of course, a profoundly religious dimension to that Nazi triumph. The mystic belief in *Volk* and *Führer*, the Nazi liturgy at the Party conferences, was indeed an attempt to create a new faith. Does that, then, corroborate what might be called the "theological theory of totalitarianism"—the view, held by the atheist Nietzsche and the Russian Orthodox Dostoevsky, that in a world without the Judeo-Christian God, people would deify the state? Both Nietzsche and Dostoevsky thought this process would be advanced by the socialists. In fact the socialists opposed it valiantly, and it triumphed in the form of anti-socialism (Nazism) or a pseudo-socialist anti-socialism (Stalinism and all of its descendants).

Karl Löwith put Nietzsche at the very center of "the revolutionary break in the thought of the nineteenth century" which unwittingly led to such totalitarian developments. For Löwith, "if the notion of man and humanity was originally connected with Christianity, then mere humaneness is called into question as soon as it loses its Christian foundation. At first, the nineteenth century believed it possible to replace Christianity with humanity and humanism (Feuerbach, Ruge, Marx) but with the result that faith was finally lost in humanity (Stirner, Kierkegaard, Nietzsche)." The "bourgeois Christian world," Löwith argued, is coming to an end, and as a result the defense of humanity becomes all the more difficult.

Dostoevsky had developed this theme, of course. In the legend of the Grand Inquisitor he told of how a totalitarian church—and he equated the Roman papacy and the Jesuits with socialism, much as Nietzsche did—substituted bread and discipline for the faith and freedom of Christ. More recently, the same theme has been elaborated by a Jesuit, Henri de Lubac (in *The Drama of Atheistic Humanism*), and by Albert Camus (*The Rebel*). Indeed, one might even read the "mass society" theories of totalitarianism as secular variants of the theological theory of Nazism and Stalinism. The rootless people of mass society, Emil Lederer and Hannah Arendt suggested, are the human basis for totalitarian movements. They huddle together in utter subservience to party and leader in order to find a substitute for the sense of community which religion once expressed.

These theories, the theological as well as the sociological, overgeneralize. They are useful in specific cases and they may even be, alas, useful in the future. God's death and/or mass society may be necessary conditions for totalitarianism; they most certainly are not sufficient conditions for it.

In the religious theory of the emergence of totalitarian society, there is a romanticization—a falsification—of the Judeo-Christian past. Religion in the nineteenth-century West was not, in the main, a bulwark of freedom and humanism tragically overwhelmed by atheists who did not understand the social consequences of their own godlessness. When Nietzsche suggests this, picturing the Christians of his time as socialists (or the socialists as Christians; it comes almost to the same thing), he was being much too kind to the churches. Indeed, Löwith implicitly concedes this point when he writes of the down-going of the "*bourgeois* Christian" world.

Second, if Nietzsche's theories have something to do with the rise of Nazism, they are irrelevant to Stalinism. He wrote of the spiritual crisis of Western society. Yet Stalinism first appeared in the least "massified," least urban and, indeed, least capitalist of capitalist societies. The Russian Orthodox Church, which was indeed a target of the Revolution, was in the Byzantine tradition of Caesaro-papism and exhibited none of that post-Enlightenment pluralism and liberalism— that "latent socialism"—which figured so prominently, and so negatively, in Nietzsche's analysis.

Third, the Nazi triumph had many preconditions; the death of God was, at most, one of them. There were the German defeat in World War I and the nationalistic resentment which peace provoked; a Weimar Republic which lacked republicans; a Depression which was the greatest economic collapse in the history of capitalism.

But when all the qualifications are made, the fact is that, under very specific historic conditions, the loneliness of a people without God can indeed lead to the search for new idols, just as Nietzsche said. Man, Suzanne Langer has written, "can adapt himself somehow to anything his imagination can cope with: but he cannot deal with Chaos." In the thirties, Chaos did indeed come to Germany and the traditional God was no longer there to help people cope with it. Under those circumstances both the theological and the sociological theories of totalitarianism turned out to be true.

One cannot be sure that Chaos is banished. Perhaps these theories will be true again.

6
THE AGNOSTIC ECONOMY

CAPITALISM, THE FIRST AGNOSTIC economic-social formation in the history of the West, was created in considerable measure by deeply religious men and women. That paradox took roughly four centuries to become painfully apparent to masses of people, and it is one of the elements in the current spiritual crisis.

That Christianity played a major role in the rise of capitalism is hardly a new or startling insight. It was clearly stated by Hegel in the *Encyclopedia* and assumed to be obvious by Marx and Engels. Then, with Max Weber's *Protestant Ethic and the Spirit of Capitalism*, it became an established cliché in social science and a commonplace for the educated. Why, at this late date, belabor the obvious yet one more time?

Because, as Hegel so well understood, the familiar is often not known at all, and that is quite true in this case. Everyone "knows" that Weber gave an "idealist" explanation of the rise of capitalism which contrasts dramatically with Marx's "materialist" theories. That misunderstanding is particularly problematic because Weber himself sometimes participated in it. Yet, Marxists like Antonio Gramsci, Franz Borkenau and Christopher Hill have come to "Weberian" conclusions by means of a rigorously Marxist analysis. And Weber the "idealist" was much more of a fatalistic determinist than Marx the "materialist." But at the same time Weber was sensitive, not simply to the aesthetic, but also to the erotic consequences of the history he described. He was one of the first moderns to realize that the religion of sexuality was part of a massive social trend.

If, then, readers will shed their stereotypes, they may discover some new perceptions in this well-worn material. I intend, however,

to avoid many of the details of Weber's thesis, which have given rise
to endless controversies over the years.* In other contexts, it might
be enormously important whether there was really a precise statistical
pattern showing that Calvinists were more significant in the rise of
capitalism than Lutherans and Catholics. But I can accept the judgment of one of Weber's most dogged critics for the purposes of this
chapter: "Agreed that Weber exaggerated, that his generalizations
tend to be sweeping. . . . in the end it is admitted that the basic premises for Weber's assertions hold good. There was a clear connection
between Protestantism and economic progress."

That is all that is being asserted here, and it leads us down some
fascinating and quite unfamiliar paths into the present and the future.

———— I ————

Weber documented the fact that early capitalism was, in part, rationalized by theologians. But why did the emergent bourgeoisie thus turn
to religious images? Why didn't it state the economic case for its existence? A forgotten Marxist classic by Franz Borkenau gives the
subtlest answer to this question.†

Borkenau began in classic Marxist fashion. In feudalism, economic
relationships were also personal relationships of dependence and fealty.
Indeed, Marx had acknowledged that the feudal society *seems* to be
more human than a capitalistic one, though it actually stunts the human
potential in an order which is rigid, parochial and hierarchical as well
as interpersonal. Still, medieval culture believed that happiness, for
both people and society, requires the subordination of the part to the
whole. "As God created the world," Thomas Aquinas wrote, "and placed
everything in its proper place and brought forth such order that the
world appears as a harmonious whole, so too must the founders of
states assign each member his proper place and so order things that
an organic, unified state articulated in itself emerges." (Almost half a
century later, the contemporary German sociologist Niklas Luhmann
made the very same reading of Aquinas from a quite different political
and theoretical perspective.)

*See Appendix L.
†See Appendix M.

That Thomist ideology was the refraction of a social structure. Under feudalism work was authoritatively allocated to individuals and classes, each group was confined to its traditional way of working and rewarded on a scale determined by the community, private property was conditioned upon the performance of social function, there was no market in land and the labor force was tied, once and for all, to one occupation. To be sure, that description is an idealization of the high Middle Ages of the thirteenth century. In earlier times, feudalism was much less structured—and theology had an Augustinian sense of the sinfulness of the world rather than a Thomistic optimism about divinely ordained orderliness. Moreover, there were times of retrogression and pessimism within feudalism after the high Middle Ages as well.

For that matter, central to Borkenau's explanation of why capitalism first spoke in theological rather than in economic terms is the fact that the dissolution of feudalism was an uneven process of fits and starts. In the Renaissance, for instance, there was a period of money and trade capitalism. The limits of fixed and assigned roles had been removed, the individual was no longer subject to the old restraints and natural talent was asserted as a basic value. In this much more uncertain society, a Nicholas of Cusa no longer argued the rational knowability of God, as Thomas had, but now stressed faith in a hidden divinity. Cusa was, Cassirer has persuasively argued, the first modern man, for whom that medieval "great chain of being" no longer existed and one had to ask whether it was possible to know God. He was a mystic, yet like Pascal he was also a mathematical genius. But the difference between him and Pascal is important too: for all his doubts, Nicholas was an optimist, Pascal a pessimist for all his certitudes.

Still, with Nicholas of Cusa the Deus Absconditus, the God of Luther and Calvin as well as of Pascal, had made a first, tentative appearance within the Catholic Church itself.

In Aquinas, politics and justice went hand in hand because both were based upon a natural law which dictated principles of measure and regulation for every species in the social whole. But in Machiavelli, politics and justice are no longer of a piece. As Ernst Cassirer put it, "The sharp knife of Machiavelli's thought has cut off all the threads by which in former generations the state was fastened to the organic whole of human existence." This dark knowledge, and the Renaissance ideal of the exceptional individual which went along with it, hardly provided the basis for a new mass morality. It expressed the response of a dazzling elite to a disintegration which was only in its very first stages. Antonio Gramsci made much the same point as he tried to explain why capitalism had failed in Italy. His own country, he said, had gone through the elite spiritual crisis of the Renaissance, but without producing the mass movement which was the Reformation.

But that still leaves our question unanswered: why was the capitalist ideology first phrased mainly (but by no means exclusively) in sacred rather than secular terms? Because, Borkenau continued, after the commercial and trade capitalism of the Renaissance—which was as far as Italy got in this period—there came what Marx called the stage of "manufacture." That does not mean, as the word suggests in a contemporary vocabulary, machine production but, rather, innovative ways of organizing traditional technology. The artisans were still artisans, only now they were grouped together and worked for an entrepreneur instead of for themselves. A society of competition and rationally organized work was replacing a system based upon cooperation and personal relationships, but much of life was still quite traditional.

The sixteenth and seventeenth centuries, Borkenau said, were a kind of "in-between" time in which feudalism had broken down but capitalism had not yet appeared in mature form. It is for this reason that the capitalist ideology first emerges in one important variant, not as a straightforward articulation of bourgeois self-interest, but as a theology which lays an enormous stress upon the sinfulness of man and the arbitrariness of God. Daily life has indeed become more "sinful" in terms of the old values, and the supreme Author of this reality has thus become much more distant and autocratic than Thomas's God. The labor process is not yet routinely capitalist; rather, it is a deviation from feudal norms. Therefore, Borkenau concludes, the sixteenth century is ready for John Calvin but not for Adam Smith.

The world is now theologically corrupt and sinful, no longer a Thomist harmony. But if this is so, then, in the absence of a "natural" law, the only rules in society are those positive laws required to place limits upon the new, egotistic forces. That, however, also means that what is not explicitly forbidden is permitted. So there is now a private sphere, not permeated by divine principles, as in Aquinas, but independent and autonomous. The sectarian believers, so often fanatically intolerant, have unwittingly laid the foundations for a liberal, bourgeois ethic in which atomistic individuals are allowed to follow their own

interests so long as they do not interfere with the corresponding freedom enjoyed by everyone else.

The atheistic Hobbes was talking about the same reality as Luther
and Calvin: the war of each against all. But how can the people be
persuaded to accept this miserable situation? Between the sixteenth
and nineteenth centuries, Braudel has shown, the living standard of
the people declined. At the same time, people had to work harder
"voluntarily" but without the support of a settled community and its
traditional institutions.

For Weber, as is well known, the Calvinist notion of work as a
"calling" or vocation (*Beruf*) was the solution to this problem. There
was now, he said, a "senseless inversion" of what is natural, a society
characterized by "the pursuit of money and only money, the strictest
avoidance of all unaffected enjoyment, the denial of hedonistic or hap-
piness-oriented perspectives, where money must be thought of as an
end in itself, irrationally transcending the 'happiness' and 'utility' of
the individual." The Calvinists, in the name of their somber theology,
rejected the erotic, as well as the theater, and "idle talk." They were
soberly purposive, ascetics in the world, contemptuous of earthly goods
and for that very reason remarkably successful in obtaining them.
Theirs just happens to be an attitude which fits perfectly into the
capitalist economy in the period of the accumulation of capital—i.e.,
when there is a vast excess of investment over consumption.

I exaggerate—or, rather, Weber did. For reasons which will become clearer in the next section, he underlined the stern and flinty
aspects of Calvinism. The theologian-sociologist Ernst Troeltsch placed
more of an emphasis upon a Calvinist value that Weber mentioned but
did not stress, "the glorification of God in action is the real test of
individual personal reality in religion." The contemporary Marxist
Christopher Hill makes something of the same point. Protestantism is
a religion of the heart, of subjectivity, and "it is essential to understand
the release and relief which [it] brought to ordinary men and women. . . ."
Luther, particularly after he sided with Protestant princes against
rebellious peasants, had turned back to a very "Catholic" authoritarianism. Still, the Calvinists also introduced a very limited but real
democracy for the elite "elders."

In short, this was not an elitist development but, as Hill puts it,
"Protestant preachers in the late sixteenth and early seventeenth centuries undertook a cultural revolution, an exercise in indoctrination,

in brainwashing, on a hitherto unprecedented scale. . . . Only the strongest religious convictions could steel men to face the sacrifices, the repressions, the loss involved; and it took generations for these attitudes to be internalized." These economic-theological links were, it must be emphasized, anything but one-to-one. Puritanism, for instance, was a precursor of British socialism as well as of British capitalism, for Winstanley, the great Leftist general, used the same values which had inspired the entrepreneurs to summon the faithful to the collective task of building a "new Jerusalem."

Weber and the Marxists, who are antagonists according to the conventional wisdom, thus recognized the same link between theology and the capitalist cultural revolution. But two Marxists, Borkenau and Lucien Goldmann, also discovered that relationship in the interior monologues of the existentialist Christian genius Blaise Pascal. In the *Pensées*, they realized, one encounters the world of Luther and Calvin, of Machiavelli and Hobbes.

"Each ego," Pascal wrote, "is the enemy of all the other egos and wants to tyrannize over them." And "All men naturally hate one another." In fragment 294 these attitudes are treated at length and quite politically. Is there justice? If there were some natural order, Pascal said, then the "most general maxim among men" would not be that each follows the mores (*mœurs*) of his homeland. "Three [geographic] degrees reverses all jurisprudence, a meridian decides the truth. . . . Truth this side of the Pyrenees, error on the other side." A few lines later: "Custom is the basis of all equity for the mere reason that it is handed down to us. That is the mystical foundation of its authority." And, in the same mood, fragment 308 announced, "The custom of seeing kings accompanied by guards, drums, officers and everything else that makes for respect and terror has the result that the king's face, even when he is alone and without his retinue, imposes respect and terror on the subjects. . . ."

This is the world of Hobbes, but with an enormous difference. Hobbes, for all his atheistic tendencies, could be matter-of-fact about the depravity of man and the necessity of power because Calvinism had already sanctified life under those conditions. But Pascal, as both a Catholic and a political actor, had gone through a much different experience from that of his English similars. He had grown up in personal contact with the turbulent shifts in politics and religion—under the very shadow of Richelieu. The French of his time had responded to the spiritual crisis of the transition from feudalism with a number of strategies: there were Libertines, who, agreeing with Calvin that the world was corrupt and without meaning, proposed therefore to enjoy it as much as possible; Jesuits, who sought a middle road which would allow the feudal rich and powerful to adapt to the emergent order; and Jansenists, Catholic puritans, Pascal's party.

The French Catholic puritans were French. That is to state, not a tautology, but the important thesis that the political and economic function of theological ideas depended in some measure upon the history and culture on which they had their impact. The Jansenists were disproportionately recruited from the *noblesse de la robe*, a bourgeois stratum which had achieved nobility through bureaucratic services to the crown and which was hostile to the *noblesse d'épée*, descendants of the warrior aristocrats of old. They had feet planted in two worlds: they were feudal since they enjoyed rights and privileges decreed by the king; they were bourgeois, both in their origin and their outlook on life. And in the seventeenth century they were threatened by the growth of royal absolutism.

In England the gentry went through an evolution in which religious ideas defined political tendencies and resulted in two victorious revolutions; in France the gentry was absorbed into the royal bureaucracy and then, in Pascal's lifetime, victimized by it. Small wonder that under such circumstances a very worldly man could become religious and that his religion would be existential and lonely rather than militant and confident. Out of this there emerged a tragic concept of humanity (found, Goldmann argues, in Racine as well as Pascal). "One will die alone," fragment 211 tells us. "It is necessary, then, to act as if one were alone." There was no longer consolation in nature, for nature had become a godless geometric space.

So there is no simple relation between capitalism and religion and yet there is an unmistakable relation. Pascal defines the social and spiritual crisis in much the same way as Calvin or Hobbes, but within a different social structure and from the point of view of defeat, of aristocratic conscience, rather than of triumph, of bourgeois power. In this in-between world of the sixteenth and seventeenth centuries the radically new was defined in terms of an ancient Christian vocabulary which was, however, given an utterly new content. And people did not become Protestants because they were capitalists or capitalists because they were Protestants: Protestantism and capitalism were reciprocally interacting causes and effects in a gigantic social transition.

This relationship between Calvinism and capitalism is a fascinating subject in itself. For Max Weber it was also an important link in a deeply pessimistic—and determinist—theory of religion and society which has affinities with both Nietzsche and Marx.

Calvinism, Weber argued, was a moment in a process which had been going on for thousands of years: the progressive "disenchantment of the world" (he borrowed the poetic phrase from Schiller). This trend, he held, culminates in a modern society which is obsessed by a functional rationality but devoid of basic values. The Calvinists had been bearers of that rationality, but within a framework of moral conscience. As time went on, the rationality triumphed, the conscience effectively disappeared and the meaningless genius of the contemporary world was at hand. In Weber's grand theory, all of this occurred within an evolutionary pattern which goes back to the very origins of human society.

The earliest forms of religion, Weber wrote in *Economy and Society*, were concerned with this world, not the beyond. Magic aims at controlling the environment and it assumes an enchanted reality which can be affected by rites and prayers. Hebrew monotheism subverts that vision by doing away with all of the intermediate spirits and focusing upon the one God. Roman Catholicism, with its trinitarian deity and its interceding saints, retreated somewhat from this austere view. But the Reformation, and particularly its Calvinist variant, carried the logic of disenchantment to its ultimate conclusion. Calvinism rejected all "magical" means, including the sacraments; it individualized salvation, created the attitude of "inner-worldly asceticism" and, above all, gave rise to a self-controlled, methodical life style as a sign of—but not a means toward—redemption.

C. V. Wedgewood gave some dramatic examples of this Calvinist "disenchantment" in her history of the Thirty Years' War:

> The Elector Palatine [a Calvinist] in particular demonstrated his disbelief in transubstantiation in the crudest manner. Loudly jeering, he tore the Host in pieces. "What a fine God you are! You think you are stronger

than I? We shall see!" In his austerely whitewashed conventions, a tin basin served for a font and each communicant was presented with his own wooden mug. The Landgrave of Hesse-Cassel took the additional precaution of having the toughest possible bread provided for the sacrament so that his people should have no doubt whatever of the material nature of what they were eating.

But why, Weber asked, did this militant disenchantment—and the rationalization of life style and economy which went along with it—occur only in the West? His answer was studded with nuances and complexities which I will largely ignore in order simply to state the relevant generalizations which arise out of all the details. For Weber, the economic-theological difference between East and West turns on those basic conceptions of God which were briefly alluded to in the first chapter of this book. Broadly speaking, the Occident believed in a personal, creator God, the Orient in an impersonal, uncreated cosmos. The Occidental belief points to a God of action, the Oriental to a God of order. In Western theology, the faithful are God's *instruments* and seek to win his pleasure; in the Eastern they are his *vessel* and try to participate in his essence. And within the West itself, the Calvinists tend more to the concept of believer as instrument, the Lutherans to that of believer as vessel.

When God is everywhere and nowhere, as in the cosmic faiths of the East, the world tends to be less a sphere in its own right, more of an emanation, or even a deceptive appearance, of divinity. When God is in his heaven and humans are on earth, as in the salvation and savior creeds of the West, there is the possibility—which Calvinism actualized—that the world will take on an importance in and of itself. For that matter, Weber insisted that there had been ironic anticipations of the Calvinist dialectic under feudalism. Catholic monks fled from the world to monasteries, which unwittingly became the most rational economic units in the society, enjoying the advantages of economies of scale, planned production and the like. A later commentator has noted that even the Cistercian monks of the twelfth century, who retreated to marginal lands in order to escape the successful worldliness of the earlier monastic communities, thereby made an—unintended—shrewd economic decision.

The Calvinists repeated this monastic paradox, only they did so as ascetics *in* the world. Weber understood that not all Eastern religions denigrated wealth and economic success: the Confucians and the

Taoists regarded possessions as good because they provided the leisure for a more contemplative life—one in which the world could be ignored. The Calvinists, in contrast, had given the world a part in the religious drama, and success did not turn them away from it but, with their rational way of life, spurred them on to greater success. So conceptions of God—not the formal economic doctrines of a religion but the human psychology implicit in a religion's vision of ultimate reality—were factors in differentiating East and West, and countries and cultures within the West itself. Other factors were at work—China was a world unto itself, the Mediterranean a culture of trade—but this implicit economic ethic of Judeo-Christianity was one of the preconditions for the "disenchantment" and "rationalization" of the world which began in Europe in the sixteenth century and was part of the capitalist cultural revolution.

For Weber that process was ominous. As the religious values decayed, all that remained of the Protestant ethic was the dedication to systematic and scientific means, but the end—the glory of God—had disappeared. The Protestant, he wrote, "whether finally, who knows—has escaped from its cage. . . . the idea of duty in one's calling prowls around our life like the ghost of dead religious beliefs." So it was that a merely functional rationality triumphed and the world became increasingly bureaucratic in all of its subsystems and irrational in its totality. It is here that one finds the similarity—and the great difference—between Max Weber and Karl Marx.

Marx, too, had analyzed capitalism as a system of irrational rationality, of growing alienation in which the prodigies of human creation take control of human beings. As Karl Löwith put it, "The rational organization of life relationships gives rise to the irrational despotism of the organization. The understanding and destruction of this reality is the basis of the theoretical and practical work of Karl Marx; its understanding is the basis of Weber's work." This is one of the reasons Weber, who played an explicitly anti-socialist role in 1918–1920, was an influence on some of the most thoughtful Marxists of the twentieth century, people like Lukacs and Merleau-Ponty.

Of equal—perhaps greater—importance is the link between Weber and Nietzsche. For Weber, the process of rationalization had, as cause and effect, the differentiation of the various spheres of human knowledge and action. Science and religion and art were, in the medieval synthesis, aspects of a whole; in the modern age inaugurated by the

Protestant ethic they are increasingly independent and autonomous spheres. The Calvinists, we have seen, pushed the Christian dualism of God-heaven and earth-man to its extreme, and the paradoxical result was to drive God out of everyday—sinful—existence, thereby constituting the world as a realm in its own right (*because*, not in spite of, its depravity). The world was kept under control for as long as that original religious spirit prevailed, but a new way of perceiving reality, which would subvert all religion, had come into being.

This meditation leads to a passage by Weber that could have been written by Nietzsche (and we know that Weber was in fact influenced by Nietzsche, particularly through his friend Georg Simmel): "The old gods, disenchanted and therefore in the form of impersonal power, rise out of their grave, strive after control over our life and begin once again their eternal struggle with one another." There is in this secularized century, Weber said, a new outburst of demoniac polytheism. But that is, of course, almost exactly what Nietzsche said in his grudging lamentation over the political consequences of the death of a God whom he ambivalently detested.

Weber, then, quite plainly described—not predicted, but described—the end of the Protestant ethic, and did so in his major work on the Protestant ethic. Even so, Anthony Giddens points out, there are more than a few scholars who ignored the fact. "The Puritans," Weber wrote, "*wanted* to be men with a vocational calling [*wollte Berufsmenschen sein*]—we *must* be men with a vocational calling." The spread of asceticism from the monastic cell to the world resulted in the "mighty cosmos" of the modern economic era, and this would dominate the life style of the people "until the last shred of fossil fuel is burned up." Then came the critical paradox: "Because asceticism transformed the world by effectuating itself in it, the external goods of this world increased and eventually achieved an irresistible power over men, as never before in history."

The Puritans had regarded possessions as a "thin coat" which could easily be cast aside; now, Weber argues, they have become a steel cage from which the spirit is flown. No one, he concludes in a powerful passage, knows who will live in that cage in the future. And then the great sociologist of modern rationality refers to Friedrich Nietzsche and his fear of the "last men," people with small souls and without vision, the unacceptable alternative to the *Übermenschen*. No one knows, Weber writes, whether at the end of this tremendous development there will be completely new prophets or the rebirth of new ideas and ideals *or*—if neither of these—a mechanistic ossification embellished with a desperate self-importance. Then the truth about the "last men" of this cultural development would be: "Specialists without spirit, hedonists without heart, these nothings imagine themselves to have climbed to a never-before-achieved stage of humanity."

So Weber ended on a note of fatalism and despair. Perhaps, he said, a new charismatic leader would save civilization from a totally rationalized and calculated destiny—this kind of speculation provided the basis for the (incorrect) charge that Weber was a precursor of Hitler—but the probability was the victory of the men of order, the *Ordnungsmenschen*. In all of this there is more than a little determinism, with bureaucratization an ineluctable fate. In Löwith's brief comment on the similarity between Marx and Weber, quoted earlier, he also succinctly defined their difference. Marx wanted to understand *and* destroy the irrational despotism of the organization; Weber wanted to understand it.

One of the reasons Marx was more hopeful than Weber was that he felt capitalism was inherently agnostic. The loss of religious faith which accompanied capitalism's success was not, for him, an ironic paradox. It was a working-through of the logic of a godless system which had been unintentionally created by men and women of militant faith.

——— I I I ———

The young Marx first spelled out that idea in an important analysis which we encountered in Chapter 4, *On the Jewish Question*. The argument is quite convoluted—at one point the truly Christian state is described as atheist—and the language pre-Marxist. But the basic insight is one which Marx deepened throughout his life and which, even more to the point, is quite true. I will purposely ignore all the complexities not relevant to the present discussion and focus on a single theme: that the capitalist society is structurally agnostic even if it was historically Protestant Christian.

Under feudalism, Marx noted, all economic and social relations are directly and immediately political. By virtue of being a duke one is the largest landowner and most prestigious person in the duchy; the carpenter works in a way specified by tradition and/or law and is paid a price determined in the same fashion; and so on. In such a society, religion is the official ideology, for the question of how God is to be worshipped is not any more private than the rights and duties of a serf are. *Everything* is public. The capitalist revolution shatters that unity. In the bourgeois democratic state, isolated and atomized individuals are equal to one another before the law, and in the new, private sphere they are unequal. The economic and the social are separated from the political.

At this point the state becomes agnostic. If the Prussians still proclaim an established Christianity, that is because Prussia is a defective bourgeois society; if the French still have some semblance of official religious observance, that is because they, too, are underdeveloped. The Americans are the very perfection of the bourgeois state. They have no established religion, faith is a private matter and yet there is a flowering of religious sentiment. Religion, in short, may in fact play an important role in the life of the people but it is no longer, as under feudalism, a critical component of the system itself.

That theme is central to the basic argument of *Das Kapital*, even though it is rarely stated explicitly. In one of the most important passages of that masterpiece, the chapter on the genesis of capitalist rent in the land, Marx makes some far-reaching methodological statements. All exploitative modes of production, he holds, seek to pump a surplus out of the direct producers. In feudalism, that surplus is sometimes realized by requiring the serf to work a certain part of the time for the lord without being paid. That is "labor rent." Under those conditions, "surplus value" is undisguised: it is unpaid labor time. Where, Marx continues, the immediate producer owns the instruments of production—in feudalism, where the serf has his own plot of land—exploitation takes on a directly political form. The serf has a personal relationship of subordination to the lord.

In contrast, it is a critical and defining characteristic of capitalism that it extracts its surplus by economic rather than political means. The "free" worker possesses only his/her labor power, which is sold on a labor market. There is a legal right not to work but the exercise of it means, for all those who are not rich, poverty or even starvation. Under feudalism, tradition—and the Church is its main keeper—and the threat of armed power force the serfs to obey. Capitalism is, however, precisely a system of indirect and disguised rule. That, among many other reasons, is why it tends to be democratic. Since the political structure is no longer the direct and immediate agency for obtaining the surplus, since the system works on the basis of economic and not political compulsion, the political can be granted a degree of relative autonomy. There can be a democratic state because the undemocratic economy is the real guarantor of the power of the rulers.

That is the source of two seemingly contradictory paradoxes. On the one hand, as we saw in Chapter 4, the capitalist state is "Christian" in that it divides life into a heaven of political equality and a this-world of economic and social inequality. It incarnates—even in the United States, where religion is disestablished—a basic theological dualism. But, on the other hand, even when a capitalist political system is officially religious, as in Prussia during Marx's youth, it is in fact atheist. Capitalism as a system does not need God any more than the model of the planets developed by Napoleon's astronomer. A feudalism populated by free-thinking serfs is impossible, since their agnosticism would undermine the very traditions which are necessary to perpetuate the system. A capitalism of free-thinking workers is more logical than a Christian (or religious) capitalism, since capitalism has jettisoned an old-fashioned, now unnecessary ideology.

All of this is critically important to Marx's analysis of capitalism, yet it is not explicitly formulated at any great length in his work. It is, however, quite clearly stated in a footnote in Volume I of *Das Kapital*. Marx tells how one of his critics had admitted that his theories applied to present-day capitalism but argued that they did not hold for the Middle Ages, when religion rather than economics had been dominant, or in ancient Greece, where politics had been the determining factor. "It is clear," Marx replies, "that the Middle Ages could not live off of Catholicism nor Greece off of politics. The manner and mode in which they support life, rather, explain why politics in Greece and religion in the Middle Ages played the key role [*die Hauptrolle*]."

That reference is cryptic but it is explained by what I have just said. Religion played the "key role" in the Middle Ages, not because it was an independent and determining factor, but because feudalism required religious faith as a fundamental motive in the functioning of the economy. The Greeks, similarly, needed civic virtue—politics— for their system to work. But now there is a new mode of production, the very first in which the economic *as* the economic is dominant. This

point ramifies in many directions—it means, contrary to the understanding of most people who call themselves Marxists, that the categories of *Das Kapital* can be applied only to capitalism—but the relevant
implication for this book is already plain enough: capitalism, unlike its
predecessor systems in the West, is structurally agnostic even if it
was historically associated with Protestant Christianity.

The knowledge of that fact has only emerged slowly, in the course
of a long history. It surfaced in different countries in different ways,
as we would expect. Bernard Groethuysen's account of the origins
of the bourgeois spirit in France is only one case in point but it can
stand as an example of a process which has occurred in every Western
country.

The French bourgeois, Groethuysen wrote, did not immediately
become an atheist, or even a Deist. And yet:

> The well-ordered life of the bourgeois seems to present fewer interstices
> through which the mysterious power of either a blind fortune or a wise
> God can penetrate. Acting in accordance with certain well-established
> maxims to which he holds fast, the bourgeois will be easily disposed to
> believe that it is he himself who makes his life. He works and saves,
> calculates and measures, reasons and anticipates. Creating order every-
> where, trying to leave nothing to chance, seeking a solid basis for his
> life, in the domain of morality as well as of economics, he will be able to
> dispense with mysterious powers.

Therefore, Groethuysen argues, even when the bourgeois remains
Catholic in France—as was often the case—it was a new Catholicism
to which he adhered. The distant terrible God of Pascal gave way to
a constitutional monarch in the heavens who ruled, not by means of
miracles, but in accordance with the law. In the old order, it was the
divine will which assigned to each person his or her rank and station
in life. "But how can one believe that God plays a role in the social
order where everything is confused and the bourgeois, born yesterday
and the child of his own deeds, raises himself above those who hold
their rank by the right of birth, people who have been selected by
divine providence above all the others?"

Groethuysen documents this shift in a careful analysis of sermons
and popular books. His conclusion is similar to Marx's: "The individual
bourgeois, this or that bourgeois, remains Catholic; but the bourgeoisie, the *bourgeois state*, will no longer be Catholic. The bourgeois,

seeing himself abandoned by the God of the Christians . . . will proceed to the conquest of power without the aid of the Church and without asking counsel of the God of the Christians; he will make his *rights* prevail and institute a new order."

Marx anticipated this development and expected that the religious morality which had motivated the masses in the early stages of capitalism would be subverted by the first society in human history which had no functional need of God. And he had, of course, his own alternative to that valueless mature capitalism. The current status of his hopes will be analyzed in Chapter 10, but for now we can make a summary contrast of Weber and Marx. The "idealist" sociologist turned out to be a technological determinist; the "materialist" revolutionary said that history remained open, that it was possible for men and women to assume control of the despotic structures which controlled them.

I simplify. Weber, the despairing prophet of the organized and soulless society, was also sensitive to the potential of aesthetic and erotic revolt within it. His insights in this area will lead us into some of the contemporary applications of his ideas.

—— I V ——

At the very beginning of religious history, Weber said, there were orgiastic cults, holy prostitution, and other manifestations of the intimate relation between the sexual and the spiritual. But the priests almost without exception favored marriage; they wanted to control and regulate this powerful drive. That, however, had some unintended consequences. As the sexual was exiled from ordinary life, it became sublimated into the erotic and, for the same reason, it became veiled. It was the feudal doctrine of courtly love which further sublimated, and even romanticized, the erotic, a process continued by the Renaissance concepts of courtesy and by the mixing of men and women in salon culture.

For that matter, as Christopher Hill shows, English Puritan rigor was, among other things, a protest against the aristocratic "property marriage" with its tolerance of infidelity. Now there was to be "a monogamous partnership, ostensibly based on mutual love, and a business partnership in the affairs of the family." In this context, the "puritanism" of the Puritans was a moment in the emergence of the ideal of romantic life.

History played the same joke on that Puritan notion of love that it did on the concept of an economic "calling." With Protestantism supplying the theological rationale for differentiating society into autonomous and independent spheres, art detaches itself from its religious and social functions and increasingly becomes a realm in its own right. More than that, as the economic structures become more relentlessly rational, art becomes a refuge for spontaneity and rebellion. It is thus no accident, Weber's analysis held, that the bohemian life style—the artist as outcast, as priest of a new aesthetic faith—comes into being precisely when capitalism triumphs. And one of the central tenets of bohemia is, of course, the liberation of sexuality from bourgeois conventions.

In the twentieth century—and Weber wrote during its first quarter, though his words resonate now—the erotic moves from the seacoasts of bohemia into the larger society. It becomes the only sphere of human existence in which modern people are in touch with primitive emotions and experiences. It therefore stands in sharp contrast to the increasingly intellectualized, refined and rationalized world and offers a kind of personal salvation from the over-organization of society. For Weber, then, the development of industrial society and the disappearance of the Protestant spirit turn into an incitement to eroticism. (This contrasts with Freud's view of civilization as the progress of repression, a concept which will be discussed in the next chapter.)

A half century after Weber's death, Daniel Bell generalized the paradox that Puritanism unwittingly paved the way for eroticism. There was, he wrote, a fundamental clash of values emerging in Western society, a product of "the 'new capitalism' of abundance which emerged in the 1920s," when the installment plan, the weapon that killed the Protestant spirit, developed. His analysis, has, I think, a pseudo-concreteness about it—the "new capitalism" did not come until after World War II, and the twenties were characterized, precisely, by inadequate consumption—yet the basic point is compelling. Capitalism today has an ethic of compulsory consumption, even hedonism, which is a prerequisite for selling its enormous output; but that output itself is created in a work process of enormous rationalization. Indeed, I would add that the morality of bohemia, of protest against that rationalization, is increasingly taking hold of the very masses who must work within the rationalized system. In the world of distribution the citizen is told to live as if there were no tomorrow, in the world of production to work as if the Protestant ethic still applied.

Bell's version of this reality refracts the experiences of the sixties, when a significant portion of college youth turned their backs, not simply on the Protestant ethic, but on capitalist motivation in any form. The children of the social upper class and upper middle class dropped out of economic competition in considerable numbers, and there were even those who argued that this process would "blue" America by opening up opportunities for the children of the—blue-collar—working class. The economic crisis of the seventies did much to undermine that attitude as college accounting departments and pre-law courses thrived. And yet that seeming return to the old ways was quite ambiguous.

To be sure, the classic economic dictum of the capitalist system—those who do not work shall not eat—remains in force for the overwhelming majority of the people. A time of relative affluence like the sixties could foster the pretense that the counterculture is an alternative to the system, but that illusion dissolves with the return of discipline associated with an economic crisis (indeed, the restoration of discipline has always been one of the functions of crisis). But not quite. In late capitalist society men and women compete for incomes and do the specialized, routinized and rationalized jobs that have to be done—but work has been robbed of any moral significance. At the same time, as Bell emphasized, a new type of work appears—the cooperative effort required in the "tertiary" sector of late capitalism, the area of the production of services and particularly of knowledge rather than goods—and this new category needs a solidaristic ethic, but none is available.

Fred Hirsch brilliantly analyzed some of these subtle changes in his *Social Limits to Growth*. Society, Hirsch said, is becoming more complex and planned (the "Weber" factor, if you will). But, and here he makes Bell's point more complex, there is now more competition, not for factory products, but for "positional" goods which cannot be produced in greater abundance without a deterioration in quality. The old-fashioned rich could enjoy a house which was isolated from the community and very private—but the moment one tries to generalize that possession, to make it available, let us say, to the entire upper middle class, one runs into an obvious limit. By definition, in a given space there can be only so many isolated and very private houses. One can proliferate washing machines almost endlessly—but not the experience of being the very first visitor to an unspoiled hideaway. Sooner or later—and in recent years sooner and sooner—that hideaway will be the site of a multinational hotel or motel. Such goods change their nature for social reasons; washing machines do not.

Under these circumstances, "management of the system has become more necessary, but the entrenchment of the individualistic ethos makes it more difficult." At the same time, as collective bargaining takes over from the market in ever-expanding areas of life, there must be some validation for the outcome of the human decisions which have replaced the "invisible hand." Keynesianism, Hirsch writes, "involved the progressive extension of explicit social organization without the support of a matching social morality—more rules for the common good, having to be prescribed and adhered to in a culture oriented increasingly to the private good."

"With the atrophy of social ties," Hirsch continues, "including those stemming from religious belief, the only remaining basis for social obligation has become civic duty to uphold a just society." In the small community there is social pressure—one does not litter because it will outrage the neighbors. But what reason is there for not littering in the alienated, gigantic, often neighborless big city? The result is the "reluctant collectivism" of Western (and above all American) society, a social order characterized by extremely individualistic values and an increasingly collectivist infrastructure.

But is there no way out of this impasse? Hirsch thinks there is, and it is an extremely important anticipation of an approach which will be generalized in Chapter 10: the possibility of political and economic decisions which make certain ethical and psychological responses, if not inevitable, then more likely. This is not, it should be made plain, the traditional philanthropic—or totalitarian—notion of forming character and personality from on high according to a preconceived model. If societal structures have made perverse and even irrational conduct likely, conscious policy can expand the freedom of individual choice so that different kinds of decisions are possible.

Hirsch's most instructive example of this dialectic has to do with education. He uses a marvelous image to develop his idea: standing on tiptoe. There is a parade and the people in the second rank of the spectators stand on tiptoe, which forces those in the third, fourth and fifth ranks to do the same. Eventually, the entire crowd is using muscle and energy in this way—and no one can see any better. The individual strategy—"I" will stand on tiptoe to gain an advantage over my neighbors—is frustrated by a social structure (the nature of a crowd).

So also with education in the post–World War II period. When that phase of capitalist development began in 1945, having a college degree was a quantifiable economic advantage. So more and more young people began to acquire a college education. When the number of such people rose from, say, 5 percent of the population to 10 percent, there were gains for the individuals and society, the former increasing their income over what it would otherwise have been, the latter benefiting from increased productivity. But when the strategy is generalized, when 40 percent of a generation begins college and 20 percent completes the course and, at the same time, the number of genuine college jobs—i.e., those which actually are performed better after such training—fails to keep pace with the supply, the investment of time and money in this area becomes both individually and socially wasteful. The educational "yield" has declined to the point that the young enter college to defend themselves against those doing the same thing, not to improve their position; and the social dividend has been swallowed up by a system of "credentialism" in which the degree has little or no relation to, or impact upon, productivity; indeed, education at this point amounts to a squandered resource.

If, then, society followed tax and other policies which made the income and wealth structure somewhat more egalitarian—if, in Christopher Jencks's terms, it reduced the rewards of success and the punishments for failure—that would make individuals more likely to respond to the new situation with freely chosen decisions to follow work strategies which would more adequately reward both them and the society as a whole. And that, not so incidentally, could also free educators from the constraint of acting as instructors in the trade schools of higher education. Indeed, it might even create the social space for a rebirth of humanistic and other "impractical" studies, which would enormously enrich the students and the society as a whole.

So Hirsch looked for economic and social policies with a psychological—and even moral—dimension which responds to the crisis caused by the decay of the Protestant ethic. Other contemporary analysts, located at every point on the political spectrum, recognize the same problem. On the Left, Robert Heilbroner fears that the decline of a voluntary, internalized work ethic will lead to a new state idolatry which will fill the religious gap left by the death of traditional Christianity. On the Right, George Gilder tries to confront the attitude that capitalism is "an edifice without an inherent foundation in morality and religion . . . [which] engenders a shallow and dubious order of human life" with a fanciful—unbelievable—reaffirmation of the Protestant ethic, but it is a sentimental, liberal "Christianity" which merely omits the cross. Moreover, as one of Gilder's critics has noted, Gilder does not trust in his own faith but buttresses it with "supply-side" tax incentives. He believes, Jerome L. Himmelstein comments, in God and Mammon at the same time.

One could go on at considerable length—the *Harvard Business Review* published an article in 1982 which acknowledged that the traditional capitalist morality was dying and proposed a technocratic substitute for it—but the central point is obvious enough. With the disappearance of the traditional Western God, the workaday world, like Pascal's cosmos, has become empty and alienated, without a transcendent justification or presence. As a result, our motivational system, from reasons for not littering to reasons for living, becomes problematic.

There are private escapes from this fate, such as the religion of sexuality. But these can hardly hold a community together and they are, as Bell shows, in contradiction to the scientific rigor which the system still requires. In the *Communist Manifesto*, Marx and Engels wrote of capitalism: "It has drowned the most heavenly ecstasies of religious fervor, of chivalrous enthusiasm, of philistine sentimentalism, in the icy waters of egotistical calculation." They were, as often was the case, quite right about the trend but a century or so off in their timing of it. The present generation is the first to live the fullness of their prophecy as an ordinary experience. And that is another dimension of the spiritual crisis of the late twentieth century.

7
DOES THE DEVIL EXIST?

"PRIMITIVE CIVILIZATIONS," Emile Durkheim wrote, "offer privileged cases because they are simple cases." "Since the facts there are simpler," he continued, "the relations between them are more apparent. The reasons with which men account for their acts have not yet been elaborated and denatured by studied reflection. . . . they offer a means of discerning the ever-present causes upon which the most essential forms of religious thought and practice depend."

That truth must be treated with care. It is possible that the simplicity of those early societies may be a function of our distance from them rather than of the societies themselves. Moreover, the cohesiveness of preliterate life is so great, the integrating force of religion so profound, that, Robert Merton notes, one tends to lose sight of the way in which God and the gods can divide, as well as unite, people. Still, with these qualifications, even a brief survey of the earliest forms of human life allows one to see the "model behind the reality," the very structures of society, in stark, dramatic fashion, with a particular emphasis upon the role of religion in establishing individual and social identity. And that helps the understanding of the complexities of the present spiritual crisis.

In the course of this overview one encounters a bitter, and contemporary, irony. In the nineteenth century, when the triumphant imperial West discovered preliterate peoples during its conquest of the world, the experience was quite positive for the conquerors. The existence of childish cultures that believed in demons was a tribute to the rationality of European humanity, that bourgeois Christian culmination of the evolutionary eons. Then came the twentieth century, with its barbaric wars, its Freudian knowledge of the savage within the civilized psyche and a modern art which asserted the relevance of African masks. The dawn of history no longer seems so remote and some suspect that, if God is dying, perhaps the Devil is not.

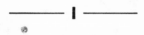

The discipline of anthropology is a cause of the present crisis as well as a means of understanding it.

It was in the nineteenth century that a notion which had been building for several centuries all but exploded inside the Western consciousness: that many of its ideas about human nature—and God— were parochial and culture-bound. "Anthropologists," Barrington Moore writes, "shook our [Western] assurance by vividly exhibiting such a variety of human customs and beliefs as to make the notion of any simple standard of moral and political judgement seem no more than a provincial rationalization of some brief phase of European history." This awareness coincided with the emergence of a new imperialism as the West, to a degree unknown before, encountered the distant societies which it was forcing into the capitalist world market.

The period was also the age of Darwin—and of the "social Darwinism" of Herbert Spencer—and that offered an escape from the corrosive effects of relativism. This was, as Lévi-Strauss puts it, "an attempt to suppress the cultural differences while pretending to recognize them. For if one treated the different states in which one found human society, the ancient and the contemporary, as *stages* or *steps* in a linear development which, departing from the same point, converges toward the same goal, then the diversity was only apparent." Not so incidentally, such a model also showed that Western capitalism was the expression of economic human nature, and Western Christianity the incarnation of religious human nature.

To be sure, there were thinkers even before the nineteenth century who had seen through this error. Vico and Herder, in the seventeenth and eighteenth centuries, saw earlier forms of society as coherent and self-contained systems which had to be judged in their own terms and not those of an alien culture. But the dominant trend, very much connected to the colonialist mentality, was to provide "scientific" explanations of the innate inferiority of preliterate (and some-times of all non-Western) peoples. Frazer's enormously influential *Golden Bough* saw them as prescientific; Lévy-Bruhl for a while even postu-lated a "prelogical" mentality.

Marx and Engels were among the first to provide an alternative to this view. They were not, let it be plainly stated, anthropological scholars; their learning in this area was quite limited.* If they do not deserve to be ignored in the history of that discipline—as happens—neither can one claim that they were major figures in it. What is significant is not their research but their attitude toward the data.

For Marx, *the* error of bourgeois thought was, precisely, to equate capitalist man with human nature. The stone tools of the early stages of humanity were, in that perspective, crude and rudimentary forms of "capital." That, Marx argued, is to engage in a crude materialism, to understand capital as a thing (any tool) rather than, as was the case, a historically specific way of using things. And, he continued, the bourgeois notion of Neolithic men and women as savage capitalists has as its analogue the Christian view that all pre-Christian religions are flawed intimations of the truths revealed in their fullness by Christi-anity.

So it was not an accident that the cross sanctified colonial conquest. Just as Nietzsche said, universalistic monotheisms make excellent im-perial religions, for they regard all other cults and creeds, not simply as different, but as wrong. It should be added that these same mono-theisms also provide a conceptual basis for an idea of the oneness of humanity which can be anti-racist and anti-colonialist. The derivation of the entire human race from two common parents, Adam and Eve, is implicitly a politically radical idea. In the nineteenth century it was, however, only implicit.

Thus anthropology is one of the causes of the present crisis in a number of ways. It is a major source of the pervasive relativism which leads people to doubt faith itself; it is also a source of a colonialist and religious anti-relativism which sees capitalism and Christianity as the absolutes by which the entire past is to be judged. The truth is, I think, the one stated with great precision by Lévi-Strauss: "there are

*See Appendix N.

no childish peoples; all peoples are adult, including those who have not kept a journal of their childhood and adolescence."

———— I I ————

If one avoids the prejudices which make anthropology part of the problem, then anthropology becomes a means of illuminating that problem. In at least three areas the experience of early human society—by analogy, contrast, or both—sheds light upon the contemporary plight: the religious role in shaping individual and group identity; the sense of the sacred; and the notion, first elaborated by Emile Durkheim, that preliterate societies reveal the secret of all religions, which is that they are society's way of worshipping itself.

Robert Bellah writes that a people needs "a relatively condensed, and therefore highly general, definition of the environment and itself. . . . Such a conception is particularly necessary in situations of stress and disturbance because it can provide the most general set of instructions as to how the system is to maintain itself and repair any damage sustained." In Neolithic societies, that function is writ large. The collective identity derived from a common ancestor provides a mythical world picture that allows the individual and the group to survive under precarious conditions.

This happens within a small-scale society in which the members are not in competition with one another but join in solidarity against the outside world, so that their mythic identity is not based on a divinity "out there," counterposed to individual and group, but pervades the life of the community. All of this is part of the process whereby men and women, in Lévi-Strauss's influential formulation, "*humanize natural laws*" through religion and "*naturalize human actions*" through magic. Nature is seen as ruled by spirits with human qualities; humans are believed to possess the power, through magic and later through prayer, to influence nature. These attitudes are particularly relevant to crisis; they are a way of dealing with "the great biological and social game which perpetually unrolls between the living and the dead." So Hegel, basing himself on Antigone, saw the distinctive function of the family in treating the corpse of the dead member, not as a meaningless "fact" of nature, but as the memorial of a conscious life which yet survives in another form. The contemporary French historian Pierre Chaunu even argues that the difference between those animals (the humans) who bury their dead and those who do not "is the most important distinction in history." A tomb is the first sure sign of the presence of the human.

This is not to suggest that religion, either at the beginning of human life or now, is simply a consolation for death, suffering and evil. In a critique of his fellow anthropologist Malinowski, Clifford Geertz writes, "Over its career, religion has probably disturbed men as much as it has cheered them; forced them into a head-on, unblinking confrontation of the fact that they are born to trouble as often as it has enabled them to avoid such a confrontation by projecting them into a sort of infantile fairy-tale world where—Malinowski again—hope cannot fail nor desire deceive." Religion may provide the basis for an identity by interpreting human existence, but this process can be a somber, life-denying phenomenon. Religious people do not avoid suffering—some of them actively seek and endure it. But for them suffering has a meaning. At the very beginning of human life, when men and women were so much more the playthings of external nature than they are now, myth and ritual were thus the means, not simply for defining an identity, but for survival itself.

All of this was accomplished within an intuition of the "holy" or the "sacred," terms which remain significant to this very day.

Durkheim, as is so often the case, pioneered the use of the concept. All religions, he said, divide the world into the "profane" and the "sacred." The best-known elaboration of the latter term was made by Rudolf Otto in *The Idea of the Holy*. The holy (sacred), he wrote, is the "real, innermost core" of every religion, from the earliest to the most modern. It refers to a mysterious, majestic, fascinating, "numinous" someone who is "wholly other." It begins with a "daemonic dread," a fear of the god(s), and gradually is transformed into a fear of God. In this process, "dread becomes worship; out of a confusion of inchoate emotions and bewildered palpitations and feelings grows 'religion' and out of a 'shudder' a holy awe."

This theory, it should be carefully noted, does not equate the primitive "shudder" of early humanity with contemporary religiosity. Otto was a devout Christian who believed his own faith to be ultimate and true. For him, the New Testament vision of the holy is "not merely the numinous in general, not even the numinous at its highest development; we must always understand it as the numinous completely permeated and sanctified with elements signifying rationality, purpose, personality, morality." It is Jesus's unique function to say that this awesome and mysterious force which is revered in fear and trembling is also "our Father," external, benevolent, gracious. That, of course, is very much in keeping with the Euro-centered, Christo-centered tradition which views Christianity as the very apex of religious evolution, the truth in its ultimate form.

Otto's analysis has all but become synonymous with the idea of the holy, but Simmel's *Sociology of Religion* is a more profound treatment of it, even if in a few pages. Nature, Simmel wrote, "often reveals in us feelings of aesthetic well-being, or fear and terror and realization of the grandeur of its superpower." Or it can produce a feeling extremely difficult to define, a sense that the world is "in secret consonance with our innermost being" (that is what Freud called the "oceanic sense"). That emotion *can* become the basis of a religion—or of a pious, religious-like attitude toward parents or homeland or social class. This piety is "religiosity in a quasi-fluid state" but it does not necessarily "coalesce into a stable form of behaviour vis-à-vis the gods, i.e. into a religion." So it is that there are "religious natures without religion."

Another view of the sacred is more prosaic. It is a way of classifying which foods can be eaten and which cannot, of keeping order in a society. "The sacred," writes the contemporary anthropologist Mary Douglas, "is constructed by the efforts of individuals to live together in society and to bind themselves to their agreed rules. It is characterized by the dangers alleged to follow upon breach of the rules. Belief in these dangers acts as a deterrent." Therefore the mystical— the inexplicable, numinous, awesome—character of the sacred is not simply a product of human emotion, of the "soul." "The reasons for any particular way of defining the sacred are embedded in the social consensus which it protects. The ultimate explanation of the sacred is that this is how the universe is constituted; it is dangerous because this is what reality is like. The only person who holds nothing sacred is the one who has no internalised norms of any community."

Emile Durkheim would have agreed. Indeed, he made the most radical claim about the social nature of religion ever argued: religion, he said, worships society.

Durkheim was deeply influenced by his studies in Germany during his formative years. When he wrote, in *The Elementary Forms of the*

Religious Life, that "it is an essential postulate of sociology that a human institution cannot rest upon an error and a lie," he was restating a basic Hegelian truth. For the purposes of this chapter, however, it is the impact of Kant upon his thought that is crucial. In a very real sense, Durkheim "socialized" Kant and made the great idealist a precursor of a radically deterministic view of human life and knowledge in which society is the key, not simply to religion, but to the very possibility of human thought itself.

Kant had argued, as Chapter 2 showed, that experience was only possible if there were *a priori* categories which permitted the human mind to order the chaotic data in a meaningful way. Now Durkheim restated that proposition sociologically:

> If men did not agree upon these essential ideas at every moment, if they did not have the same conception of time, space, cause, number, etc., all contact between their minds would be impossible and with that, all life together. This seems to be the origin of the exceptional authority which is inherent in reason and makes us accept it with confidence. *It is the very authority of society transferring itself to a certain manner of thought which is the indispensable condition of all common action* [emphasis added].

The rules of reason are a precondition, not simply of experience but of communication and therefore of society; a social necessity thus undergirds our notions of time and space, and since society is thus the key to language—to humanity itself—it is awesome, Holy.

In arguing this hypothesis, Durkheim was attacking all of the theories which said that the earliest humans worshipped nature. The natural objects—plants, animals—which figured in their religions, he argued, were actually symbols of a nonvisible reality. The totems of the Australian aborigines (Durkheim took totemic religions as the focus of his analysis) were "the material from under which the imagination represents this immaterial substance, this energy diffused through all sorts of heterogeneous things, which alone is the real object of the cult." The Sioux call this force *wakan,* the Iroquois, *orenda,* the Melanesians *mana,* but the definition is the same: " 'a force altogether distinct from physical power which acts in all ways for good and evil. . . .' " "All life," the Sioux say, "is 'wakan.' So also is everything which exhibits power, whether in action, as the winds and drifting clouds, or in passive endurance, as the boulder by the wayside."

What is the basis of this mysterious force? It is society, which "is to its members what a god is to his worshippers. In fact, a god is, first of all, a being whom men think of as superior to themselves, and upon whom they feel that they depend. Now society also gives us this sensation of perpetual dependence." And indeed, this translation of social relations into religious symbols is a prime source of political authority. Society's hold "is due much less to the physical supremacy of which it has the privilege than to the moral authority with which it is invested." Simmel made the same point in even more dramatic fashion. The unity of the group, which is the basis of the religious transcendentals, "must only too often seem like a miracle."

Durkheim's thesis ramifies in many directions. Jürgen Habermas suggests that he and the American George Herbert Mead were precursors of twentieth-century linguistic philosophy with its understanding that language is the articulation of a way of living. More to the point of this chapter, Durkheim made morality itself dependent upon that social sense of the sacred. He therefore thought that an irreligious society would be an immoral society, lacking all transcendental reasons for ethical behavior. People must, he said in the conclusion of *The Elementary Forms of the Religious Life*, celebrate their unity, their trust, through rituals and commemorations. But then Durkheim recognized that at the present time "the great things of the past which filled our fathers with enthusiasm do not excite the same ardour in us." "In a word," he wrote, "the old gods are growing old or are already dead and others are not yet born." However, he was confident that there would be a new time of religious effervescence, for "if there are no gospels that are immortal . . . neither is there any reason for believing that humanity is incapable of inventing new ones."

So the "simple case" of preliterate religion proves, in Durkheim's view, that human nature itself is religious. This, Mary Douglas comments, is a sophisticated version of what she learned at Sunday School and from the Catholic Truth Society: "if primitive man is religious, this is proof that modern irreligion fails to meet the requirements of our nature." It is not so simple as that. In the nineteenth century the West looked down upon primitive faiths with contempt; now, at the end of a tormented twentieth century, it sometimes views them with nostalgia. Only, I would argue, there is no way back, and one of the reasons is that those "primitives" learned and transformed themselves. They are a dynamic clue to their own disappearance.

The "simple case" was itself the product of complex change.

The "Neolithic revolution" is often defined as the point at which humans ceased to be exclusively hunters, fishers, and gleaners and began to grow food and domesticate animals. It was, Klaus Eder theorizes, the cause and effect of a cognitive, as well as an economic, revolution, and the former had much to do with religious concepts. Paleolithic peoples—"Stone Age" men and women, in the popular phrase—had an impoverished religious view of the world in which natural forces were, at the most sophisticated, only rudimentary spirits. With Neolithic agriculture, settled communities appeared and humans began to shape their environment rather than accept it as a mysterious given. A "magic" reality in which one cajoles enchanted powers gives way to a mythic cosmos which possesses a kind of order and in which personalized gods are no longer merely arbitrary. The humanization of nature is at hand, and analogy is the great intellectual tool for understanding the universe.

The social relations of family and tribe are projected upon the screen of the world; there is an endless reciprocity and similarity between humans and the universe. Jürgen Habermas notes that this "gives each perceptible element its meaningful place. It thereby absorbs the insecurities of a society which, by virtue of its very low level of development of the forces of production, is hardly able to control its environment. In the mythical world, all entities are seen as being of the same species: individual man as well as substances like rocks and plants, animals and gods."

In such a system, religion does not legitimize the existing order; it constitutes it. The "simple case," then, represents a gigantic advance, and the myths allow humans to deal with much more complexity than ever before. Still, there is only a "domestic mode of production" and morality is situational, applying to a family or a tribe but not beyond its frontiers. Then, in "early high culture," religion and society as cause and effect of each other achieve a new level of economic-religious sophistication. Roles which had once been different functions of a relatively homogeneous whole take on a life of their own; there are chiefs, kings, priests. What happens on earth is then refracted in heaven as the gods become even more human and, like mortals, submit to a division of labor. This is a critical moment, for now there is a distinction between the sacred (which once explained everything) and the secular.

Eder emphasizes the cognitive aspect of this change, too. In early high culture there is the labor of artisans, the first abstract, intentional form of man's interaction with nature. Indeed, nature is no longer a given; it is becoming a human product, a second, created, nature. There is thus an intellectual transition from the logic of perceptible qualities to the logic of (human) forms. Yet, for all of these changes, the gods still remain identified with a people even if the latter is more complexly organized than ever before. It is with the appearance of "developed high culture" that divinity also escapes from the particular. This is the time of the universalistic, monotheistic God. It marks one of the great divides in human history.

In the first millennium before the Christian Era, all of the ancient centers of culture went through the experience of a religious rejection of the world. Man and society were seen negatively, and the invisible realm of the divine was the truly real and valuable. Why? "The" answer has not been identified as yet, but a further increase in social and economic complexity was certainly a factor. The earliest forms of society, Sahlins writes, lived at an exceedingly low level of material existence, yet since subsistence was their purpose, they were not poor. Poverty, he continues, only comes into existence when consumption has become an end in itself, there is a surplus and it is unevenly divided up. At this point, productive capacity increases and poverty therefore becomes possible.

Habermas elaborates this notion:

As soon as the organization of societal labor is separated from kinship relations, resources can be more easily mobilized and effectively coordinated. But this expansion of material reproduction is accomplished at the price of dismantling the system organized around families and replacing it with a stratified class society. That which, from the point of view of the system, presents itself as an integration of society on a higher level of expanded production means, in terms of social integration, *an increase in social inequality*, massive economic exploitation and juridically cloaked repression of the dependent classes.

The dualistic religions which emerged in developed high culture were able to legitimize this new situation: the miseries of this world would be made good in the next. That is not to suggest that some mysterious and teleological providence summoned up monotheistic theologies *because* they were needed to play a political and social role. Rather, a societal transformation which was reciprocally economic and religious had radically redefined the religious function in society. Moreover, there was an exceedingly important ambiguity in this development: it rationalized the established power *and* it made possible a subversive threat against it.

God no longer belonged to a particular tribe or a city. And therefore the religious community ceased to be ethnic and, on principle at least, was opened up to all believers. As a result religion became, for the first time, subjective and personal, which made prayer possible. To be sure, there had been rites and ceremonies and collective incantations almost from the beginning of human life, but those were social and political acts, which is why people could worship the gods of whatever place they found themselves in. Now, however, prayer as the communication between the individual and God made sense. And with the emergence of conscience came the possibility of a conflict between the collective identity sponsored by the state and the ego identity of the believer responsible to God.

With the Reformation, that conflict became a crucial aspect of life. In theory, one's personal relation with God now took precedence over the Church as well as the state. In fact, Luther was, we have seen, quite "Catholic" in his political authoritarianism, particularly after the peasant revolts. And, in any case, the first generations of this internalized faith were as stern with themselves as any pope had ever been. Still, the scrupulous ascetics had established a libertarian principle: that the individual, not the community and certainly not the priest, shaped his or her relation to God. So when God became a liberal and then began to die, people discovered that they were all alone within their sovereign selves in a disenchanted world.

This history makes it clear that there is no going back to the religious innocence of preliterate society. If it shows that religion is a constituent as well as a product of social change, it nevertheless makes it plain that myths cannot be willed back into existence when the social structure of the human mind has left them behind. Durkheim may well be right that humans are irrepressibly creative in the sphere of religion;

there is no way of disproving it. But what one can say is that the societal basis for the old faiths—the political creed of Judeo-Christianity as well the Neolithic cosmos—has been destroyed.

But if the preliterate model of religion cannot survive in contemporary society, it can, and did, act as a stimulus to society's imagination. The bourgeois, imperial Christian faith of the nineteenth century went down, and the skeptical, alienated men and women of the twentieth century faced the sophisticated barbarism of war and totalitarianism. At that point, the primitive became a prime constituent of the modern.

——— **I V** ———

Art and religion both speak in symbols about the invisible meaning of the visible. It should come as no surprise, then, that the histories of beauty and of God are closely linked.

At the very beginning of human time, Hegel argued in the *Aesthetics*, art and religion were one. They both were manifestations of the wonder men and women felt toward the world. Indeed, at this point spiritual and aesthetic meanings are identical with nature itself. But then the sense of awe detaches itself from immediate objects and creates a symbolic realm in its own right (much as the magic manipulation of reality turns into the mythic interpretation of reality). Yet there are limits to that symbolism and they are encountered in every culture. For once a culture has probed all of its possibilities, filling and overfilling its gallery of symbols, then art must "turn *against* the subject matter which had previously been the only valid one." So, for example, Cervantes turned against the feudal culture and its ideal of the knight.

The modern age—Hegel is speaking in the 1820s, long before the advent of modern art—represents a unique point in this process. The nation and the age no longer provide the artists with a subject matter. Analysis and criticism have taken over what had once been the province of art—much as they usurp God's functions, one might add. The aesthetic consciousness is therefore a *tabula rasa*. "The artist now stands above the historic [*bestimmten*] and consecrated forms and figures, moving freely for himself, independent of the content and mode of perception in which the consciousness of the holy and eternal was once present to the eyes."

In a related passage, Hegel wrote:

> In the beginning art permitted a mysterious, secret surmise to continue to exist, a yearning, because its representations did not completely exhaust its content. . . . But if the complete content is now achieved, the reawakened spirit turns back from objectivity into itself and recoils from itself. Such an age is ours. One can hold that art will continue to progress and will fulfill itself, but its form has ceased to be the highest need of the spirit. We may well find the Greek representations of the gods admirable and see God the father, Christ and Mary marvelously well presented. But that does not help for we no longer genuflect to them.

Part of Hegel's analysis was clearly wrong. The idea that art had exhausted itself, that it no longer responded to spiritual needs (sometimes referred to as the "end of the art period" theory), is hardly borne out by the painting, music and writing of the past century and a half. But the rest contains a remarkable anticipation of the aesthetic future: the artist, freed from both objective and cultural limitations, turning inward; the liberation of form from subject; the irrelevance of traditional sacred art. Something like that did happen, preparing the way for the impact of the primitive upon the modern: no longer committed to, and confined within, the forms of his/her own culture, the modern artist was now open to communications from the distant past. The primitive, which was once seen in aesthetic terms as an undeveloped and inept perception of things moderns see clearly, was now redefined—sometimes much too romantically—as an awareness of a reality unknown to the present. In this perspective, history had progressed from wisdom to coarseness, not the other way around.

José Ortega y Gasset understood one aspect of this process. He analyzed modern art within his own theory of mass society (a theory which, it should be noted, is quite faulty, even if the flaws do not vitiate the point cited here). There had been, he said, a separation brought about by modern art: between the elite, who could comprehend it, and the masses, who could not. As a conservative, Ortega was contemptuous of the democratic pretensions of the masses, in aesthetics as well as politics. Still, his reactionary prejudices led him to a most illuminating analogy: "Up until now," Ortega wrote, "the eyes of the painter have revolved around each object, maintaining a servile orbit. . . . We deal now with a Copernican revolution comparable to the one promoted in philosophy by Descartes, Hume and Kant." Now the world was determined by the artist's eyes, not the other way around.

That is Hegel's point, updated by a thinker who had actually seen nonobjective paintings. The liberation of art from objectivity is part of that incredible and massive process described in Chapter 2: the most scientific and technological culture the world has even known has created the most intense subjectivity in human history. But the fate of art and religion diverged: the latter was rudely shouldered out of its traditional domains, the former broke through to a new inner space and even followed the anthropologists back to the beginning of time.

André Malraux dealt with many of these trends in *The Voices of Silence*, a book which is remarkable for the poetry of its writing as well as for the power of its insights. Modern society, he said, lives in "the twilight of the absolute." It was because of this relativization of consciousness that the Aztec social order was no longer seen as "mere savagery but a cruel culture." "In civilizations whose unity was based on a supreme Truth," he commented later on, "art nourished the best in man by the loftiest type of fiction. But once a collective faith was shattered, fiction had for its province not an ideal world but a world of untrammeled imagination." On the one hand, this opened up the artist to a new subject matter—himself/herself; on the other, it changed the aesthetic view of the past. Earlier, "a great Egyptian work of art was admitted in proportion to its congruity, subtle as this might be, with the Mediterranean tradition; we, on the contrary, admire the further it diverges from that tradition."

To be sure, as Renato Poggioli has pointed out, the Romantics had their own cult of the past, their Medievalism and Orientalism, their fascination with the exotic and even the "barbaric." But the new art—Poggioli describes it as the "avant garde"—was concerned mainly with the most distant past. It arose, not so incidentally, at the same time as anthropology was beginning to establish itself as a discipline and, in Poggioli's formulation, turned its artistic eye "almost exclusively to negroid sculpture and the art of savages, prehistoric graffiti and pre-Columbian Indian art. . . ."

This shift in point of view was part of a process which transformed the nature of the artist as well as of art. Bourgeois culture was unlike the Christian Middle Ages or even the absolute monarchies. Those periods had seen the artist expressing the supreme values of the society and therefore living in a certain consonance with both the rulers and the mass. But, Malraux wrote, the new capitalism tried to make art "pander to a social order which was rapidly losing its awareness of . . . [supreme] values. The bourgeois, now in the saddle, wanted a world made to his measure, devoid of intimations and owing allegiance to nothing that transcended it; but such a world was abhorrent to the artist, whose conception of the scheme of things involved a transcendent value—his art." "On the whole face of the globe," Malraux writes a little later about capitalist industrialism, "the civilization that has conquered it has failed to build a temple or a tomb."

So there came, Malraux went on, that radical separation of the artist and society which Weber also defined: "The outcast artist had taken his place in history; haunted henceforth by visions of his own absolute, while confronted by a culture growing ever less sure of itself, the artist came to find in his very ostracism the source of an amazing fertility." And, later: "Once civilization had ceased being under the sway of the gods, and the affinity of the various accents of different arts was recognized, *all* art emerged as a *continuum*, a world existing in its own right, and it was as a whole that art acquired, in the eyes of a certain category of men, the power of refashioning the scheme of things and setting up its transient eternity against man's more transient life."

This "transient eternity" was a kind of religious conception and modern art was, in a metaphorical sense, a religious movement. It has had its saints and saviors, its men and women who suffered scorn and exile in their lives and resurrection after death. So it was, as Poggioli pointed out, that a Georges Rouault, the modern artist with perhaps the greatest religious faith, could only express his conviction "through a deformation not only of the images but even the icons" of his belief. The Virgins and Christs and God the Fathers of the old order were, as Hegel was probably the first to understand, impossible; the painting itself, as Malraux stressed, had become the artist's only real act of religious conviction.

But, as Irving Howe documented in a brilliant essay, that aesthetic faith was short-lived, precarious and, above all, subject to assimilation by the voraciousness of contemporary society. But, then, that is the fate of all the willed absolutes, from the revolutionary cults of the French Revolution to the present. Moreover, as Malraux (and Howe) understand, there was a terrifying and even sinister aspect to the artistic rediscovery of the relevance of the primitive. "Many of our representations," Malraux wrote, "call in question not only painting as we know it but man as he is today. For what all the painted idols and Polynesian forms of the Autun tympanum are challenging is, primarily, Western optimism." The nineteenth-century visionaries who most stimulate us now, he continued, belong to a "limbo of negations" and "had little faith in traditional man and no more faith in the 'coming man.'" And with war, totalitarianism, the discovery of the subconscious, "the diabolical principle . . . which was more or less subtly present in all savage art, was coming to the fore again. . . . And the more ground the new devils gain in Europe, the more her art tends to draw on earlier cultures which, too, were plagued by their contemporary demons."

This phenomenon is, Irving Howe rightly points out, ambiguous. On the one hand it is true that modern man—along with modern art—has been opened up to a vast range of experience and discovered relevancy in cultures once seen as childish. But there is in this also a "plenitude of sophistication narrowing into decadence. The search for meaning through extreme states of being reveals a yearning for the primal: for surely man cannot be bored even at the moment of his creation!" And that yearning can lead to "another, more ambiguous and perhaps sinister kind of primitivism: the kind that draws us with the prospect not of health but of decay, the primitive as atavistic, an abandonment of civilization and thereby, perhaps, of its discontents." We will shortly explore one of the most frightening of these revivals of the primitive: Hitler's racism.

For now, it is enough to say that modern art and anthropology are linked in that each, in its own way, announced the death of God, the rediscovery of the gods and the possibility that if divinity was in its final throes the Devil was not.

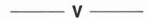

V

Sigmund Freud attempted to develop a scientific and secular theory to explain, among many other things, the persistence of the diabolic in the modern world.

Freud, as he himself readily conceded, was not the first to probe the dark underworld of the human consciousness. Artists had been doing so for centuries, and it was no accident that one of his central discoveries was named after a character in a Greek play written long before the Christian Era. Indeed, Freud was not even the intellectual pioneer who declared that all forms of affection, including the maternal and platonic, were expressions of the same drive as that which is found in sexual love: Schopenhauer had made that argument in the mid-nineteenth century in *The World as Will and Representation*. Not so incidentally, in making that point Schopenhauer was elaborating an irrationalist philosophy which would be taken up by a disciple greater than the master, Friedrich Nietzsche, with the consequences outlined in Chapter 5.

What Freud did was not to recognize a fact but to do so in a systematic and natural scientific way. It was no longer the poet's or the philosopher's intuition which probed the unconscious; it was that very rational methodology which was supposed to liberate humans from their archaic superstitions which now demonstrated their tenacious survival in the modern world. Freud was an heir of the Enlightenment (not only in his faith in reason but in his contempt for the masses as well) and, as one of his most optimistic books, *The Future of an Illusion*, makes clear, wanted to free society from its religious "obsession." Some of his followers have even radicalized his theory and made it compatible with the dream of a socialist future which Freud always rejected. And yet, in a century which has seen two catastrophic world wars and the emergence of totalitarian societies, his analyses sometimes tended to support an illiberal cynicism about humanity.

In developing his ideas on the primitive origins of religion as they continue to affect a sophisticated technological age, Freud constantly had recourse to a basic analogy: between the psychic evolution of the individual and that of societies and civilizations. That was not a new idea, either. The notion of "species being" (*Gattungswesen*) was a staple idea of the German classical philosophy, worked out by Kant and central to Marx. Humanity, it was said, advanced as a collectivity: the zero concept, which was once a daring intellectual breakthrough of Indian and Mayan thinkers, became a subject for schoolchildren; the growing complexity of the division of labor socialized the ability of men and women to master their external environment. But Freud gave a new meaning to that perception. The whole history of psychic evolution, from the primitive reaches to the present day, coexisted within the psychological structure of modern man, and this was one of the reasons for the persistence of religion.

In one mood, Freud, the heir of the Enlightenment, argued that humanity would eventually grow up, turning from myths and religion to science. In the twentieth century, he said, "the time has probably come, as it does in analytic treatment, for replacing the effects of repression by the results of rational operation of the intellect." To paraphrase: just as the psychoanalysis of an individual allows him/her to integrate the id into the ego and thereby vitiates the need for the obsessional and hysterical defenses built up against the id, so the psychoanalysis of a culture allows it to do away with the religious neurosis and to face up to reality even when that is profoundly disturbing. Indeed, Freud thought that the people had for a long time nullified some of the worst demands of the religions that repressed them, forcing the priests to meet them halfway. "God's kindness," he wrote, "must lay a restraining hand on His justice. . . . It is no secret that the priests could keep the masses submissive to religion only by making such large concessions . . . to the instinctual nature of man."

In *The Future of an Illusion*, Freud even attacked the Voltairean proposition that the masses needed a faith. Reason, he said, speaks softly "but it does not rest until it has gained a hearing. Finally, after a countless succession of rebuffs, it succeeds. This is one of the few points on which one may be optimistic about mankind." "Our God Logos," he went on, "will fulfill whichever of these wishes nature outside us allows, but he will do it gradually, only in the unforeseeable future, and for a new generation of men." Logos, which the Gospel of John had identified with God and Christ, was now scientific reason, and it would be the salvation of the human psyche as well as a means for the mastering of external nature.

With the rise of Nazi totalitarianism—which led to his exile from Vienna—Freud changed. The optimism of *The Future of an Illusion* (1927) gives way to the deep pessimism of *Civilization and Its Discontents* (1930) and *Moses and Monotheism* (1939). To be sure, an early book, *Totem and Taboo* (1913), had anticipated some of the themes of the last decade of Freud's life, but now he was not engaged in a rather careless speculation about anthropology, as in that earlier work, but was confronting a monstrous political reality.*

*See Appendix O.

He had realized, Freud said, that "nothing once formed in the mind could ever perish, that everything survives in one way or another, and is capable of being brought to light again, as, for instance, when regression extends far back enough." "We must conclude," he wrote in *Moses and Monotheism*, "that the mental residue of primitive times has become a heritage which, with each new generation, needs only to be awakened, not to be reacquired." There was thus the possibility—the danger—of the "return of the repressed." Freud felt that in Stalinism "progress had concluded an alliance with barbarism" while in Nazism "the retrogression into all but prehistoric barbarism . . . [came] independently of any progressive idea."

Indeed, this regression toward the primitive was in some ways made more probable by the advance of civilization itself, for that advance was purchased at the price of such instinctual repression that it could well culminate in an archaic scream of outraged protest against itself. There is, Freud the conservative argued, "an inborn tendency to negligence, irregularity and untrustworthiness in their work" in men and women. Civilization had to put that down with the aid of religion, so it should not come as a surprise that the most sophisticated—and consequently the most repressed—society should awaken the most primitive instincts.

That profoundly pessimistic vision of history was challenged from within the Freudian camp by one of its most disconcerting heretics. Wilhelm Reich, a one-time disciple whom Freud had admired, tried to synthesize psychoanalysis and Marxism. For him, the instinctual repression described by Freud was made necessary not by human nature but by certain forms of exploitative society. It was only with the passing of the earliest—and freest—forms of human life, Reich argued, that the institution of authoritarian patriarchy was created as an apparatus of repression. And with the triumph of communism, he concluded, the social and economic need for psychological repression would end. The classless society would be a time of erotic liberation.

Herbert Marcuse made a much subtler critique of Freud on this count. He distinguished between "basic" repression and "the 'modifications' of the instincts necessary for the perpetuation of the human race in civilization," and "*surplus repression*," the repression necessitated by social domination. This is an ingenious psychological analogy to Marx's distinction, made in Volume I of *Das Kapital*, between the direction and planning inherent in any form of social production (which will continue under socialism) and the historically specific forms of direction and planning needed to defend class rule within antagonistic systems. Where Marcuse and Reich are compelling, I think, is in their insistence on viewing the "return of the repressed" in historic terms rather than seeing it, as Freud did, as an expression of human nature and an expression of the very structure of the human psyche itself.

Certainly there was an obvious primitivism and barbarism in Nazism. There were the pseudo-religious rites of Nuremberg, the myth of racial superiority and the monstrously irrational but scientifically organized crime of genocide against the Jews. Does Freud explain this? Only in part. As he himself conceded, the "return of the repressed" takes place under certain historical conditions. A Germany which had never gone through a genuine bourgeois revolution and therefore was a sort of feudalistic capitalism faced the greatest economic and social crisis in history in the early thirties. Under *those* circumstances and in *German* culture, there was indeed a return of the repressed.

Moreover, there is another, Marxist, explanation of these events which is both relevant and implicitly critical of Freud. Marx, it will be remembered, always insisted that there was a "primitive" and irrational aspect to a capitalism which he also regarded as the very triumph of science. Bourgeois consciousness, he wrote in *Das Kapital*, is "fetishistic": commodities take on a spooky life of their own, humans are turned into wooden figures, things are spiritualized and spirits reified. And in the opening lines of the *Manifesto* Marx even said that the alternative for the future was either communism *or* "barbarism." He did not predict the rise of fascism (I think it would have astounded him); but he did provide a social, economic and historical theory of sophisticated primitivism.

Finally, another Freudian heretic, C. G. Jung, provided some fascinating glimpses of these great historic trends as they were refracted in the lives of individual patients.

Not that Jung was a clinician who eschewed grand theory. Far from it. If anything, he insisted on the archaism within the modern psyche even more than Freud. There was, he said, a "collective unconscious" which contained "archetypes," "forms of images . . . which occur practically all over the earth as constituents of myths and at the same time as autochthonous, individual products of unconscious origin." Why does the primitive continue to exist in the time of the modern? Jung would answer: Because the primitive is still there in our collective unconscious, and our individual and private dreams are usually made of the stuff of myths, even if we do not know it. I do not, however, want to get into the controversy over that theory. What concerns me is Jung's reports on his psychoanalytic practice, for they suggest one way in which the current religious crisis has an impact upon individual psyches.

"During the past thirty years," Jung wrote in 1932:

> people from all over the civilized countries of the earth have consulted me. . . . Among all my patients in the second half of life—that is to say, over thirty-five—there has not been one whose problem in the last resort was not that of finding a religious outlook on life. It is safe to say that every one of them fell ill because he had lost what the living religions of every age have given to their followers and none of them has been really healed who did not regain his religious outlook. This of course has nothing whatever to do with a particular creed or membership of a church.

And then Jung went on to say:

> It seems to me that, side by side with the decline of religious life, the neuroses grow noticeably more frequent. There are as yet no statistics with actual figures to prove this increase. But of one thing I am sure, that everywhere the mental state of European man shows an alarming lack of balance. We are living undeniably in a period of the greatest restlessness, nervous tension, confusion and disorientation of outlook.

The psychological consequences of the death of God, then, ramify in many directions. There are the shudders of individual impiety, the monstrous primitivism of Nazism at a time of economic collapse, the chic primitivism of a bored affluence. And there is no reason to think that the repressed has stopped returning. No one knows, for instance, what anxieties the eighties will provoke. In all of this, there is a cruel paradox. We cannot, this chapter has suggested, go back to the gods of preliterate society or, I would add, even to the God of our grandparents. But it is not simply that the evil those gods and that God once exorcised remains; our fetishes, just as Marx said, are now the work of a technological irrationality. So, simultaneously with the death of God, unbelieving geniuses, both artists and scientists, have invoked demons to explain what is happening in an agnostic age.

8
GOD'S CHRISTIAN BURIAL

POLITICS, SOCIAL STRUCTURE, economics, psychology, anthropology and art all responded to the death of God. So did religion.

Basically, there were two ways in which the faithful tried to cope with an increasingly godless world. There were those who accepted it and sought to build a Christian enclave within it or even to baptize atheism. That was the strategy of some of the most thoughtful Protestants. And there were those—Roman Catholics and American fundamentalists who regarded Rome as the Whore of Babylon—who declared modernity anathema and affirmed the old truths in the teeth of the new reality. There were analogous tendencies within Judaism (Orthodoxy, Conservativism and Reform) but the singular Jewish contribution came from the "non-Jewish Jews" (Marx, Freud) who had left the synagogue but not the prophetic tradition and were architects of the modern, agnostic spirit.

In surveying some of these theologies, I am not concerned with their truth or falsehood. Rather, how did these developments affect the capacity of religion to play the societal role it had fulfilled for more than two thousand years in Western civilization?

———— I ————

There is a marvelously symbolic anecdote about Friedrich Schleiermacher, the dominant Protestant theologian of the nineteenth century. On his deathbed he wanted to receive communion but the doctor would not allow him to take wine. So he received it in the form of bread and water, a fact which his twentieth-century critic (and admirer) Karl

Barth regarded as an epiphany. Wasn't this incident a fitting end for the man who had diluted the Christian faith?

And yet it could be argued that Schleiermacher simply faced up to the new relation between religion and society. There were those, he said, who thought that faith was based upon the fear of the uncontrollable in nature. But "increasingly, man is learning to understand or destroy these gods of nature by pitting them against one another. He is destined soon to be a smiling spectator at this game, its victor and lord. Consequently, the more man has triumphed over nature, religion's previous objects of worship have become less and less appropriate." Under these circumstances the theologian had to speak to "the cultured among those who scorn religion" (that is the subtitle of Schleiermacher's most influential work, *On Religion*).

Schleiermacher's tactic for dealing with this new situation was in keeping with the Romanticism of the turn of the nineteenth century. Humans, he said, want to be individual—but they also yearn to "surrender to something greater, to absorb oneself in it, and to feel both grasped and determined by it." Therefore religion was "the feeling of absolute dependence."

> True faith is to know oneself in possession of religion. In contrast what people ordinarily call "faith"—adopting what somebody else has said or done, trying to think or feel as another has thought or felt—is an undignified and burdensome service indeed! Some say it is the apex of religion. Actually, it is something to be shunned by anyone who wishes to move on into the sanctuary of religion. Such faith is nothing but an echo.

Miracles, Schleiermacher said, are not so much objective events as events perceived by someone who is religious. It is the mind-set, the feeling, not the fact, that is decisive. So the doctrines about God and immortality are unimportant; what is crucial is the state of consciousness they evoke. This attitude, I will suggest in the next chapter, defines what many—perhaps most—people in the West today mean by religion.

But if Schleiermacher's theories anticipated the popular, sentimental religiosity that came a century later, his optimism was of his time and place and therefore deeply flawed. He wrote of millions groaning under the burden of "meaningless mechanical labor." This, he said, was a tremendous hindrance to religion. But the time was coming when it would only be necessary to "speak a magic word or press a button" to have all those routine tasks performed. At that point, everyone would be able to become a contemplative. This hope, Schleiermacher's twentieth-century successors would rudely realize, was not to be fulfilled, and the liberal theology which went with it therefore became problematic.

But even before events falsified part of Schleiermacher's message, his contemporary and colleague Hegel was subjecting him to a savage criticism. If, Hegel said, religion is defined as an emotion, and particularly as a reverent sense of dependence, then "a dog is the best Christian," since he experiences that feeling more than any human. The Reformation, Hegel wrote in the *Phenomenology*, had been a great advance, with its stress on inner faith and its rejection of the external trappings of Catholicism. But Schleiermacher, he continued, was the Protestant principle run wild. He made religion into something for "virtuosos of enthusiasm" and that was analogous to thinking that one could have art without a work of art, that the aesthetic intention was everything and the aesthetic creation nothing, the religious emotion all and religion nothing.

Religion, Hegel argued, had lived in two worlds, the mystical and the rational, the theological and the philosophical. But now the Enlightenment attacked the former with the latter, and as a result faith lost its content and was driven out of its kingdom as reason took over all of its functions. Insofar as religion tried to persist under these conditions, he concluded, it turned into a "pure yearning" (*reines Sehnen*) and dedicated itself to an "empty beyond" since the this-world had been expropriated by science.

Feuerbach was even more damaging to Schleiermacher: he congratulated the theologian on having discovered the basic truth of atheistic humanism, that God is an expression of human feeling. And indeed, Schleiermacher was a brief stop on Friedrich Engels's voyage to disbelief. For David Friedrich Strauss, whose *Life of Jesus* had such an impact upon the mid-century, Schleiermacher's logic led to a new, humanist religion completely independent of Christianity.

And yet, if Hegel's critique of Schleiermacher is the work of an authentic, and angry, genius, what was his alternative to the religion of feeling? A religion of such an intricate rationality that it could not possibly serve as the basis for the faith of masses of people (or even for the elite). It was, ironically, a deeply Christian man, Søren Kierkegaard, who grasped how radical this situation was. A twentieth-century thinker marooned in the nineteenth century, he understood the profundity of the Christian crisis before anyone else.

Christianity, Kierkegaard wrote in his *Attack upon "Christendom,"* is over, finished. To be sure, there are "millions of Christians, Christian states and countries, a Christian world, thousands of mercantile priests, but faith . . . ?" There is, rather, an "apostasy from Christianity" which is not open and honest but takes the form of a dilution of Christianity from within. The freethinkers, Kierkegaard continues, are at least plainspoken. They say that Christianity is nothing but a myth. The official Christians agree, but they do not dare to speak openly, perhaps even to themselves.

This "official Christianity is a perfectly charming and elegant invention for very sensibly making this life as enjoyable as possible, more enjoyable than the pagan could have it." It has

taken occasion from some sentences in the New Testament (this doctrine of a cross and anguish and horror and shuddering before eternity) to compose with free poetic license a lovely idyll, with procreating of children and waltzes, where everything is "so joyful, so joyful, so joyful," where the priest (a kind of leader of the town band) is willing, for money, to let Christianity (the doctrine of dying unto the world) furnish the music for weddings and christenings, where everything in this (according to the teachings of Christianity a vale of tears and a penitentiary), this glorious world (yea, according to the New Testament is in a time of probation relating to an accounting and judgment) a foretaste of the still more joyful eternity which the priests guarantee to those families which by their devotion to him have evinced a sense for the eternal.

Kierkegaard thus had a vivid, angry sense of the hypocrisy of the official—bourgeois—Christianity of the nineteenth century. In this, as Karl Löwith has remarked, he resembles Marx. The Danish theologian and the German socialist both saw "a world determined by merchandise and money, and . . . an existence shot through with irony and the 'drudgery' of boredom." And Kierkegaard, like Marx, can only be understood in terms of the society he abominated. His austere and demanding Christianity was reminiscent of Luther and Calvin, only there was no longer a public for such a message. The Protestantism of early capitalism was a creed of renunciation and discipline appropriate to a time of the primitive accumulation of capital and the need to favor investment over consumption. But the Protestantism of the triumphant, confident capitalism of the nineteenth century became a comfortable faith for a complacent middle class. That was the development that horrified Kierkegaard.

That transition was not simply European. In America, H. Richard Niebuhr had suggested, the bourgeoisification of Calvin was carried to the extreme. From Jonathan Edwards through William Ellery Channing and then beyond, theology eliminated the problem of evil: "the Puritan passion for perfection has become a seeking after the kingdom of health and mental peace and its comforts." In his enormously influential Divinity School address of 1838, Emerson argued "the moral sentiment" as "the essence of all religion," and William James defined religion as *"the feelings, acts and experiences of individual men in their solitude so far as they apprehend themselves to stand in relation to whatever they consider divine."* Religion, the nineteenth-century American Evangelicals said, echoing Schleiermacher, was the province of the heart—which created a haven for it where science could not intrude.

So Schleiermacher and his religion of feeling triumphed everywhere, and on one crucial count Kierkegaard had to agree with him. He, too, made the private, individual decision the critical measure of the authenticity of faith. Of course he insisted that feeling alone was not enough; he spoke of the cross and death and punishment. And yet, he made a virtue out of a necessity. He said that Christianity by its very nature could not be a mass religion—that the salt lost its savor when it was shared by millions—at the very time that Christianity was indeed beginning to lose its capacity to speak to the masses. And it was not an accident that Kierkegaard's greatest influence was achieved, not only when liberal, middle-class Christianity had been shattered by the upheavals of the twentieth century, but at a time when there seemed to be no religious community, when lonely men and women, many of them atheist or agnostic, some of them Christian, could respond to the plea for an individual and existential commitment. Kierkegaard is a theologian for an age in which religion is more and more a *credo quia absurdum.*

I anticipate. For now, the first response of theology to the death of the traditional God was to say, in effect, that he didn't matter that much after all, that the essential thing was to continue feeling the emotions which had once been associated with his worship. This was a Romantic religiosity—but, as Nietzsche understood so well in his attack on Strauss, it was a tamed, middle-class, complacent Romanticism. Kierkegaard protested magnificently but it took a new century to get him a hearing. Meanwhile the Roman Catholics and American fundamentalists tried a different tack: they sought to excommunicate the present and the future.

——— I I ———

It was Pius IX—the legendary Pio Nono—who defined the intransigent Catholic position which was to prevail until the late 1950s and John XXIII. He was the leader of a feudal organization in a post-feudal world, of a cosmopolitan church in a nationalist age, a conservative confronting a rising working-class movement. His church had, Antonio Gramsci remarked, once been the keeper of the world view of an entire society; it was now reduced to being one institution among many, and a beleaguered one at that. As Hans Küng described the situation, "In modern times, one attack after another had been made on the bulwark of the Church. On Lutheranism and Calvinism there followed Jansenism, Gallicanism and princely absolutism; with the beginning of the new age came the French Revolution, the Napoleonic Wars; and after all these, atheistic materialism, liberalism and socialism. . . . innumerable educated people had left the Church, and the proletarian masses were abandoning it."

The response? "There had to be a consolidation around the Roman center and an unflinching rejection of the spirit of the age. . . ." Liberal Protestantism adapted itself to new trends; "integralist" Catholicism insisted that one had to accept tradition, narrowly defined, in every one of its particulars, that the slightest deviation set one on a slippery slope that ended in atheism.

Pius IX was not simply a theologian but a temporal sovereign as well, and his political experience reinforced—perhaps even created—his religious theories. He began as a liberal and Mazzini had even invited him to become the head of a new, humanist religion. The revolutionary wrote the new Pontiff that "beliefs are dead, Catholicism is lost in despotism; Protestantism is losing itself in anarchy. Look around you: you will find superstitious men or hypocrites but not believers. . . . But humanity cannot live without heaven. The social idea is nothing but the consequence of the religious idea." For the conservatives, the fact that the Pope could even flirt with such notions was appalling. "Warm of heart and weak of intellect," Metternich wrote, "he has allowed himself to be taken and ensnared . . . and if matters follow their natural course, he will be driven out of Rome."

He was driven out of Rome in the revolutionary year of 1848. When he returned in 1850, he was completely dependent upon Napoleon III and engaged in an ultimately unsuccessful struggle to find a stable political base. It was this experience, a sympathetic biographer of Pio Nono has argued, that accounted for his ideological shift. It led him to a kind of "domino" theory: liberty leads to Mazzini, Mazzini to the religion of humanity, the religion of humanity to the persecution of the Church and to atheism. So it was that in 1864 Pius IX issued his famous Syllabus of Errors and the encyclical Quanta Cura. The eightieth proposition condemned in the Syllabus is the most famous. It is forbidden, the Syllabus declared, to teach that "the Roman Pontiff can and should reconcile and harmonize himself with progress, with liberalism and with recent civilization." E. Y. Hales, Pius's friendly biographer, tries to restrict the sweep of this proposition, arguing that it really meant to interdict only some specifically Italian outrages. It was not understood in that way. It was seen—and not unfairly—as a Catholic declaration of war against the entire modern world.

Pope Leo XIII, who succeeded Pius IX, softened that stance somewhat—but only somewhat. He first attacked the "plague" of socialism in the encyclical Quod Apostolici Muneris, a document which, as Hans Küng remarked, recognized "only the dangers and not the positive concerns of socialism." It was only thirteen years after that document that he issued his famous Rerum Novarum (1891), in which he posed a Catholic alternative to socialism. But, to cite Küng again, that attempt to relate to the rising worker's movement was "forty years too late," appearing when much of the European proletariat had abandoned religious faith. And Leo maintained his predecessor's emphasis on Thomism as the one and only Catholic philosophy, thus continuing the narrowing of Catholic intellectual life.

But even though evaluating Leo's papacy is a complex matter, those very complexities highlight an important point made by Gramsci (that a Marxist would be so sensitive to trends within Catholicism is partly explained by two facts: Gramsci was an Italian and a genius). Even in reactionary periods, he argued, there was always a popular, democratic, "modern" tendency within the Church. If it seemed, under

Pius IX and Pius X, that integralism had totally carried the day and that the modern world had been decisively abjured, there was nevertheless a counter-movement, one which surfaced in Italy after World War I and then, after Gramsci's death, inspired the Christian Democratic and Christian socialist trends after World War II. Leo XIII provided a papal basis for these currents, just as Pius IX and Pius X were the spiritual fathers of Catholic reaction.

When Leo died, Pius X made up for whatever momentum had been lost during the liberal interregnum, returning with a vengeance to the themes pursued by Pius IX. He was worried by the influence of Kant and Schleiermacher, by the appearance of Catholic intellectuals who examined the psychological and subjective bases of faith and were not satisfied by the neo-Thomist "proofs" of the truth of Catholic doctrine. Religion, one group of Italian priests told the Pope, "cannot be imposed by means of a syllogism . . . cannot be imposed from without by reasoned arguments. The soul must first seek [the Church's truths] through its own free action . . . under the stimulus of its own religious experience. . . ." The Holy Father was appalled. In 1907, he published the decree Lamentabili, and the encyclical Pascendi, denouncing all "modernist" innovations. There was even an anti-modernist oath, binding on the Catholic clergy until Vatican II, which demanded a sworn statement that God's existence could be proved. Pius XII, in many ways the last Pope of the nineteenth century even though he did not die until 1958, declared his anti-modernist predecessor a saint of the Church.

In fact, as Leszek Kolakowski pointed out, in all this the Church was "step by step losing control over cultural life and repelling the educated classes." It had already alienated the workers so that the European church was reduced, in Gramsci's biting phrase, "to the superstition of peasants, the sick, the aging and women." Not so incidentally, the American Catholic Church was an exception to this trend. The Irish workers who were its militant core remained faithful, in considerable measure because their nationalism and religion were identical, and the educated Catholics, only a generation removed from steerage, were therefore grateful to have a comfortable theological ghetto in a difficult and alien world.

"American exceptionalism" was also at work among the Protestant fundamentalists in America. (The name "fundamentalism" was not used until the first decades of the twentieth century but the religious tendency which grew into that identification was, of course, much older.) Just like the Church of Rome they, too, tried to turn their collective backs upon modernity and all of its pomps.

The fundamentalists were never quite sure whether the United States was Zion or Babylon, whether to remake this country in a Christian image or to become internal exiles within its godless borders. In the nineteenth and early twentieth centuries, the first, reformist, tactic often prevailed. In the first decade of this century, for instance, the *Christian Herald*, which grew out of the "premillennial" theology that led to fundamentalism, endorsed unions, worked for laws curbing women's and children's labor, sought better treatment of blacks and immigrants and was a militant advocate of peace. In that phase, the deeply religious Evangelicals embraced science—they were proud of being "Baconians"—and, as was fitting in democratic America, were exponents of the philosophy of "common sense."

But then, after World War I, the obscurantist, "Manichean" element in this theology came to the fore. In the 1890s, the Southern Populist Tom Watson opposed anti-black and anti-Catholic sentiment; by the time of the war, he was one of the leading racists in the nation, anti-Semitic as well as anti-Catholic and anti-black. And in the twenties, William Jennings Bryan, once the Great Commoner, spent his time, in Richard Hofstadter's words, "attacking freedom of thought, and promoting Prohibition, while his erstwhile followers celebrated him, no doubt inaccurately, as 'the greatest Klansman of our time.' " At the Scopes trial, Bryan led the fundamentalist charge against the Devil's party of Charles Darwin and was routed by Clarence Darrow. That defeat—followed almost immediately by Bryan's death—drove the fundamentalist *Kulturkampf* to the margins of the society for the next forty years.

Why this dramatic shift? Seymour Martin Lipsett and Earl Raab suggest an answer which will bear very much on my analysis of the revival of the Christian Right in the seventies and eighties. Between 1890 and 1920, they argue, traditional Protestantism went from being a majority culture to the status of a minority culture. Industrialization, urbanization and massive immigration transformed the social structure—the very ethos—of the country. The militant fundamentalism of the twenties, then, was a backlash, a sign of defeat, of dispossession. In this, it was literally a "reactionary" movement, just as Pio Nono's Catholicism had been.

It would, of course, be absurd to equate the fundamentalists and the Catholics. The latter were the heirs of a sophisticated culture, and there were serious and profound scholars, like Etienne Gilson and Jacques Maritain, who turned Thomism into a subtle and complex theory (Maritain even developed an ingenious Thomist analysis of modern art). This was light-years distant from Biblical literalism and its struggle with Darwin. And yet, the basic mind-set of the Catholic and fundamentalist responses to modernity was the same (and in recent years in the United States the Catholic and Protestant Right have made an alliance). More to the point of this book, both movements failed. It was—it is—impossible to pray a rationalist, technological civilization out of existence.

For this reason it is of some moment that there is a link, strange as it may seem, between the fundamentalists and one of the most austere dialectical theologians of the twentieth century, Karl Barth. His neo-orthodoxy, for all its extraordinary intellectual richness, was, like fundamentalism, an attempt to will faith in a world in which it was no longer reasonable. The crisis, in short, afflicted erudite geniuses as well as simple folk.

Thus it was that Karl Barth wrote a theology for a God who is no longer there.

——— I I I ———

Barth had begun as a liberal and an optimist. But then, preaching sermons in a small Swiss church within earshot of the battles in Alsace during World War I, he found the times tumbling in upon him. He turned to Kierkegaard and Dostoevsky as well as to Luther and Calvin. As Alec Vidler describes this conversion, Barth concluded that "men would never come to hear the authentic Word of the true God . . . till they had discovered that all their last questions were unanswerable questions, and that all the alleys they went down in their enlightenment, proved to be blind alleys. It was only the blind, and those who knew themselves to be blind, who could receive their sight."

So Barth declared war on both of the dominant Christian strategies of the nineteenth century, the Protestant as well as the Catholic. Schleiermacher and all his progeny—for he was, Barth conceded, "the church father of the nineteenth century"—were wrong in reducing

God to human emotion. Indeed, in a remarkable essay on Feuerbach written long after his World War I conversion, Barth held that the first German atheist was, in a very real sense, the logical culmination of all of the Christian anthropologies which began with Hegel and Schleiermacher. And he was also opposed to the anti-modernist Catholicism of Pius X, with its insistence that the existence of the transcendent God was not just knowable by reason but could even be proved.

All of these attitudes emerged in Barth's commentary on Saint Paul's Epistle to the Romans. That book was not simply a landmark in its theological content; it was also extremely innovative in its form. It was not scholarly and exegetical but impassioned and expressionistic, very much of a piece with the artistic and literary styles of the postwar period. "For all faith is both simple and difficult," he wrote, "for all it is a leap into the void. And it is possible for all, only because it is equally impossible for all." Christianity had arrived in the twentieth century.

I simplify, of course. Barth himself has stressed that he changed his views over time, and the Preface to the second edition of the *Epistle to the Romans* (1922) argued that even the basic structure of the first edition (1919) had been changed. And some time later on, in his *Church Dogmatics* (which appeared between 1932 and 1950), he was to stress the value of traditional Scholasticism and Thomism in a way which made some Catholic theologians quite happy. He did not, wrote one of them, Hans Urs von Balthasar, turn Baudelaire, Nietzsche and Rilke into modern church fathers, as some of the more trendy religious thinkers did. But even with all of these intricacies, the basic thrust of Barth's work was quite consistent after the change brought about by World War I, always expressing a sense of the utter transcendence of God. Pascal's Deus Absconditus, the hidden God who no longer inhabits our scientific world, had non-appeared once again.

To be sure, Barth continued the dialogue with Schleiermacher all of his life. He praised his social liberalism and insisted upon the depth of his Christian commitment. Moreover, Barth recognized that Schleiermacher had tried to formulate his Christianity in such a way that it could enter into his culture, his time and place. But his great limitation, Barth said, was that he considered religion from the point of view of religious consciousness, of human subjectivity, rather than as an outpouring of the Holy Spirit. He therefore ignored the Word of God which the Spirit communicated—and ultimately could find no basis to demonstrate the unique character of the revealed truth of Jesus Christ. Schleiermacher makes the experience of men and women critical; Barth places his emphasis upon the Word of God.

Here is a characteristic statement of the Barthian theme from the *Epistle to the Romans* (it is translated from the sixth edition):

> Religion, so far from being the place where the healthy harmony of human life is lauded, is instead the place where it appears diseased, discordant and disrupted. Religion is not the sure ground upon which human culture safely rests; it is the place where civilization and its partner barbarism are rendered fundamentally questionable. . . . Religion poses no solution of the problem of life; rather, it makes that problem a wholly insoluble enigma. Religion neither discovers the problem nor solves it; what it does is to dissolve the truth that it can be solved.

For Barth then, as Peter Berger remarked, the error of the liberal theologians was to "think that there is some innate capacity of men to experience the divine. There is no such capacity. Only the Word itself gives the capacity to affirm it." The believer, Barth himself said, like Luther "loves the deus absconditus." That God is indirectly revealed to humanity in Jesus Christ, but if Jesus is seen *within* history, then he is only a problem or a myth. He brings the world of the Father, "but we who stand in this concrete world know nothing, and are incapable of knowing anything, of that other world." Balthasar very shrewdly intuits a consequence of this line of thought. In such an analysis "the hardcore center of Christianity, the Incarnation, now becomes impossible. If the divine touches the world only tangentially, if the only relationship between God and the world is that of an infinite qualitative difference, then there can be no such thing as a *life* of Christ. All there can really be is a *death* of Christ. . . ." It was this approach which led Edward Schillebeeckx, a contemporary Catholic scholar of enormous erudition, to comment that "if God is indeed the 'Wholly Other' without a recognizable immanence in our world, then we would revere him best by saying nothing about him."

It is at this point that we encounter a remarkable anomaly. The young Barth, prior to his great change, was, as I have noted, a Christian socialist. One might think that having developed a theology in which God was so distant from the world, knowable only through revelation in Christ and therefore outside of normal human affairs,

Barth would have been a political quietist. And since there was a very strong German Protestant tradition emphasizing precisely such an attitude—Luther believed in obedience to the law, and "Render to Caesar the things that are Caesar's" was taken with the utmost seriousness by German theologians—it would seem logical for Barth to have taken it up.

Indeed, in the very first edition of the *Epistle to the Romans*, Barth was explicitly political and even—writing in the tumultuous year of 1919—revolutionary. Perhaps, he said, strikes and general strikes and street fights would be necessary—though no Christian should ever exalt them. But, he went on in an extremely condensed statement, one was "social democratic, but not for the social gospel."* For the Barth of the first edition, and the Barth of all subsequent editions, the New Testament was a shattering revelation of God, not a statement on politics, even if the recognition of that God could have profound political consequences in a person's life.

So it was that Barth not only organized the "Confessing Church" against Nazism in 1933–34 and was expelled from his professorship in Bonn in 1935. More than that, he charged that it was precisely because the liberal Protestants and the Roman Catholics had lost a sense of the transcendence of God that many of them were ready to make a compromise with a man like Hitler. He drew activist and anti-fascist conclusions from his vision of the distant Deus Absconditus. To understand how that could be, one must develop a subtle and complex analysis of the relationship between a theology (or any ideology) and actual politics.

The politics, economics and social structure of an age leave their mark upon its theologies, but that does not determine or predict the politics of its theologians. Barth—and Reinhold Niebuhr in the United States—were Leftists, even if it might seem that their view of a distant God should lead to quietism. There were—there are—fundamentalists who see Christ as a hunted rebel and those who see him as an absolute monarch. Their interpretations are their own just as much as fundamentalism itself is part of a larger cultural tendency and not the random choice of so many individuals. These complications are particularly important when the question concerns a genius like Barth, who signs the trends of his time with his own unique signature.

---

*This is an extremely free translation, American in its use of the phrase "social gospel," of *"Sozialdemokratisch, aber nicht religiös-sozial!"*.

It was a most heterodox Marxist, Ernst Bloch, who understood best how truly dialectical Barth's vision was. In that vision, Bloch wrote, God is made grotesquely distant from man and Christ, as mediator, is all but exiled from Christianity. And yet, Bloch continued, that was also a defense of God's awe against the trivialization of a theological liberalism. Moreover, Barth's Deus Absconditus, his distant, all but disappeared God is the analogue to the Homo Absconditus of Marx, that hidden, repressed human potential which one intuits precisely in the distortions and alienations of it.

And yet Barth was a creature of those times as well as one of their creators. He had contempt for the "death of God" theologians of the 1960s. Their doctrine, he wrote, was "idiotic," "the ultimate and fairest fruit of the glorious existential theology. . . ." And yet, willy-nilly, he, too, made the decision of faith in faith a critical dimension of faith. After World War II, the growing Western stratum of the college-educated middle class became interested in such abstruse matters. The death of God became a fad.

───── I V ─────

In 1963, an Anglican bishop wrote a theological best-seller. The book was *Honest to God*, the author Bishop J. A. T. Robinson. This was the volume that made the work of a number of sophisticated thinkers—in particular Rudolf Bultmann, Paul Tillich and Dietrich Bonhoeffer—the topics of cocktail-party conversation.

Bultmann's "demythologizing" of the New Testament made statements which challenged Christianity more than most atheist attacks upon it, but in the name of Christianity. The New Testament, Bultmann wrote in a famous essay, speaks of a cosmology of earth, heaven and hell. "All of this is the language of mythology and the origins of various themes can be easily traced in the contemporary mythology of Jewish Apocalyptics and in the redemption myths of Gnosticism. To this extent, *the Kerygma is incredible to modern man for he is convinced that the mythical view of the world is obsolete*."*

Thus Bultmann argued that human control of the external world

---

*"Kerygma" comes from the Greek word for the content of what the herald proclaims.

has proceeded to such a point that "it is no longer possible for anyone seriously to hold the New Testament view of the world—in fact, there is no one who does." That does not mean, however, that one can reduce the Gospel to a few principles in religion and ethics as the liberal theologians have done. For in that case, the Kerygma is no longer the proclamation of "the decisive act of God in Christ." And yet, if Bultmann insisted upon the importance of Christ and God, they come to one solely through faith: "To every other eye than the eye of faith the action of God is hidden. Only the 'natural' happening is generally visible and ascertainable. In it is accomplished the hidden act of God." This is of a piece with Karl Barth's militant supernaturalism (Barth once refused an invitation to give the Gifford Lecture on the grounds that he was opposed to all *natural* theology).

Yet if revelation is central for Bultmann, what, precisely, has been revealed? On this count, he is not too clear. The Resurrection, which he takes as a central Christian theme, was "the rise of faith in the risen lord"—but does that mean that Christ rose from the dead or not? Edward Schillebeeckx credits Bultmann and his co-thinkers for rejecting "a sort of empiricist objectivism in which, apart from the act of faith—and so without any faith experience—people were supposed to be able to see the resurrected Jesus." But that should not be taken to imply what Bultmann does imply, "that the resurrection was achieved not in the person of Jesus but only in the believing disciples, as it were. 'Resurrection' is then more a symbolic expression for the renewal of life for the disciples." Can there be, Schillebeeckx asks, a Jesus Kerygma in the absence of a historical Jesus?

But then the point is, precisely, that by the mid-twentieth century views which would have been proclaimed as heresy fifty years earlier were being espoused by respected, even revered, theologians. In the mid-sixties, for instance, Reinhold Niebuhr told a journalist that "there are very few theologians today who believe the Resurrection actually happened." Karl Rahner, a Catholic moderate, spoke of eternal life in this way: "It does not mean that things continue on after death as though, as Feuerbach put it, we only change horses and then ride on. . . ." Today no person serious about theology would be disturbed that in thus redefining the doctrine of the afterlife Rahner appeals to the authority of the atheist Ludwig Feuerbach.

Indeed, Alasdair MacIntyre, in an influential essay on the controversy over Bishop Robinson's book, rightly noted that Bultmann's "Jesus Kerygma" is in reality a "theistic existentialism" in which it is not at all clear that "the existentialism is more than nominally theistic." In Bultmann's reading, Christian "mythology conceals rather than conveys the message that man is prey to an inauthentic existence, that Jesus summons him to a decision, by which he can face up to his being as that of one who is going to die and so begin to live authentically." But all that can be found in the writings of Bultmann's one-time colleague Martin Heidegger, to whom he dedicated his first volume of essays. There are obvious similarities between *Being and Time* and the New Testament, yet Sartre, departing from Heidegger, arrived at an existential Marxism, not Christianity, and Heidegger eventually decided that it was wrong to raise the question of God at all.

These redefinitions of ancient doctrines also complicate the empirical analysis of religious belief. For instance, a 1981 survey of 112 Protestant and Catholic theology professors showed a surprising degree of orthodoxy. Ninety-nine percent of the respondents said they believed in God, 88 percent in immortal life, 83 percent in final judgment. However, it is quite probable that, for a significant number of these people, God, immortal life and final judgment were defined in a way that nineteenth-century Christians would have regarded as blasphemous. So when the same percentage confess belief in God in 1981 as did in 1881, that may conceal a transition from the God who spoke to Moses from the burning bush to Paul Tillich's "ground of being." Moreover, even though 83 percent of those respondents said they believed in final judgment, only 50 percent accepted the doctrine of hell. The rejection of eternal torment is hardly new—Origen had his version of such a rejection in the third century—but what is revealing is the way theologians privately and inconsistently decide which church truths they will accept. And it is of some moment that only 56 percent of the respondents had, over a decade, tried to convert someone.

One Protestant scholar described the situation this way: "For contemporary theological thought the Bible would be no more erroneous if there were no God; the Resurrection of Christ in Barth's theology would be no more unverifiable if God did not exist; and Tillich's 'Protestant principle' would be no more keneotic if there were no 'ground of being.' " But then Tillich is a special and important case. If some theologians refined the definition of God to the vanishing point, Tillich saw religion absolutely everywhere. But, as any Hegelian would easily understand, there is not much difference between a God who is no-where and a God who is everywhere.

Tillich was fairly well known, not simply among the theologians, but also among that growing stratum of the college-educated well before the fashionable interest in theology in the sixties. Moreover, he had long understood that the philosophic and theological crisis of the age was also political. The great catalyst of bourgeois thought, he wrote before World War II, is the *"problem of freedom and authority,"* of finding some substitute for the myths that once had integrated human society. Yet, as he remarked in a later book, religion remained "the meaning-giving substance of culture and culture is the totality of forms in which the basic concern of religion expresses itself." But how, then, to conceptualize religion so that it can survive in a demythol-ogized time?

Anyone, Tillich said—whether a believer or a skeptical sociolo-gist—who defines religion "as man's relation to divine beings" would be incapable of understanding religion at all. If you ask the question of whether God exists, you thereby guarantee that you will never be able to answer it. Indeed, atheism is the proper reply to those who talk about the "existence" of God. The problem, Tillich argued—and this dovetails with the social scientists who deny that there has really been a secularization of Western society, who will be discussed in the next chapter—goes back to Thomas Aquinas, who broke with the Augustinian tradition and sought to know God by way of things (this is the argument "by analogy" which Barth rejected, too, defining it as *the* theological sin of Roman Catholicism). "The bible, consequently, became a collection of true proofs rather than being a guide book to contemplation. . . ." It had been the great merit of the Jews, Tillich went on, to have broken utterly with the myths of soil, blood, family and nation, to have perceived the universality of God. Tillich then took this concept of universalism to its logical conclusion.

Religion, he said, "is being ultimately concerned about that which should be our ultimate concern. This means that faith is the state of being grasped by an ultimate concern and God is the name for the content of that concern." Therefore religion "is at home everywhere, namely in the depths of all functions of man's spiritual life. Religion is the dimension of depth in all of them. . . . What does the metaphor *depth* mean? It means that the religious aspect points to that which is ultimate, infinite, unconditional in man's spiritual life. Religion, in the largest and most basic sense of the word, is ultimate concern."

This definition can obviously be attacked, as Hans Albert has argued, as an example of "immunization strategies," of propositions which are compatible with any fact situation, as the basis of a "crypto-atheism." But then it is precisely this ambiguity which made Tillich's message so welcome to that educated public. Jerald Bauer, the dean of the Chicago Divinity School (Tillich's last chair), caught that aspect of his thought:

> You see, all his life he has been speaking to the people on the borderline of religion, people who were outside the church but leaning toward it, but *now* the people who are in the church, even those of us in theology, find *ourselves* to be also on the borderline of religion. The people who are on the borderline are growing in number everywhere. They are the people for whom Tillich's theology is made, so Tillich now has more to say than ever.

Max Weber was, of course, dead long before this social stratum appeared, and he was talking about a somewhat different phenomenon, yet these words from *The Economic Ethics of the World Religions* might have a contemporary relevance. He wrote of intellectuals who "among other sensations which they enjoy also want to enjoy a 'religious' situation as an 'experience,' desiring, so to speak, to outfit their inner decor stylishly with guaranteed old items. . . ." The intellectuals had in the past, Weber concluded, been very important, but this dilettante religiosity would never be the source of a religious renewal. Clearly Tillich cannot be blamed for his audience—but his social and political impact cannot be analyzed apart from it, either.

Dietrich Bonhoeffer has suffered from some of the same problems of being overenthusiastically interpreted. Yet he was in some ways the most traditionally Christian of the three Protestant thinkers discussed here. He, like Bultmann and Tillich and every serious Christian and Jew of the past two centuries, faced the problem of how to speak of God in a Western world which no longer required him as a "working hypothesis" (Bonhoeffer uses that famous phrase in one of his letters). But he, differing somewhat from Bultmann and Tillich, insisted upon a specifically Christian content even if he saw the need to present it in a radically new way.

"Our whole nineteen-hundred-year-old Christian preaching and theology," he wrote in a letter about a year before his martyrdom at the hands of the Nazis, "rest on the 'religious *a priori*' of mankind. 'Christianity' has always been a form—perhaps the true form—of 're- ligion.' But if one day it becomes clear that this *a priori* does not exist at all, but was a historically conditioned and transient form of human self-expression, and if therefore man becomes radically religionless— and I think that it is already more or less the case . . . what does that mean for 'Christianity'?"

Typically, Bonhoeffer then asks whether Christ cannot become "the lord of the religionless as well? Are there religionless Christians?" This can be interpreted in that stylish, comforting way in which reli- gious fashions are expressed on the "borderline of religion." Bonhoeffer was, I think, talking of a much more profound attempt to maintain Christian faith in a culture which was hostile to it. Indeed, in his strictures on Bultmann he had said that religion (the institutional church, the traditional metaphysics, the historical baggage of nineteen hundred years) could not be made into "a precondition for faith." But then Bonhoeffer rejected—somewhat crudely—the secular salvations of psychoanalysis and existentialism, and he clearly underestimated the degree to which anxiety had reached the "ordinary man."

In short, Bonhoeffer failed to answer his own question—but his enormous value is that he had the clarity and courage to pose it in the first place. From Schleiermacher to Bonhoeffer, Bultmann and Tillich, Protestant theology wrestled with the problem of how to find a place for God in a world in which he no longer existed. During most of that period the Catholic Church evaded the issue altogether, or at least the official church did. Then, with the papacy of John XXIII, the modern world stormed into the last citadel of pre-nineteenth-century culture.

As I remarked earlier, Catholicism was never reduced to its "in- tegralist," pre- and anti-modern version. Despite the vigilance and authoritarianism of Pius IX, Pius X and Pius XII (Pius XI was no radical but, as Gramsci pointed out at the time, was something of a "modernizer" if not a modernist), there was a kind of underground church of the liberal and Left catechumens which continued to exist. After World War II there were the worker priests in France (the future John XXIII, then a diplomat in Paris, encountered them), the Jesuit and Dominican theologians like Lubac and Congar, who wrote not only on religious topics (Lubac on the supernatural) but on political issues as well (Lubac made an extraordinarily sympathetic assessment of the sworn foe of Catholicism, P. J. Proudhon). There were also those, like Jean-Yves Calvez, who sought that which was good and Christian in Marx.

In Germany, Küng was a most learned liberal, Metz a scholarly radical, Balthasar sought a Catholic dialogue with Barth. In Holland there was a remarkably creative church producing thinkers like Schillebeeckx. Even in the United States—where Catholicism was still quite orthodox and, not so incidentally, had kept much more of a hold on the people than the European church—there were stirrings. The journal *Cross Current*, which began in the fifties, published theological innovators from Europe as well as from the United States. And, quite ironically, it was an aristocratic and politically conservative Jesuit, John Courtney Murray, S. J., who brilliantly formulated a democratic and civil-libertarian theology. Murray was silenced by Cardinal Spellman in the 1950s—and was a spiritual father of the Vatican II pronouncements on freedom. There was another stunning reversal in Latin America (which is not in the purview of this book), where theological openness combined with political radicalism to produce a "theology of liberation" (for instance, José Miranda's *Marx and the Bible*).

The Catholic theologians traveled down the same road as the Protestants, appreciated the latter's work, but remained somewhat more traditional in their insistence on the historicity of Jesus. Even so, Hans Küng agreed with Tillich (and Barth and Bultmann) that the God "out there" of Greek thought and medieval Scholasticism—the God whose "existence" one "proved'—was meaningless for modern man. There must be a "modern secular understanding" of God *in* the world; the Catholics must learn from Hegel's identification of God with history. Küng also believed that Rome had, in narrow and sectarian fashion, failed to understand the Chinese conception of God, and therefore lost a chance to bring an entire culture into the ambit of the faith.

And yet, Schillebeeckx still insisted upon the historicity of Jesus and the Resurrection. That was done, it should be noted, within the framework of a very radical book on Jesus, one which eventually brought a threat of disciplinary action by the Congregation for the Doctrine of the Faith. (After John's revolution there was a theological Thermidor.) Schillebeeckx, for instance, laid great stress upon the importance of the Christian "movement" which predated and shaped the New Testament account of Jesus, and therefore argued that the interpretation of Scripture rightly changed over time in response to current events.

Newman had smuggled something like that conception into the nine-teenth-century church, but he managed to do so mainly because many of the orthodox reinterpreted his point out of existence. And, of considerable moment, Schillebeeckx's stress upon the role of the Christian people in the formation of the New Testament reinforces the argument in favor of a greater role for the late-twentieth-century laity (and a diminished role for hierarchs, a consideration which may have occurred to the Congregation for the Doctrine of the Faith).

However, Schillebeeckx attacked the notion that the images of Jesus are "purely mythical conceptions, the real nonmythical content of which is nothing other than our own historically new religious experience (with Jesus still seen of course as exemplar and animator at the time)." Even so, the openness to new ideas about both God and Christ is striking in Schillebeeckx as well as in Küng. And if there were any doubt about the departure involved, the response of Catholics in the West removed it. With the disintegration of traditional Catholicism, large numbers of priests and nuns renounced their vocations, new recruits declined precipitously and in the United States, the country with the highest percentage of religious attendance (mass, communion, confession) in the West, churchgoing dropped and 25 percent of the college-educated laity left their religion completely.

It was in this context that the "death of God" theology made a considerable journalistic impact upon the popular consciousness, even receiving the mid-cult imprimatur of a *Time* cover study at Easter 1966. The death-of-God theologians, one of them said, do not mark the loss "of the idols, or of the God of theism, but of the God of the Christian tradition. And this group persists, in the face of both bewilderment and fury, in calling itself Christian." Tillich, Thomas Altizer wrote, did not go far enough. He only "translates the transcendent Beyond into an immanent 'depth' as a means of making the Christian faith meaningful to our time," and in this he resembles the German philosopher (and Catholic) Schelling. The theologian, Altizer said, "must exist outside of the Church; he can neither proclaim the Word, celebrate the sacrament nor rejoice in the presence of the Holy Spirit. Before contemporary theology can become itself, it must first exist in silence."

There was, to be sure, an aspect of trendiness in all of this; the death-of-God theology had a cultural half-life, at least in the popular mind, approximately equal to that of the miniskirt. This, one suspects, was one of the reasons Karl Barth was so contemptuous of the movement. Yet that is, I think, a mistaken attitude. The death-of-God theology is not a new content but a paradoxical rhetoric which expresses a theological content which had been developing throughout the twentieth century. The innovators of that content, like Barth, might have grumbled at the rhetoric, but that should not disguise the fact that they made straight the way for that kind of language.

A German theologian (who also teaches in the United States), Dorothee Sölle, gave one of the best explanations of the seriousness of the paradox of a death-of-God theology. She wrote that for those people who believe in the traditional God, he has obviously not died; for those who do not believe in any God, he has not died because he never existed. But for those who emerge out of that traditional Christian faith which is disappearing, there is "the new experience of God which characterizes our contemporary situation, the experience of the individual who finds himself insecure and alone in a completely changed world and society." There is therefore the need for a "post-theistic theology." Pascal's anguished perception of the Deus Absconditus has now become the reality for an entire stratum of people, for the serious Christians in the time of the vanishing of the religious *a priori*.

Therefore, Sölle wrote in another book, one must "believe in God atheistically" (*Atheistisch an Gott glauben*). "This paradoxical expression means that belief is here understood as a way of life which springs up without any supernatural, otherworldly image of a heavenly being, without the peace and trust that such an image can bestow, a way of life which is thus without any metaphysical advantage as against the non-Christians in which, nevertheless, one holds fast to the cause of Christ in the world." Secularization, Sölle holds, is not the antithesis of Christianity but its essence, that which marks it off from all other religions. For the Christians "desacralized, de-Godded and profaned the world" so much that pious heathens regarded them as atheists. (Sölle is one of a number of theologians who have attempted to develop a "political theology." This very important, and quite recent, trend will be discussed in Chapter 10.)

Some considered such attitudes preposterous. "If a hundred, or even fifty, years ago," Max Horkheimer said, "one had asserted that the dominant religions of Europe would be able to continue existing without expressly affirming belief in God, there would have been shaking of heads and laughter. Today we have come so far that there are bishops who question the traditional belief in an almighty God and are yet accepted as functionaries of the Church and as Christians."

But could it not be said, then, that these developments only mark the death of the old, used-up God, the "out there" God of Greek thought and medieval theology? Yes, of course. As a theological proposition that idea can be debated by theologians. As a social, historical and political thesis it must be subjected to a secular scrutiny which makes it more complex than many of the theologians and sociologists realize. That Greek–Judeo-Christian notion of God was an ideological basis of Western civilization from at least the time of Constantine to the twentieth century. As such, it helped express individual and collective identities. This more than a millennium of theological-political interrelationship is not an accident, or an experience which can be easily abandoned as one searches for new gods or new definitions of the old God. For that old God was a political figure of great importance and people trusted him, usually because he counseled patience and obedience, occasionally because he was a revolutionary.

Now, there is a new political-theological situation. Ernest Troeltsch, the sociologist-theologian, wrote before the novel doctrines described in this chapter came to the fore. But he had an understanding of what the shift in religion's social position might mean. Medieval Catholicism, he wrote, after permeating its society, had then been unable to cope with the capitalist world. Protestantism had accepted that world but proposed to limit its materialism with an ethic of social responsibility which was against luxury, the worship of Mammon, etc. And now *neither* can function as the cement of a society. And he wrote in 1922:

> Today, because of the extremely advanced differentiation of the common life, it is quite conceivable that the religion and the political-economic-social have separated themselves from one another and that the solving of problems found in the latter sphere is the responsibility of a completely *profane* . . . reform. Dreamers, ideologues and theorists must come to terms with this fact and find a purely *sociological* attitude toward the whole problem (an ethic of the secular society).

In short, God defined by the most serious Protestant and Catholic theologians of the twentieth century is obviously incapable of playing the political and social role of the God whom they rightly declare obsolete. He is too problematic, subjective, existential for that. I think it is quite likely that the way to save the possibility of faith was to move in the direction they took. But that does not change the fact that they did help to kill—or at a minimum recognized the death of—the old God. They have sincerely and sometimes brilliantly—and, I would assume, unwittingly—done the work of Nietzsche in the name of Christ, providing a Christian burial for the dead God.

9

THE RISEN GOD
OF SOCIOLOGY

THE FACTS, IT HAS BEEN wisely said, are never given. They are always taken.

It is for this reason that I have postponed a central point until now: that God—or, more precisely, the Judeo-Christian God of Western politics and society—is in fact dying or dead. It was necessary first to define exactly who this God is, politically, socially, economically, psychologically, aesthetically. Only then can we decide whether or not he is dying and, if so, analyze the earthly consequences of that heavenly event. More precisely, it is impossible to determine what the data are in this case if one does not have some criteria of relevance which allow us to recognize the data in the first place. That preliminary labor, which constitutes the bulk of this book, is now finished. It is therefore possible to confront the most sophisticated defenders of the deity. Not the theologians: the sociologists.

There is an enormous irony in the fact that God is in his heaven in the social sciences—or at least in a very important sector of the social sciences—even as he seems to be vanishing from the altars. Sociology is, after all, one of the disciplines which did so much to relativize human consciousness. And that sense of the relative character of all the moralities and deities has been a major force in subverting the universal lordship of the Judeo-Christian God. But sociology is also a weapon for the defense of (a) new God(s) who (has) have risen from the tomb of the dead divinity. The born-again sociologists say much that is interesting and true in the course of their defense of their newly risen God, and they shred a number of straw men. But they do not refute the proposition which is central to my argument: that the death of the Judeo-Christian God, the only God Western culture has known for almost five millennia, is an event of enormous political importance.

First of all, how does one determine the "facts" about religion? People tend to be even more inconsistent in this area of life than in politics, which makes it hard to say whether anyone is religious or not. "The creed of the Englishman," Alasdair MacIntyre writes, "is that there is no God and that it is wise to pray to him from time to time."

In surveys of a London borough done first in 1945 and then repeated in 1960, MacIntyre shows, 40 percent of the people who attended Anglican services did not believe in life after death, at least a quarter of the "doubters, agnostics and atheists" prayed and over 20 percent of them thought that Christ was more than a man. But, then, who can blame the rank and file for such contradictions when a significant percentage of the theology professors, as the last chapter documented, believe in the final judgment but not in hell?

Given these vagaries, how does one measure "religion" in order to determine whether it is coming or going? In a useful analysis, Charles Glock has suggested that there are at least five dimensions of religious commitment, and individuals and societies can be seen as more or less religious depending upon which one of them is considered central. There are the experience of God, the theological content of a definition of God (ideology), ritual, intellectual knowledge about these things and, perhaps most difficult of all to describe precisely, the "consequential" dimension, the impact that religion has upon individual and social behavior.

Two of Glock's colleagues, Joseph Faulkner and Gordon De Jong, then did an empirical study of his five dimensions based on a survey of college students in 1964. They found that the five dimensions correlated with one another (for instance, a person with a strong experience of God was more likely to be ritually observant than one who had not had such an encounter). The most significant of the dimensions in terms of predicting the others was the ideological; the least significant, the consequential. Those who believed most deeply were most likely to participate in the four other dimensions.

These statistics are imprinted with the sign of Western culture, which has been, as we have noted from time to time, the civilization of the personal, knowable God and is thus marked off from the "cosmic" faiths of the East. Yet even though Max Weber has demonstrated the connection between that particularly Western religious ideology and Western economic and social structure, this is precisely the dimension which is ignored by the sociologists who deny that God is dying. I, on the contrary, will try to show that the replacement of God the Father by God the friend, not to mention God the satyr, signals, not a divine continuity in which this or that detail has been changed, but a basic change in the conditions of human life.

In making that point, however, one must take great care to recognize that religiosity is cyclical. In 1950, for instance, the editors of *Partisan Review*, the quintessential journal of anti-Stalinist Marxism for the thirties generation, announced: "One of the most significant tendencies of our time, especially in this decade, has been the new turn toward religion among intellectuals and the growing despair with secular attitudes and perspectives in not a few circles that lay claim to the leadership of culture." A scant sixteen years later, that *Time* cover story was asking Middle America whether or not God had died.

So I do not for a moment assert that God vanished one fine morning or will do so in the near future. "God is dead," to quote Nietzsche again on this count, "but, given what man is, there will probably be thousands of years in which people will see his shadow in some cave." I am somewhat more precise than Nietzsche. Though there have been, and will again be, "awakenings" of faith in the Judeo-Christian God, they have been, and will be, of declining intensity. The revival of the 1950s which captured the attention of the editors was, Samuel Huntington rightly observes, "very marginal in its impact compared to that of the 1740s." The traditional God, I assert, is disappearing in crooked, but unmistakable, ways.

In documenting this thesis, the nationality of the numbers I am presenting is American. That is a complicating factor of considerable moment.

The American experience, in this area as in so many others, is quite exceptional. America, Edmund Burke shrewdly said, "is the dissidence of dissent, and the Protestantism of the Protestant religion." The frontier turned European churches into sects—and then the establishment of an ordered society transformed sects into churches. As

Huntington puts it, "America is unique in the world in the number of religious bodies to which it has given birth since the early seventeenth century" even though it "produced no significant theologian between Jonathan Edwards and Reinhold Niebuhr. . . ." This exuberant pluralism led to the "Americanization" of religion, since the national creed was the only one accepted by all the churches and sects. But it also promoted Biblical literalism—and the only fundamentalist movement in the West—because there was no established church to interpret the Holy Scriptures authoritatively.

Were it not for the United States and Canada, Walter Dean Burnham documents, there would be a one-to-one relationship between economic development and secularization (measured crudely by church attendance, which declines as the GNP rises) in the world. This, Burnham suggests, has political consequences for this country. For instance, a significant portion of the constituencies which are quite religious in the United States (the poor, minorities, Protestants) tend to have Leftist counterparts in Europe. By a great margin, more Americans believe in life after death than do the citizens of any other Western nation. Is this one of the reasons the American welfare state is the cheapest and least extensive in the West? If there is more than one life, a national health system is not so important; if there is only one life, it is a necessity.

Most paradoxical of all, America has always been as secular as it is religious; or, rather, it has always been simultaneously very secular and very religious. Religion in this country has generally been a mile wide and an inch deep, pervasive but not too important as a belief. Tocqueville was one of the first to see that.

The nation began with a theocratic dream of a "city on the hill" in the Massachusetts Bay Colony but quickly moved toward tolerance. Even in Virginia, where there was an established church, the fight against the Crown began as a struggle for religious freedom led by, among others, the young Patrick Henry. And even though the Revolution had roots in the eighteenth-century "awakening," it was led by *philosophes*, occurred at a time when religion was at a low ebb and drove the Tory Anglicans out of the country. But then there was a new, typically American surge of religious fervor, the Second Great Awakening in the New England of the turn of the century. After that, in the first decades of the nineteenth century, evangelism—primarily

Baptist and Methodist—swept across Kentucky, Tennessee and southern Ohio. These typically American churches were frontier institutions, democratic, uncontrolled by hierarchies.

Tocqueville came to America during that religious surge in the early nineteenth century. And yet, as he himself intuited, secularism was powerful even then. In the early days of the Republic there was resistance to any notion that this country was "Christian." In 1810, Congress passed a law which provided that the mail should be delivered seven days a week in order to emphasize that the government did not keep the Sabbath holy, whatever the churches might do. That commitment to public services on Sunday was confirmed in 1825, and in 1829 a Senate committee declared that irreligion had the same rights as religion. To proclaim Sunday a day of rest, the committee said, would be unjust to both non-Christians and the irreligious.

Religion itself, for all of its ubiquity, had strangely secular qualities. Tocqueville noticed the indifference of the American faithful to religious doctrine. This quality, he said, did not diminish "the fervour of each for the cult he had chosen"—but it did make each remarkably tolerant of the other churches (Roman Catholicism was often an exception to this rule because it was suspected of being systemically and structurally intolerant, hostile to democracy). The sermons, Tocqueville wrote, concerned morality, not dogma. Later on, when Max Weber visited America, he came to much the same conclusion. Church membership, he commented in *The Protestant Sects and the Spirit of Capitalism*, was something required of a good businessman who wanted to establish his credit-worthiness. You can believe anything you want, a salesman told him—as long as you believe something.

Historically, then, religion played a particularly diffuse role in America; it was everywhere and nowhere. That trend, Lipsett writes, was then further accentuated by urbanization and industrialization, which broke up the old, homogeneous communities. Gerhard Lenski, one of the sociological defenders of religion, made the same discovery in his empirical study of contemporary urban churches: the cities, bringing together so many diverse kinds of people, require that they tolerate one another's faiths. But perhaps the shrewdest recent application of this paradigm is found in the book that summarized the great "religious revival" of the 1950s, Will Herberg's *Protestant, Catholic, Jew*.

That decade was the period of the highest level of church attendance in American history (49 percent average weekly attendance). Yet Herberg understood the paradox which was later traced by Lipsett back to nineteenth-century American history. "America," Herberg wrote, "seems to be at once the most religious and the most secular of nations." There were, he argued, secular reasons for religious observance: "With the religious community as the primary context of self-identification and social location, and with Protestantism, Catholicism and Judaism as the three culturally diverse representatives of the same 'spiritual values', it becomes virtually mandatory for the American to place himself in one or another of these groups."

That trend, Herberg continued, was also influenced by one of the great social facts of the fifties: the baby boom. Parents with younger children often join a church, not so much out of great religious commitment, but because they believe that the young should have some form of religious (moral) education. There was, Herberg said, a "faith in faith" which was also part of the American "civil religion." These perceptions were, I think, telling and complex, but they dealt with a volatile subject matter. The seemingly pious fifties were followed by the turbulent sixties. The Roman Catholic Church, a rather orthodox, mainstream faith, lost 25 percent of its college graduates in the period immediately following Paul VI's 1967 reaffirmation of the traditional teaching with regard to birth control; between the mid-sixties and the mid-seventies, the number of Catholics attending mass declined from 71 percent to 50 percent.

Yet even this new tendency was quite ambiguous. At the same time that official Catholicism—and mainstream Protestantism—witnessed a significant decline in terms of the traditional indices (church attendance, membership, etc.), the fundamentalists grew, "new" religions, usually Eastern in origin, proliferated, and a charismatic movement appeared within the normally staid American Catholic Church. Herberg's account of the religious revival was the conversation piece of the fifties and early sixties; Dean Kelley's *Why the Conservative Churches Are Growing* was widely discussed in the early seventies. There was a similar shift in terms of the perception of "civil religion."

In a sense, "civil religion" in the United States is as old as the Republic itself. It was, however, during the Civil War that this national creed acquired a powerful set of symbols, a liturgy of the patriotic faith. In the "Battle Hymn of the Republic" there was, as Michael Linesch has noted, a "civil millenarianism":

> I have seen him in the watch fires of a hundred circling
>   camps,
> They have builded him an altar in the evening dews and
>   damps,
> I have read his righteous sentence by the dim and flaring
>   lamps,
> His day is marching on.

Indeed, Linesch notes that the Confederate soldiers could have sung the very same verses had they been written for their side.

The Civil War also produced a genuine American martyr, a Christ figure of the democratic religion who died to make men free, Abraham Lincoln. The "Battle Hymn" reverberated for at least a century. In an influential paper of 1965 (published in 1967), Robert Bellah interpreted the religious imagery of the Kennedy and Johnson administrations in terms of an American tradition with more than a century of history behind it and even saw the trend as the point of departure for new ideological transformations as the world groped toward some kind of international order. This religion, Bellah understood, could provide a royal road to triviality, as in Eisenhower's statement that "our government makes no sense unless it is founded in a deeply felt religious faith—and I don't care what it is." But, Bellah also noted, the religion was enduring and sometimes profound.

Bellah delivered his paper on civil religion at the point when the escalation of the war in Vietnam was beginning to do more to undermine that Americanized faith than any event in our history. The God of civil religion, Martin Marty commented a little later, died along with the God of traditional religion. More broadly, the rapidity of the two transitions I have just described—from the religious revival of the fifties to the secular humanism of the sixties, from the civil religion of the early Kennedy-Johnson years to the attack on patriotism in the antiwar movement of the late sixties and early seventies—emphasizes again the cyclical nature of the statistics.

So what are the "American" qualifications which our particular history requires when we are generalizing from the experience in this country to that of the West as a whole? On the one hand, it can be fairly said that a drop in the more obvious forms of religious observance in the United States—church attendance, for instance—would suggest that these trends are probably *more* advanced in the other late capitalist societies of European origin. Since the American numbers describe the most religious Western nation in terms of conventional church faith, they make a particularly strong case. In this country, one survey showed, 85 percent of the people believe in heaven—as against 50 percent for the Swiss and 39 percent for the French—and 56 percent say they think religion is "very important," compared with 17 percent in West Germany and Scandinavia (and 12 percent in Japan).

At the same time, the reader has already been warned that such facts must be taken with a grain of salt. God and heaven, we have seen, have always been treated more casually in the United States than in most other Western nations. It is important, then, to distinguish between religious rhetoric and religious belief. That is one reason that I will focus on one survey—*The Impact of Belief*, a report commissioned by the Connecticut Mutual Life Insurance Company and published in 1981. By dealing with a single, comprehensive source, I hope to avoid many of the definitional problems which arise when one picks and chooses among the endless data. Moreover, *The Impact of Belief* is enthusiastic about its findings and interprets them as proving that "the impact of religious belief reaches far beyond the realm of politics and has penetrated virtually every dimension of American experience. This force is rapidly becoming a more powerful factor in American life than whether someone is liberal or conservative, male or female, young or old, or a blue collar or a white collar worker." Since this conclusion is diametrically opposed to my own, if I can make my case from its numbers that certainly guarantees that I have not used statistics biased in my favor.

In addition, the Connecticut Mutual analysis corroborates trends identified in other studies. For instance, it quite closely parallels the results of a *New York Times* poll published at Christmas 1981 and the figures in a 1980 book by George Gallup, Jr., and David Poling. Not so incidentally, both the Gallup-Poling book and the *New York Times* article also purported to document the persistence, or even growth, of religious faith in the United States. Clearly, then, we are in a situation where people with opposite readings can reach a consensus on the raw data. It is one of the most striking cases of the difference between seeing a glass as half full or half empty.

Connecticut Mutual asked eight questions of a weighted sample of the population. There were approximately sixteen hundred respondents. It also mailed a questionnaire to 4,383 leaders and received 1,762 answers. The latter were treated separately from the poll data on general public attitudes. The eight questions put to the general public asked whether the respondent (1) feels that God loves him or her; (2) engages in prayer; (3) attends religious service; (4) reads the Bible; (5) has had a "religious experience"; (6) participates in a church social activity; (7) encourages others to turn to religion; (8) listens to a religious broadcast. Those who said they "frequently" did seven or eight of these activities were in the "highest" category of religious commitment; positive answers to five or six items put an individual in the "high" category; three or four described a "moderate"; one or two was categorized as "low" and zero was the "lowest" on the scale of religious commitment.

Given this measure, 10 percent of the sample were in the highest, 16 percent high, 24 percent moderate, 32 percent low and 18 percent lowest. For Connecticut Mutual, the fact that 26 percent of the American people were in the top two categories "identifies a cohesive and powerful group of Americans approximately 45 million strong [as a percentage of the 174 million Americans over 14 years of age] as 'intensely religious.' . . ." There is another way of looking at the same figures. The number of Americans with zero positive responses to the eight questions was almost twice as high as those at the highest level of commitment (18 percent as against 10 percent). Fully one-half of the population were found with no more than two positive responses (18 percent with zero, 32 percent with one or two "religious" answers). And three-quarters of the people were positive about half or fewer of the questions (adding the 24 percent of moderates to the 32 of low and the 18 percent of lowest). Since the Gallup Poll found 59 percent of the American people to be church members, belonging to a church must be compatible with moderate, low—or perhaps even zero—religious commitment.

Clearly, however, it would be difficult to settle the argument between my interpretation of the statistics and that of *The Impact of Belief* since there is no objective criterion for determining whether the glass is half full (their reading) or half empty (my thesis). However, this report provides other figures which do, I think, offer the possibility of an even more persuasive rejection of the conclusions it draws from them.

The analysis which resolves the impasse is dynamic: that is, deals with characteristics of religious people, and our knowledge about whether those characteristics are, in general, increasing or waning. It discovers that the most religious people belong to groups which have been least affected by the cultural revolution of modernity. Since that revolution continues to proceed apace, the religious attitudes found in those groups are not simply held by a declining percentage of the population but have less and less social and political weight.

Who are the most committed religious people according to *The Impact of Belief*? They are disproportionately older, Southern, black, female and low-income, with low levels of education and from small cities and rural areas. The Connecticut Mutual study attempts to deal with the age-distribution statistics by arguing that they represent, not a progressive decline in religion over the generations, but a life-cycle pattern within each generation. This was demonstrated, the report says, because 75 percent of the people in *every* age group said that religion would become more important to them if they knew they had only six months to live. That strikes me as an extremely casual way to settle a major question. However, without elaborate argument, I will simply assume that the age distribution of religious belief is a function of both a life-cycle pattern *and* the fact that recent generations have been born into a more secular society. The basis for this assumption is to be found in the evidence all the other data about the characteristics of the highly committed religious people provide as to the importance of cultural effects which have been intensifying over time. And this suggests intra- as well as inter-generational differences.

The South is over-represented at the highest level of religious commitment (35 percent, against 28 percent in the Midwest, 22 percent in the West and 17 percent in the Northeast) because it is more black, poorer and less educated than the other regions. Those sociological determinants, I would suggest, are the most important discovered by the Connecticut Mutual research. Why is it that the blacks (and, in the *New York Times* Christmas 1981 survey, the Hispanics in New York City) are so much more religious than the whites? As a result of discrimination, black people (and Hispanics) have been disproportionately excluded from the most "modern"—scientific, technological—sectors of the society. Indeed, while a participant-observer in the civil-rights movement of the fifties and sixties, I argued that "soul" was less an innate quality of black people than a characteristic of all groups who had not been through the capitalist cultural revolution. Since the enormous immigrations into the United States in recent years—from Mexico, Central America and the Caribbean—have been heavily composed of precisely such people, a part of the religiosity showing up in the polls is an import which is likely to be assimilated into the more secular patterns dominant in America over a generation or two.

The education and income figures—which are obviously related to one another—refract the same cultural-social trends. The more money and the more education one has, the more likely it is that one has been exposed to secular cultural influences—for instance, that one has been to a college where the Bible is studied, even if under the direction of a deeply religious professor, as history, sociology or literature and not simply as the revealed Word of God. So it was that *The Impact of Belief* also found out that "leaders" in the United States were less likely to consider themselves religious than the people as a whole: 74 percent for the public, 66 percent for the leaders. And that last figure is obviously affected by the fact that one of the leadership groups surveyed was religious leaders, 100 percent of whom considered themselves to be religious. Indeed, the spectrum of opinion among leaders corroborates the general thesis being urged here: 100 percent of the religious leaders define themselves as religious, 80 percent of the business leaders, 67 percent in the military, 64 percent in voluntary associations, 64 percent in news media, 63 percent in education, 57 percent in government (*sic!*), 53 percent in law and justice and 50 percent in science. The sciences and humanities—the areas most affected by the cultural revolution of the past several centuries—are thus the least religious areas.

There is one large exception to the data just reported and it will be quite relevant to the argument of the next chapter. On almost all issues, the leaders are more secular (or liberal) than the public. But when it was asked, "Do you agree or disagree that the government ought to make sure everyone has a good standard of living," 69 percent of the public agreed—and only 31 percent of the leaders. This is one more confirmation of a familiar pattern: higher degrees of liberalism and tolerance on social issues among the better-educated with higher incomes; higher degrees of concern for economic issues among the middle and lower levels of the educational-occupational structure. The politics of economic conservatism and social liberalism as practiced by Jerry Brown, John Anderson and more than a few Democratic liberals in flight from liberalism after the 1980 elections are based on this reality.

On moral issues, the Connecticut Mutual statistics present America as more traditional than do other (and, to my mind, better) studies, but the same age, class and education determinants are still at work. For instance, 54 percent of the general public thinks that heterosexual cohabitation without marriage is not a moral issue—but at the lowest level of religious commitment we find 83 percent with that position, at the highest level 16 percent. And similar differences show up on the income and education scales. Even more striking are the findings of Everett Ladd (a neoconservative political scientist). They show an almost one-to-one relationship between attitudes on adultery, homosexuality, premarital sex and the like and levels of education.

What do all these figures have to do with the statistical debate over secularization? They indicate that the internal social and cultural processes in the United States—when prescinded from immigrants with different kinds of societal backgrounds, that is—are eroding the social sources of faith in the most religious groups (black, poor, Southern, women). Women are an important case in point. They show up in the Connecticut Mutual study as almost twice as likely to be at the "highest" or "high" level of commitment (34 percent for women, 19 percent for men). But, Thomas Luckmann points out, women who work resemble men who work more than they do housewives in these matters. And, it is well known, the percentage of working women has dramatically increased since World War II and is still on the rise.

There is, it should be noted, a seeming exception to this trend. The recruits to "countercultural" religions in recent years—the Jesus People, Children of God, Unification Church, Hare Krishna—are disproportionately young and male and come from comfortable, middle-class families with relatively high levels of education. But there is no reason to think that the counterculture, even in these rare cases where it is institutionalized, offers anything like an alternative faith for American (or Western) society. The major social determinants affecting the future of religion in America are, I believe, the ones unwittingly defined in the Connecticut Mutual study. And they predict further secularization.

But isn't my thesis contradicted by the clear evidence of the revival of the religious—mainly fundamentalist—Right in the seventies and eighties? Kevin Phillips, one of the shrewdest interpreters of American electoral patterns, has even talked of a "Fourth Great Awakening," one more of those bursts of revivalist energy which dot American history. Two issues have to be kept quite separate in dealing with this question. There is no doubt that the political mobilization of a religious constituency containing millions of people can have a major impact on American society. Phillips's analysis of election returns showed that Jimmy Carter's winning the Southern Baptist vote was a factor in his victory in 1976, and his losing it a cause of his defeat in 1980. It is a deplorable fact that groups like the Moral Majority can make a difference in American politics. But that does not begin to prove that there is a religious revival in the United States, that the trends revealed in the Connecticut Mutual report have been reversed. Indeed, the Moral Majority candidates did rather poorly in the Congressional election of 1982.

Phillips estimates that there are 75 million *members* in the denominations (including "traditional" Catholics) which lean to the Right; *The Impact of Belief* found 45 million *individuals* over fourteen years of age who took religion seriously. If one makes the plausible assumption that at least some of the denomination members are less than passionate in their individual commitment, those figures are not far apart (and Phillips himself has cited the Connecticut Mutual numbers).

In a sense, it would be surprising if there were not such a sizable religious minority in the United States. After all, when it was a majority, not too long ago, it succeeded in passing the Prohibition Amendment to the Constitution. One of the reasons the present development seems to herald a radical new turn is that fundamentalism withdrew from the political arena after the fiasco of the Scopes trial in 1925 and did not really return to activism until the Goldwater movement of the sixties. What happened at that point was that a traditional minority in America suddenly became quite visible again. But there is no evidence that this meant a move toward religion on the part of people who had previously been indifferent.

There are scholars who argue that the reactivated fundamentalists are more "middle-class" than previously, which would undercut the normal link between class and theological rigor. But here the Connecticut Mutual data are unambiguous. The more money and education a person has, the less likely he or she is to be deeply committed to a faith. More broadly, the more people find themselves in the "modern" sector of the society, the more likely it is that they will be secular. We have seen how women change their attitudes when they enter the paid labor market. Thus the steady increase in female labor-market participation signals a further secularization of America.

Moreover, even the newly reactivated fundamentalists are more secular than before. In the sixties, when this tendency first reappeared, Richard Hofstadter commented that it showed "that ascetic Protestantism remains a significant undercurrent in contemporary America and that its followers have found newfangled ways of reaffirming some of their convictions. They cannot bring back Prohibition or keep evolution entirely out of the schools. They have been unable to defend school prayer or prevent *Life* magazine from featuring a topless bathing suit." That, it might be argued, was the sixties, the heyday of the counterculture. But then George Marsden, who has written the most important scholarly study of fundamentalism, notes that in the eighties this movement has become "more secularized" than its predecessors. That, Marsden wrote, was one of the reasons they could now make an alliance "with the once-despised Catholics."

The Moral Majority and related groups, then, do not demonstrate that there has been a quantitative or qualitative increase in religion in the United States. So I repeat my thesis: the data in the Connecticut Mutual study demonstrate that traditional religion will persist in the foreseeable future as a declining force, that the death agony of God, which has lasted for a century at least, is still in process.

With that said, we can now turn to the risen God of the sociologists.

———— I I ————

There is a basic, underlying theme in most of the sociological defenses of religion. One God is indeed dying, it is conceded: the historically specific Judeo-Christian deity who has presided over Western civilization. But as he expires, another God, other gods, take his place, not the least because human beings are, in their very essence, religious. God is dead—long live God!

"The rise of what has classically been considered non-belief in the modern world," Robert Bellah writes in his version of this argument, "has been connected with an enormous expansion of just that class among whom non-belief has always been a problem: the self-conscious intellectuals. . . . This vast increase in literacy and education in the past two centuries has been intimately related to the rise of anti-authoritarianism as a major cultural theme." This shift, brought about by the emergence of a vastly enlarged stratum of literate people, may indeed mark "the decline of the external control system of religion and the decline of traditional religious belief. But religion as that symbolic form through which man comes to terms with the antinomies of his own being has not declined, indeed cannot decline unless man's nature ceases to be problematic to him."

To begin with, Bellah's definition of religion is so broad that it would include a serious Marxist atheism (I am not referring to Stalinist or neo-Stalinist cults but to authentic Marxism) and, for that matter, all variants of atheistic humanism. They, too, provide "symbolic form[s] through which man comes to terms with the antinomies of his own being." It is certainly true, as Ernst Bloch has written, that "the real metaphysical questions last longer than the mythological, transcendental answers which the churches of the rulers give to them. They do not vanish with the churches." But wouldn't the vanishing of the churches be a matter of some moment for the sociologist? Wouldn't the emergence of nonsupernatural transcendentals as the basis of social integration signal one of the greatest transformations in the conditions of Western life?

Second, it is not true that intellectuals have normally constituted "that class among whom non-belief has always been a problem." The intellectuals, Weber pointed out long ago, have often been the agents, the bearers, of religion. That this is not true in the present (which Weber also recognized) is explained, not by the innate qualities of the intellectuals and the literate, but by the specific character of *modern* culture. It is not simply the vast increase in literacy over the past two centuries which is the problem—but everything else that occurred in those two centuries, the process which caused intellectuals, in Lionel Trilling's phrase, to adopt the stance of the "opposing self" with an "intense and adverse imagination of the culture in which it had its being."

Finally, Bellah skirts an abyss. He concedes the possibility that society may indeed be undergoing "the decline of the external control system of religion and the decline of traditional religious belief." But there will be symbolic forms after that event, and therefore it is not that religion has declined but that one of its phases has merely given way to another. It is like writing that the French Revolution did not change the reality of "government" but "only" marked a transition from absolutist "government" to bourgeois democratic "government." That a historically specific Judeo-Christian faith is being replaced by a much more diffuse, private and often undefinable feeling, that the "external control system" of religion is in question, is precisely what is critical. That one can, by the very broad definition of "religion," subsume this millennial shift under it trivializes a cultural revolution.

Talcott Parsons took a somewhat different path to Bellah's conclusions in an analysis which was rich, insightful and flawed. He acknowledged that he was "being deliberately paradoxical in attributing to the concept secularization what has often been held to be its opposite, namely not the loss of commitment to religious values and the like, but the institutionalization of such values, and other components of religious orientation in evolving cultural and social systems." This is not, Parsons held, the most irreligious of times; it is the most religious age that has ever been.

To reach that paradoxical conclusion, Parsons developed a concept that had been introduced into sociological theory by the first great defender of the proposition that humans are essentially religious, Emile Durkheim. In *The Division of Labor in Society*, Durkheim made a tremendously influential distinction between two forms of social solidarity. In the early stages of society, Durkheim said, solidarity was "organic." The system was "segmented" into units which resembled one another; the whole was an accumulation of segments. This led to "ethnic types and not to personal types" and, romantic theories of primitive holism notwithstanding, required harsh rules to keep everyone in line. "Mechanical" solidarity develops with the increasing complexity of the economy and is based on a division of labor and specialization.

Parsons applied this concept to the history of religion, which he interpreted as a process, not of secularization, but of *differentiation*. Originally, at the dawn of human history, the religious and nonreligious were fused. But with growing complexity, the sacred was differentiated from the profane. However, even in Judaism, a very advanced form of religion, faith was identified with a people. It was Christianity—and Saint Paul in particular—which separated belief and ethnicity and, at the same time, also challenged Rome's political gods. Since it was now possible to be a Christian *and* a Roman, this opened up the way for converts who would not have otherwise been available to the new religion.

In medieval Christendom a new stage developed. Many peoples and states and societies existed under the roof of a single creed. And

those societies "were the first in history to have a basic religious uniformity for a very large population as a whole." Religion did not sub-
jugate society—the political order was not theocratic—but it dominated
indirectly, by means of values which were shared by both the Church
and the ruling class. It is indeed true that many of the theories of
secularization take this model of medieval society as a norm for invid-
ious (by secularists) or nostalgic (usually, but not always, by conservatives) comparisons. But even within that medieval unity, Parsons
noted, there was further differentiation. The Cluniac Reform and its
establishment of a celibate clergy institutionalized the separateness of
the Church from the society.

The Protestant Reformation was, obviously, a new and important
moment in this process of differentiation. When the religious wars
finally ended, they left behind a religious pluralism *within* Christianity
itself. And just as Christianity eventually assimilated the Jewish and
Roman traditions which it had originally opposed, so here Protestantism and Catholicism turned out to be separate branches of an intact
Christianity.

What is happening in twentieth-century America is, Parsons concluded, simply one more step in the differentiation of religion, not the
end of religion. There are new problems, like nuclear weapons, which
do not fit into the old theological (and moral) categories. At the same
time, religion, like the family, has become private, a matter of individual choice. Indeed, society is, in a very real sense, becoming more
religious, as the power of the civil-rights and anti-poverty movements
of the sixties demonstrated. These seemingly secular attempts to deal
with social and economic problems make religious values truly effective
in society, something that never happened in "holier" times.

In a sense, Parsons's grand theory provides an explanation for
the American "faith in faith" which Will Herberg described in more
empirical terms. "The contemporary Catholic, Protestant or Jew,"
Parsons wrote, "may, with variations within his own broader faith,
even for Catholics, be a believer in the wider societal moral community . . . and . . . this common belongingness means sharing a religious orientation at the level of *civil religion*." For Parsons, then, at
the beginning only kinsmen, with a common ancestor, belonged to the
same moral community. Subsequently, through a process of societal
differentiation, faith spread to a complex ethnic group (the Jews), freed
itself from ethnicity in a universal church of many nations (the Chris-

tian Middle Ages), became plural within a common framework (Protestantism) and now provides a morality for secular movements which
may not even recognize their own religiosity.

In part, I agree. There is indeed a common heritage within the
West—it will be described in the next chapter—which provides the
possibility for motivating men and women in the late twentieth and
the twenty-first centuries. For Weber, at his most pessimistic, there
could be no morality without formal religion. For Parsons, at his most
optimistic, morality can survive the passing of institutional religion.
That is true and important. But Parsons tends to treat the possibility
he describes as a providential inevitability. One must question, I think,
whether social differentiation is the agency of mysterious purpose in
human history.

It is indeed true that the civil-rights and anti-poverty movements
of the sixties were permeated by Judeo-Christian values, even if some
of those who acted upon them were atheistic humanists. But how,
then, does one deal with the facts that the anti-poverty "religion" came
to an end in a decade or so, and that the civil-rights movement—which
did indeed have the aspect of a "beloved community"—fragmented in
the late sixties? The Judeo-Christian God had the great advantage of
being eternal and therefore immunized from the vicissitudes of politics.
But when "religion" simply becomes a synonym for any deeply held
altruistic commitment, religions will come and go like fashions and
fads.

Even more important, Parsons is much too complacent about the
privatizing of religion. It is of considerable moment that, a recent
survey found, "many young people seem comfortable with a solitary,
personal approach to matters of faith. . . ." A similar theme was sounded
by Philip Hammond when he wrote that "decisions about the higher
good are always 'religious' in character, but this is the point: these
latter decisions are no longer made by churches." But if religion has
been, precisely, a critical force for integrating people in a society around
shared—and sacred—norms, what happens when it becomes private?
It may endure in some sense, yet it forfeits a role it has played in the
West for more than four millennia.

By claiming social potency for such a "religion," Parsons is to
sociology what Tillich is to theology. Both are realistic enough to con-
cede the decline of the traditional faith. And both treat the shadow of
the dead God as if it were the glory of the living God when he was in

his heaven. Alvin Gouldner, who wrote a radical critique of Parsons's sociology of religion, put it quite well: "The Parsonian 'sacred' thus no longer has an icon, a cult, or a God. It is an unexplained protoplasmic *sentiment*, a hungry piety that may reach out and endow anything with a touch of divinity."

This profound flaw is not resolved by saying that religion is simply becoming more differentiated, like the family. For the family is, in its contemporary evolution, as problematic an institution as the Church, and the crisis of both is clearly interrelated. One does not have to be an anti-feminist reactionary, like the historian Pierre Chaunu, to see, as he does, that the dramatic fall in the birth rate in the post–World War II West is cause and effect of the drop in religious commitment.

However, there is yet another sociological argument in favor of the notion that God cannot die. Like Parsons, Thomas Luckmann understands that, as society evolved, "what were originally total life values became part-time norms." But he then goes on to defend the continuing relevance of religion in phenomenological, rather than sociological, terms. There were adumbrations of this theory in Kant, Hegel, the Marxist Max Adler and George Herbert Mead, and it was brought into the social sciences by Alfred Schutz. Luckmann's *Invisible Religion* is an extremely powerful statement of it.

For ethical relations to exist, Luckmann says, there must be "the moral unity of a biography." Each person knows that in the course of everyday life he/she "meets witnesses of his past, as well as potential witnesses of his future, conduct. He is and will be reminded of his past. Indeed, he can be taken to task for actions he may have forgotten already." It is this social dimension of personality, Luckmann holds, that makes of humans something more than isolated organisms, atoms of a mere subjectivity. The self emerges from a cooperative construction of reality and morality, from a transcending of the individual. It is this sense of transcendence, inherent in the human *qua* human, which is the realm of religion.

That community is a precondition of humanity and/or morality is quite true. So is the claim that in the past, religion in the West—but not necessarily, say, in Confucianism—articulated that community in transcendental terms. But this does not mean that only religion can accomplish such a task or, even if that were true, guarantee that it will be able to do so in the future. These sociologists are often rich in insights yet they make a curious error, given their discipline: they define religion in such a vague, ahistorical way that it becomes a useless concept for the analysis of society.

For instance, at one point Robert Bellah complains that, had the Enlightenment occurred in Zen Buddhist culture, the outcome would have been different, since that culture never believed in a God "out there" as the West did. So, he asserts, why can't the West now take up a Zen-like religiousness and thus annul the unfortunate effects of the Enlightenment? Was it, then, an accident that the Enlightenment occurred in a culture that believed in a God "out there"? We have seen that one of the reasons for the scientific revolution in the seventeenth-century West was, precisely, a theological heritage which had inculcated the notion of an objective order of things in a culture and motivated scientists to give glory to God through the exploration of his creation. The West will have to continue living with the Enlightenment, which is, for better or worse, inside its mind and eyes and soul, and consequently with the dying of the only God it has ever known, the God "out there."

There is another sociological theory which makes the same kind of point as those raised by Luckmann and Parsons but in a much different way. Thinkers like Pitirim Sorokin and Arnold Toynbee take entire civilizations and centuries of human society as their basic unit of analysis in this area. And they conclude (Sorokin) that the "sensate" culture of the twentieth-century West will be driven to a new spirituality, or (Toynbee) that the collapse of Western culture will provide a salutary shock which will revive and even strengthen Christianity. These kinds of speculation cover such an immense period of time and are compatible with so many outcomes that they read like Nostradamus in the language of social science. So my objection to these theories, as to Luckmann's and Parsons's, is that they are utterly lacking in a sense of the historically specific, for all their learned reference to history.

If I thus reject the ahistorical optimism of the born-again sociologists, I share their hope that the values of Judeo-Christianity will indeed survive the dying of God—*but not in religious form.* For now, let me turn to a much more pessimistic thinker, Niklas Luhmann. For him it is not simply the Western God who is dying but the very possibility of integrating a society on the basis of moral values. He is a Nietzschean for the age of systems theory and computers.

Durkheim, Luhmann holds, showed that the classic Western notion of society as a whole composed of parts no longer applies. For each individual and family to feel linked to an order which was their own existence writ large, it was indeed necessary that the segments resemble one another. But with the development of a world society in which there are no longer national boundaries in science, economics, technology—or even love affairs—the old "organic" system of social integration has become obsolete and irrelevant. In the past, what held societies together were norms—which is where religion functioned— and people's ability to learn to deal with the unexpected or the disappointing by changing. The latter process—Luhmann calls it "cognitive" integration—was subordinate, and the normative was dominant, not least because the normative is easier to institutionalize: it is simpler to tell people to act in the traditional way than to argue that they must change their behavior in order to adapt to new circumstances. The cognitive approach tries to change itself when the world does not correspond to its expectations; the normative tries to change the world to make it conform to expectations.

But now—and here is the critical parting of the ways with Parsons and Luckmann—specialization and differentiation have gone so far, creating a world system of systems, that normative integration is no longer possible. There is not a whole composed of similar parts. Rather, the various subsystems (economic, scientific, technological) seek to reduce the infinite complexity of the environment, to achieve an "inner environment" of peace and predictability and thus to give the entire system an ability to cope with even more change. But there cannot be a normative ideology for the entire world—indeed, it is questionable whether the world can be organized democratically—and there is no one value system which can function within all of the disparate, highly specialized subsystems.

Indeed, in his book *The Function of Religion*, Luhmann defines secularization as "the *social-structural* relevance of the *privatizing* of religious decision." That is, he views the new personal and subjective religions, which inspire Parsons and Bellah with such hope, as *the* sign of the secular, of a society in which "on the general, societal level religion is no longer functionally necessary but is only summoned to be 'helpful' in certain situations."

More recently, Bellah has recognized some of the weaknesses in his earlier, and excessively enthusiastic, interpretation of countercultural faith. To be sure, he still insists that the 1960s witnessed "an upwelling of mystical religiosity." But now he is more sensitive to the distortions of this form of consciousness, "its inner volatility and incoherence, its extreme weakness in social and political organization, and above all its particular form of compromise with the world, namely its closeness to psychological man in his pursuit of self-centered experiences in preference to any form of social loyalty or commitment." For that matter, Bellah concluded that what was needed was a revival of "church religion" of a traditional type. But Luhmann would argue that, in the age of the functional specialization of the planet Earth, hopes for such an old-fashioned, almost pre-modern, revival are bound to be disappointed.

There is, I think, real power in this argument. But when one considers the centuries of travail which were required to move from tribal to city to national consciousness, and then asks how we are now to move to an integrated planetary consciousness in which being human is more important than being American or Christian or Islamic or Buddhist, the issues are staggering. If I agree with Luhmann that traditional religion in the West is no longer able to provide a normative, integrating consciousness for its various national societies, much less for the globe as a whole, I disagree profoundly with his assumption that his description of how the various subsystems function provides the basis of *social* integration. There is no subjectivity in Luhmann's system, no human integration; there is only the system itself. In addition to finding this abhorrent, I do not think that it will work as a way of holding society together.

God, I argue against Parsons and Luckmann, may indeed survive in some new persona but not as the integrating norm of Western society; values, I hold against Luhmann, may endure, and if they do not a globe integrated by systems will be inhuman. Am I, then, saying that there once was a religious time which is the measure of our contemporary faithlessness and immorality? No. And perhaps.

No, because the last four or five centuries have indeed seen—in the West and, even though much less so, in the rest of the world—an increase in the recognition given to simple humanity (longer life, greater literacy, more rights created through struggle). Parsons is, on this count, right: America in the twentieth century treats human nature better than Aquinas's thirteenth century, even if we are much less sure what human nature is. And Freud was right when he wrote, "It is doubtful whether men were in general happier at a time when religious doctrines held unrestricted sway; more moral they certainly were not."

Moreover, it is useless to measure the moralities of different systems against one another. That is dividing apples by oranges. But one can say, as Marx did, that the destruction of the religiously integrated system of feudalism by capitalism made a much higher level of social morality possible, even though the defeated society was holistic and the triumphant order was alienated. Similarly, the question of decadence today does not have to do with whether our agnostic age is "better than" the thirteenth century. It has to do with whether or not the death of God opens up new possibilities for morality—*both* religious and nonreligious. The benchmark of our decadence is not what was in the past but what might be in the future.

If the empty heavens signal a failure to find larger meanings in a society hoist on its own ingenuity, then the death of God is indeed a decadence. The mindless, and self-destructive, hedonism which would result from such an eventuality might make us nostalgic for the old absolutes—for some, this has already happened—but absolutes cannot be brought back from the grave we have dug for them. Moreover, the lingering shadow of the dead God, which the born-again sociologists mistake for God himself, is not enough. Religiosity, as S. S. Acquaviva has pointed out, is indeed surviving the decline of religion. But religiosity does not provide the norms to integrate a society, much less a civilization. Therefore the present crisis demands something unprecedented: a united front of believers and atheists in search of a common transcendental which is neither supernatural nor anti-supernatural.

10
PROLEGOMENA
TO A
POLITICAL MORALITY

CAN WESTERN SOCIETY CREATE transcendental common values in its everyday experience? Values which are not based upon—yet not counterposed to—the supernatural?

That is the question posed by this book. It is both huge and limited, and it is important to stress the latter aspect at the very outset of this chapter. I have simply evaded the problem raised in Chapter 9: whether and how it is possible to look forward to an integrating, normative consciousness on a planetary scale. I have done so, not because I consider the matter unimportant, but because it is of such tremendous significance, so complex, so uninvestigated, that I do not want to hazard what would necessarily be a superficial response to it. Thus, my self-imposed limitation does not spring from a parochial, Western-centered attitude. And I see this treatment of the issue of religion, society and values as a Western contribution—a Western prolegomena—in a dialogue that must become global.

But even after I have thus eliminated the majority of the world from my analysis, the question I have posed is so formidable that my answer to it will be inadequate, sketchy, perhaps more unsatisfying to me than to my readers. In addition to all the other complications, there is a generic difficulty, one that I have alluded to in earlier books. The Devil, as John Milton found out, is a fascinating figure of enormous dramatic power; but making God interesting is quite hard. So in the modern world it is easier to identify the devils, the evils, the wrongs, than to imagine how things might be made whole again. The bad is palpable and present; the good to come can seem merely dreamy. Demythologizing is second nature to the modern mind; affirming is most emphatically not.

197

However, men and women cannot decently live by demythologies alone. Yet there is no way back to what Paul Ricoeur calls a "primitive naïveté" because "something has been lost, irremediably lost: immediacy of belief." And there is no easy way forward to new transcendentals, for these, I suggest, must first exist as a commonplace before they can be stated as a dazzling truth. But if all these contraries are valid, how do we escape from their intersection in the contemporary spiritual crisis?

I am not sure we will. I have some ideas on how we might.

It has been demonstrated that the political God of Judeo-Christian tradition is in his death agony. There may be a new God, or a new version of the old God, or new gods, but the functions of the historic divinity of the Western heavens are going, going, almost gone. This has meant, we have seen, the loss of

- that philosophy for non-philosophers that made an intolerable life tolerable for the great mass of the people and thus contributed both to civil peace and to the passive acceptance of injustice;
- God the conservative, who legitimized established institutions, and that much rarer persona, God the radical, who legitimized the overthrow of those institutions;
- the transcendent symbols and sacraments of human community;
- a spiritual dimension for the pursuit of daily bread;
- a major source of personal and social identity.

Judeo-Christianity, as the theologian-sociologist Ernst Troeltsch was candid enough to realize, cannot fill up this social void (I prescind from its relevance for individuals). Functional differentiation and specialization have gone so far, and the social system is so diversified and complex, that the tradition is becoming more and more ceremonial in nations which are historically Judeo-Christian in ideology. Even in the Jewish state of Israel, the modern sectors are generally secular, and fundamentalism flourishes among the poorer, un-Westernized Mediterranean immigrants of the last generation.

If, then, the coherent profundities of Judaism and Christianity are incapable of providing the integrative consciousness for modern

Western society, it is preposterous to think that superficial counter-cultures or fashionable gurus will accomplish this task.

Another, much more serious, solution is to turn back to a fundamentalist version of either Judaism or Christianity. My rejection of that strategy is not based on the fact that some—but by no means all—of the Christian and Jewish fundamentalists in the United States in the late seventies and the eighties are politically reactionary. Rather, I view the fundamentalist tactic as a way of surviving in societies in which the religious *a priori* has vanished. That approach can work for some people over a long stretch of time—the Catholic Church followed a version of it for more than a century, from Pius IX through Pius XII—and it may provide comfort to a remnant. But it cannot replace God the politician.

On the other side, there are sophisticated theologians and philosophers, such as Schillebeeckx, Küng, Bultmann and Moltman, who are searching for a modern—demythologized—image of God, no longer the God "out there" of the West. They may, or may not, succeed, but their new vision of God is, precisely, a radical revision of the Judeo-Christian deity in social, as well as theological, terms.

My first conclusion, then, is that the basic religious tradition of the West can no longer, as a *religious* tradition, provide the core values of Western society. And my second proposition is that Western society needs transcendentals.

Note carefully: *needs* transcendentals. That does not mean that they will necessarily be created (and discovered in the process of being created). Niklas Luhmann's prophecy of the future might well turn out to be true. It could be that the process of functional specialization has gone so far that, particularly from the point of view of an emergent world society, we are entering a time when norms and values in the old sense have become irrelevant. At such a stage, the only criteria for choice would be based on technical appropriateness. The problem is that there can be rational programs for madness—the careful organization of the Holocaust is a monstrous case in point—and science is not its own excuse for being.

Such a "value-free" society could develop—it would rest, of course, on that most dubious value, the notion that individuals and societies can and should be value-free. Therefore, I am making a normative statement about norms. A moral consciousness, a sense of right and wrong and of the purpose of life, is desirable for society even if it is not inevitable. In making this assertion I am speaking from within the Marxist tradition. Marx was a furious foe of moralizing, a vice he rightly thought was rampant among the socialists of the nineteenth century. But he has been misunderstood—and sometimes maliciously—as a foe of morality, which is something else again. If he was naïve with regard to the ease with which socialist values would replace religious values among the masses, he was profoundly committed to the notion of a society organized around values.

Indeed, Lucien Goldmann is not entirely wrong to argue, in *Le Dieu caché*, that there is a kind of Pascalian wager in Marx: that the proletariat will, through struggle, create a transcendental of this world, called socialism. I disagree with Goldmann to the extent that he equates Marxism and religion, for I insist that, in Western Judeo-Christianity at least, religion involves reference to, belief in, a supernatural order. But if Marx demanded, at the very outset of his career as a revolutionary, that the movement abandon all religious trappings, he certainly believed all of his life that socialism would be the functional equivalent of religion.

Roger Garaudy, the French Marxist, understood one important aspect of this proposition. "Transcendence," Garaudy wrote, can mean "belief in a world beyond, in the supernatural, with the irrationality, the miracles, the mystery, and finally the deception that these notions carry with them." But, Garaudy went on, there is another meaning: "The claim to transcendence is the actual human experience that man, though belonging to nature, is different from things and animals and that man, forever able to progress, is never complete." In short, the autobiographical statement made in Chapter 1—that I, like religious people, feel a sense of awe in the communion of the universe, but without a religious interpretation of the origin of that communion—could have implications that go far beyond any individual. The serious atheistic humanist and the serious religious humanist are, I suspect, talking about the same reality in different languages. That those languages differ is not a minor detail to be forgotten by reducing antagonistic philosophies to a vague emotion. Such a promiscuous ecumenicism is, of course, empty of content. But that common emotion does offer a common point of political departure.

Ernst Bloch, as Chapter 8 noted, contrasted the Marxist Homo Absconditus to the Barthian Deus Absconditus. Just as religious people have been forced to sense God in his absence, so the Left has had to discover hope in defeat, to see in alienated, shattered humanity a negative definition of what might be. Here, too, there is a community of feeling.

If, however, the Left, both atheist and religious, has been forced to learn bitter and humiliating lessons, if Marx's optimism has to be qualified, then, so does Weber's pessimism and all of its lesser variants. It is not that functional differentiation and rationalization inexorably destroy human values. Rather, differentiation and rationalization programmed by elites—corporate-democratic in the West, totalitarian-"Communist" in the East—impoverish the spiritual lives of the people. Both Nietzsche, that most poetic of philosophers, and Weber, that austere polymath of a social scientist, had to resort to theories of the return of the demons and gods in order to explain the modern predicament. That will not do. The machines and structures of late capitalist (and mature Communist) society may sometimes seem to behave as mysteriously as storms and floods, but they remain human creations, not fates.

Yet the Nietzschean-Weberian nihilism does have the merit of being profound even if it is one-sided. This is not the case with Panglossian liberalism, which congratulates itself on having rejected the visionary alternative to the present crisis offered by Marx. But, then, in a fit of utter utopianism disguised as pragmatism, such liberalism reaffirms a faith in gradual, incremental change which, even more mystically than the Hegelian providence, will stop the ground from quaking under its feet. As a result, these liberals do not understand that it is the culture—not simply the economy or the polity, but the culture—which is going out of control. "A change to a new type of music," Plato said in the *Republic*, "is something to beware of as a hazard of all our fortunes. For the modes of music are never disturbed without unsettling of the most fundamental political and social conventions. . . ."

The music—not what is said but what is felt, the soundtrack of everyday life—is changing. Nietzsche, who understood Greek society in terms of the transition from Dionysus to Apollo, saw that, as we know. And the death of God has indeed pointed toward the death of all the higher values. For hundreds of years those values were, consciously or not, rooted in the assumption of an absolute order in the universe, guaranteed by God. When God and morality and religion were relativized by the new scientific, historical, sociological and an-

thropological consciousness of the nineteenth century, a good part of
traditional Western culture was undermined. And when, in the twentieth century, it became increasingly difficult to believe in optimistic
theories of liberal or socialist progress, the crisis became all the more
severe. I do not think that it is an overgeneralization of the evidence
presented in this book to say that masses of people in the West no
longer know what they believe.

In a conversation with the Indian leader Nehru André Malraux
posed the question in much the same way as I have. He told Nehru,
"I believe that the civilization of machines is the first civilization without a supreme value for the majority of people. There are traces of
values—many. . . . But the distinguishing characteristic of a civilization of action is, undoubtedly, that everyone be possessed by action.
Action against contemplation; a human life, and perhaps the instant,
against eternity. . . . It remains to know whether a civilization can be
merely a civilization of questions or of the instant, if it can for a long
time base its values upon something other than a religion."

My answer is clear by now: there is no way back—or forward—
to a religious integration of society on the model of Judeo-Christianity
in any of its manifestations. But there is a need for the transcendental.
That is why the conflict between religious and atheistic humanism must
now be ended.

That is the basis for the radical change in the relationship between
atheism and agnosticism on the one side, and religion on the other,
described in Chapter 4.

In the nineteenth century those two sides were at war with each
other, and for good reason. Science was undermining religion as it had
been traditionally understood; both middle-class and working-class
atheism were on the rise; and the difference between faith and anti-
faith was often overtly political. In the Catholic and Lutheran countries
of Europe, there were bitter battles against the established religion,
and in more open societies, like England, against the established church.
There was a "cultural war" in progress and, on the whole, the atheists, agnostics and dissident religionists waged a good and necessary
struggle.

That conflict has been over for some time and a strident, anti-
clerical atheism is as dated and irrelevant as the intransigent anti-
modernism of Pope Pius IX. Even more to the point, atheist and
agnostic humanists should be as appalled by *de facto* atheism in late

capitalist society as should people of religious faith. It is a thoughtless, normless, selfish, hedonistic individualism. If Herbert Marcuse was sometimes imprecise about this trend, he was accurate about the way it functioned from 1945 to 1970: binding people to the status quo with the "golden chains" of mass society, creating a passive, infinitely manipulable stratum which provides any technocratic regime a mindless measure of political security. *De facto* atheism relates to the Promethean atheism of a Marx as a mouse relates to a lion.

Even more to the point of the present chapter, serious atheists and agnostics now share a common cause with serious believers: a concern for values as such, for a vision of individual and social meaningfulness which goes beyond the latest consumer or cultural fad. An Orthodox Jewish rabbi understood this fact quite well in a *Commentary* symposium on *The Condition of Jewish Belief* in the 1960s. "It is not modern thought which poses the challenge to Jewish belief," Eliezer Berkovits wrote, "but the failure on the part of most Jews to think seriously about human experience and the human condition in our times and to do so from a position of rootedness in their ówn historic tradition."

That absence of serious thought about the human condition is, I would suggest, the common enemy of faith and anti-faith during the time of the death of the traditional Western God. Jacques Maritain, the Catholic neo-Thomist, articulated some of the implications of that fact in some of his writings after World War II (at the very end of his life, Maritain became more conservative, which does not alter the value of his earlier opinions). World thought, Maritain said at a UNESCO conference in Mexico in 1947, has been rightly called *"Babelism,"* a cacophony of unresolved and warring ideologies. And since, as he explicitly recognized in another book, there was no longer the possibility that a single faith or philosophy could organize society, how were men and women to act together in unity?

There could be, Maritain rightly commented, no consensus on basic philosophic issues and world views. That was the problem, not the solution. But there could be a coming together on "common practical notions," "not in the affirmation of the same conception of the world, man and knowledge but on the affirmation of the same set of convictions concerning action." If this was not an ideological agreement, it was something more than a joint program for action since it involved "a sort of common residue, a sort of unwritten common law, at the point of practical convergence of extremely different theoretical ideologies and spiritual traditions." This, Maritain rightly concluded, was a development of "major importance."

Many of those hopes for a practical ideological convergence on a world scale were shattered soon after that UNESCO meeting by the eruption of the Cold War and, later on, by a colonial revolution which sought to appropriate Western technology in a context of anti-Western values. Thus, it is clear that the proposals being made here are problematic and will require a great deal of time—they are certainly not to be the task of a single generation, but of generations. And this is true even if the difficulties of seeking such a practical spiritual consensus are somewhat less within the West, with its common traditions, than in the world as a whole.

There is some recent history which gives one reason to hope, despite all of these difficulties. The Catholic Church, as Chapter 8 detailed, was not only anti-modernist but also anti-socialist from the mid-nineteenth to the mid-twentieth century. That ideological intransigence was sometimes modified in national practice—Catholics in England voted by a majority for the British Labor Party long before Pope John XXIII—but it was a major factor in European—and Canadian—political life. In America, one of the reasons a mass socialist movement never developed was the hostility of the Church, particularly as it was transmitted through Irish-American workers in the labor movement. It was, however, in France that this conflict was most bitter. The Church had fought the Revolution and then the Republic. The Left was, therefore, religiously fervid in its anti-clericalism.

Immediately after World War II, the Christian Democratic trend, which had been something of an undergound and dissident movement in European Catholicism, became a significant force in Italy, France and West Germany. In some measure this was because the Church was now, for the most pragmatic of reasons, attempting to come to terms with the modern world and its political forms. Under the Fourth Republic, the French Christian Democrats, the Popular Republican Movement (MRP), had moved steadily to the Right, but in the early years of 1945–47 it had a democratic, and even social-democratic, appeal. The French Confederation of Christian Workers (CFTC) was established, parallel to the MRP. This union was committed to Christian (mainly Catholic) social ideals and was anti-socialist as well as anti-Communist.

But over the years, the CFTC evolved more and more in a socialist direction, eventually dropping all of the references to Catholic social teaching and changing its name to the French Confederation of Democratic Workers (CFDT). Even more important to my argument, the socialism adopted by the CFDT bore the signs of the Federation's Christian origins. The Catholic Church, as Chapters 6 and 8 showed, was never really comfortable in capitalist society. Its golden age had been the thousand or so years when it was the dominant spiritual and ideological force within feudalism. In the period of the rise of capitalism, Catholicism was therefore in general a reactionary force, particularly in comparison with Calvinist Protestantism. The Church, so to speak, opposed the new system for the wrong reasons. But then, after World War II, that implicit Catholic anti-capitalism expressed itself through democratic and labor organizations, counterposing a communitarian ideal to the centralization, bureaucracy and merely technical rationality of late capitalist society.

In the process, Catholic Leftists helped the secular socialists rediscover some of their own history. In the period of the emergence of the socialist movement—the first half of the nineteenth century—most of the working-class dreams of a new society were decentralist and communitarian. This can be clearly seen in some of Marx's early writings—not only the *Economic and Philosophical Manuscripts* of 1844–45 but also in *The German Ideology*, the first programatic statement of Marxism—and it permeated his thought throughout his life. Moreover, this decentralist tendency was particularly marked in France as the Proudhonists struggled for cooperatives and the unions, suspicious of politicians, took on a syndicalist hue.

Stalinism, that fateful corruption and inversion of the socialist ideal, forgot this history, and so did many democratic socialists who came to see the welfare state, and only the welfare state, as the fulfillment of their ideal. In the years right after World War II, European socialism came to stand for centralized nationalization and planning, and if that conception was modified in the 1950s, it was in the direction of an even greater accommodation to welfare-statism and technocracy. The student movements of the sixties, culminating in the events of May 1968 in Paris, rejected both the Stalinist anti-socialist "socialism" and the statism of the social democrats. And so, in a much more complex and enduring way, did the trade-unionists of the CFDT. When they became a part of the new socialist movement led by François

Mitterrand in the seventies, they were the carriers of a distinctive idea of socialism: worker-managed, decentralized, communitarian. And that trend can now be found in almost all of the socialist parties of Europe.

That French experience might even serve as a model for the consensus being proposed here. It did not involve the CFDT in a repudiation of its origins and an acceptance of the secular, anti-clerical socialism which Catholics had always fought in France. Rather, it meant that both the traditional socialists and the new socialists changed themselves, that in the process of uniting they discovered (rediscovered) new (old) values. I am suggesting something like that as a political-spiritual project for all of Western society. It is not that the religious people are being offered a gracious opportunity to surrender all of their principles. Rather, they are being urged to bring those of their religious principles which are relevant to a secular politics into that politics, to enrich it and to broaden it.

There are religious people right now who have something like that perspective. In Germany, their work is often described as "political theology." This does not mean, Dorothee Sölle explains,

> that theology is going to exchange its subject matter with political science . . . or that there is a concrete political program which is derived from faith, a kind of social gospel. . . . There is no specifically Christian solution to the problems of the world. Political theology is rather a theological hermeneutic which, in contrast to the ontological or existential readings of theology, opens up an interpretative horizon in which politics is seen as the all-embracing and decisive sphere in which the Christian truth becomes a praxis . . .
>
> There are housing arrangements which systematically destroy the mother-child relationship; there are modes of organizing labor which define the relation of the strong to the weak in Darwinistic fashion and therefore atrophy potentialities for helpfulness, sympathy or fairness which are said to be not wanted in production. If these circumstances are changed, if the housing becomes humane, the production cooperative, then the *possibility* of another life is at hand [emphasis added]. No more—and no less.

Political theology rightly understands that privatization is the great enemy of religion in the modern world—not, as some sociologists think, its salvation. All those theologies which accept that premise—even the radical existential theologies in their search for authenticity—are,

Johann Baptist Metz stresses, uncritically affirming the bourgeois norm of the private man. At the same time, these thinkers are not uncritical of the secular Left. For Jürgen Moltmann, there is a "deep schism in the modern age" because "in the past two centuries a Christian faith in God without hope for the future of the world has called forth a secular hope for the future of the world without faith in God."

That secularism, Moltmann argues, was often the agency of an inhumane, instrumental rationality, which is true enough (although Moltmann, like so many Europeans, faults socialism for the sins of the anti-socialism that was, and is, Stalinism). That insistence upon communitarianism—as opposed to collectivism—is, I think, part of the unique contribution which the religious can make to the atheists in the sphere of politics. I assume it is quite clear by now that I do not think that any religion, even the most liberated, is capable of becoming the integrating force of a world society in the way that Catholicism integrated the Middle Ages and Protestantism integrated much of early capitalism. I *do* think that there is an enormous—and distinctive—contribution which a revivified religion can make in its political united front with atheistic humanism.

That explains the paradox that the decline in religious commitment, as conventionally measured by a drop in church attendance, a relaxation of doctrinal rigor and the like, might actually signal a deepening of religion. In Troeltsch's famous distinction, sects based on deep and personal faith give way to churches which are routine and conventional. But, as many of the participants in the Catholic transformations of the past two decades stated explicitly, it is now possible that churches can become more sectlike in the good sense of the term: more serious and radical about their faith. If that were to happen, then churches sparsely filled with truly devout people might be a sign of religious growth much more significant than the packed houses of worship in the 1950s. That would also mean that the religious commitment to the consensus ideology I am trying to evoke here could become all the more profound.

But what about that ideology? I have spoken thus far of the functional need for it, but what is it that will fulfill that function? My next conclusion provides the outline of an answer.

In a society in which the legitimacy of political power is no longer cloaked in the aura of God, why obey the law? Why die for the common good? That is a question which Hobbes and all the political realists could never answer. Modern societies cannot motivate their citizens through a return to the *Gemeinschaft* of the earliest time. That romantic notion, sometimes celebrated in the counterculture of the sixties, is not simply impossible (unless the 95 percent of humanity dependent on modern methods of production were eliminated); it is also reactionary. Those totally integrated communities, as Durkheim well understood, were extremely repressive. And in that other romantic utopia—usually, but not always, the dream of conservatives—the Middle Ages, infinitely richer and more diverse than preliterate times, life was still not only simply nasty, brutish and short but also organized around relationships of hierarchy and subordination.*

A return to those past times is impossible and undesirable. Therefore, contemporary societies cannot integrate themselves and provide an identity for their members in terms of a traditional and objective ideology which the individual finds, in a finished form, counterposed to himself/herself and through which he/she works out his/her personal identity. Rather, the legitimacy of modern political structures can arise only out of the participation of all of the members of the society in the elaboration of the rules which bind them. This is, of course, an ideal that has existed at least since the bourgeois revolution, and it was a commonplace in the German classical philosophy almost two hundred years ago. But social and economic inequality subverted the theoretical equality of all the citizens. It will be remembered that Marx equated the dualism of the Judeo-Christian vision of earth and heaven with the split in capitalist society between juridical equality (its heaven) and actual inequality (its this-world). Marx said that in order to make the bourgeois ideal come true, bringing its heaven to earth, it would be necessary to go beyond bourgeois society. Marx was right.

With these qualifications (which will be elaborated and explored in the next section), the first principle of the new consensus is: no law is binding unless the people have had an effective participation in its formulation.

The second principle has to do with community. If society continues its process of functional specialization without concern for community, then effective participation is impossible and so is that common experience which alone can provide the basis for common values.

---

*I am indebted for some of the ideas underlying this section to the writings of Jürgen Habermas. (See Appendix P.)

Therefore, communitarianism is an essential component, in both theory and practice, of the new transcendental.

Third, there must be an expansion of moral motivation based on solidarity. One does not move quickly from a society which has spent four hundred years exalting greed and gain to one in which altruistic reasons for action become dominant. But capitalism is now the chief source of the mindless, *de facto* atheism which is the enemy of both atheistic humanism and religious faith in the West. If people cannot find reasons outside of themselves and their immediate interests to behave in a compassionate way, then they will obviously not find transcendental values, either. Clearly, the consensus of which I speak cannot be proclaimed by some new messiah. Either it will be found by modern people in the course of common action or else it will never exist at all.

Fourth, even if I imagine this consensus as arising in the West, it must be universal. Luhmann is right: a world society is in the process of becoming a fact. Our economics, science and technology long ago shattered national and regional borders. Our consciousness, as usual, lags well behind, and so do our politics. If a global identity is to become a part of the day-to-day consciousness of men and women, it will happen through a long and painful process. Perhaps it will not happen at all, and the catastrophic nihilism of a Nietzsche, or the technocratic nihilism of a Luhmann, will come to pass. But if there are alternatives to those possibilities—a question which will not be settled within the life of anyone now living on the earth—they require, not an ethnic or a national identity, but a human identity.

These four main elements of a new integrating consciousness are, quite obviously, clichés of Western thought. That is their strength and their weakness. It is their weakness because they have either become routine or else pieties that the youngest cynic knows are observed only in the breach. It will, therefore, be extremely difficult to get people to take them seriously—and taking them seriously is the precondition of their resurrection from the dead. But their commonplace and faded character is also a strength. It marks them as part of that "common residue," that "unwritten common law," which Jacques Maritain evoked. These are value judgments, in short, which can be arrived at within the framework of practically every serious Western tradition, secular as well as religious. The figures of Adam and Eve, for example, are the common patrimony of Christians and Jews and symbolically express that universality of the human, that common origin of all races and peoples, which is also central to atheistic humanism.

So what will turn these principles, threadbare from misuse, into the vital norms of a truly human—and therefore genuinely spiritual—society? Politics. Or nothing.

———— I I ————

I take democratic socialism as the point of departure in a search for the moral reformation of the Western world.

Democratic socialism? Isn't that calling upon a cliché to revive the other clichés? Can one seriously propose that an idea and an ideal that had lost its freshness before this century began can be the key to a spiritual revival in the next century? Of course not. If democratic socialism were today what it was a hundred years ago, it would be totally irrelevant to the project I propose. But the socialists have learned. I am not talking about the socialism of the 1890s or of the 1930s—which contained considerable truth and significant, if unwitting, falsehood—but the socialism of the 1980s. And I assume that it, too, will be superseded. Note: it is urged here as a point of departure, not as a finished answer to all problems.

In some ways, it would be simpler for me not to raise a point certain to invite so much misunderstanding. And yet, merely to argue for a desirable social-moral consensus in the broad terms of the preceding section would be to make an almost empty assertion. The constituent elements of my proposal, as I have already noted, have been around for hundreds of years (but not, of course, within the analytic context put forward here). There is only one way to rescue them from the fate of pompous wishes: to show that there is a creditable politics which can turn them from fine sentiments into a practical reality. That means exploring the present and future in terms of the relationship between spiritual crisis and social-economic structure.

I assume that this book has laid to rest any vulgar Marxist—or any other simplistic determinist—theory that the relationship between religion and social-economic structure is one-to-one, that the former is epiphenomenon and the latter the "real" reality. We have seen that spiritual values act as cause as well as respond as effect and are scattered among all the gradations of reciprocal interaction in between.

And yet, when all of the complications are acknowledged, the fact remains that it is useless to talk about that spiritual crisis and its possible resolution without suggesting, not simply a politics, but a politics which confronts social and economic structures.

For instance, Chapter 6 outlined the unintended consequences which turned a capitalism created by pious men and women into the first agnostic society in Western history. One of the causes of norm-lessness in the society, if this analysis is correct, is a system which has no way to value community. The corporate calculus counts a park-ing lot or an office building as "worth" more than a church or a neigh-borhood, as long as it will yield a higher profit. This logic is not always followed to absurd consequences—no one has seriously proposed to replace Notre Dame de Paris with a skyscraper—but most of the time it is pursued to antisocial, and anti-communitarian, consequences. Therefore, I would argue, anyone who is serious about the spiritual crisis of late-twentieth-century Western society must also propose po-litically feasible economic alternatives to the structural sources of the crisis.

More broadly, post-bourgeois society will resemble pre-bourgeois society in a way which will make ideology—visions of the world, values, culture—more politically and socially important than during the last four hundred years in the West. In the classic capitalist model of society, there was an autonomous economic and social order which reproduced itself according to its own laws and did not—like feudalism, with its authoritative allocation of social roles and its "just" price— require political intervention. So it was, as I argued in Chapter 6, that capitalism relied on economic rather than political coercion and helped create the "liberal" (in the European sense of the word) state.

It was this transient—four hundred years long, yet historically transient—state of affairs that allowed Adam Smith, Marx in some careless moments and many Marxists habitually, to develop a "base-superstructure" theory in which religion (along with politics and ev-erything else having to do with values and ideas) was seen as a mere reflection of the basic economic and social relations. In this view, all faiths and creeds were matters of secondary and derived importance. The analysis was superficial even applied to the liberal phase of cap-italism but had a certain plausibility, because its overgeneralizations did seem to describe some of those transient facts. That is clearly no longer the case. In every Western society, including those politically directed by conservatives elected to undo precisely this trend, the state has intervened more and more in the economy and social structure. That is not because the conservatives betrayed their principles or the liberals and socialists were bent on creating a leviathan. The intervention grew out of the increasing complexity, and the national and international interdependence, of late capitalism. Ronald Reagan, sincerely committed to the balanced budget and simultaneously presiding over the largest budget deficit in history, is a paradigmatic case in point.

Therefore, the choice before late capitalist society is not whether there will be the politicalization of economic decisions—that matter has been settled for some time—but, rather, who will make those decisions, how and for what purposes. There was a time when leaders could at least pretend that an "invisible hand" was allocating resources and rewards. That time is now past. Visible hands are trying to systematize and computerize those decisions. *But on the basis of what values?* When the market system destroyed the human community it did so impersonally, and society could thereby (wrongly) deny moral responsibility for the actions of its most powerful members. By what norms and criteria will the conscious, political decision about preserving, or destroying, a neighborhood now be made?

If this analysis is accurate, then values—or values disguised insidiously as the commands of technological imperatives—are going to affect our lives more in the future than they have in the four hundred years of the immediate (and not so immediate) past. It is for this reason that I regard the issue of social structure and spiritual values as of critical importance. In making democratic socialism the point of departure, I am building upon the analyses of one of the subtlest Marxists who ever lived. Perhaps more than any other thinker in the Marxist tradition, Antonio Gramsci understood the enormous importance of religion and religious values for the future of socialism. I go back to his work for two reasons: it has a relevance to the future which is now unfolding half a century after his death; and it shows that the socialist tradition was concerned with these matters long ago, that it has a historic claim in this area.

In the first volume of the *Prison Notebooks (Quaderni del carcere), Historical Materialsim,* Gramsci made an extraordinary analysis of Marxism (socialism) as a movement of "moral and intellectual reform."* From this vantage he saw it as the continuation of the reform of mass consciousness which was undertaken first by the Protestant Reformation and then by the French Revolution. As an Italian, he was sadly conscious that his country's fate had been profoundly affected precisely by the failure of that reform. The Renaissance had been an affair of high culture which did not reach out to the masses. Erasmus had arrogantly said that "where Luther appears, culture dies." And yet, it was out of the primitiveness of the Reformation that there came "the German classical philosophy and the vast cultural movement which gave birth to the modern world."

The Italian liberals, Gramsci continued, were like Erasmus. Croce and his friends disdained a truly popular cultural movement. It was Marxism "which represented, and represents, a historic process analogous to the Reformation and thus stands in contrast to liberalism. The latter produces a Renaissance strictly limited to small groups of intellectuals. . . ." In saying this, Gramsci was not being romantic. If he believed that "all men are philosophers," that philosophy was not simply an activity of the elite, he had a profound, even anguished, sense of the limitation of such mass philosophy. It was composed, first of all, of a language "which is a totality of concepts and specific ideas, not simply of grammatical rules devoid of content." Then it was made up of "common sense" and "good sense," the latter being somewhat more critical and counterposed to the former. And finally, the philosophy of the people was based "on the religion of the masses and in the entire system of belief, superstition, opinion, ways of seeing and acting which are part of what is generally called 'folklore.' "

Religion, as a part of this philosophy, is not, however, philosophy, because it cannot be reduced to a coherent unity. It is a "conception of the world and a norm of correct conduct." Moreover, in a subordinate social class there are often two philosophies: the one taken from high culture and honored in words, and the one which informs the actual behavior of the class. The Catholic Church, Gramsci continued with a sort of grudging admiration, had always fought resolutely against any tendency toward creating two religions, one for the elite, the other for the masses. Socialism had to be at least as daring. It had to un-

---

*In Italian, *la riforma* means "reform"; La Riforma, the Reformation. As the text will make clear, Gramsci clearly intended the analogy to be between socialism and the Protestant Reformation.

derstand that when its theories and ideals became part of the mass movement they would necessarily be vulgarized. Indeed, Marxism had to fight a difficult war on two very different fronts. On the one hand it had "to combat modern ideologies in their most refined form in order to be able to constitute its own group of independent intellectuals"; on the other hand it had to "educate the broad mass whose culture was [in Italy] medieval."

This reformation was not, however, simply a matter of preaching a new socialist morality. As long as anti-socialist ideologies were the official view of the society, they would permeate the popular mind and accentuate that contradiction between nominal philosophy and the philosophy which informed action. The moral and intellectual change required a struggle for political "hegemony" (a famous Gramscian word), for the permeation of society by socialist values, which would open up the possibility of a unity of theory and practice. Gramsci also formulated one of the central points of this chapter some fifty years ago: "To create a new culture does not merely mean that individuals make 'original' discoveries. It means in particular diffusing critically truths which have already been discovered, 'socializing' them, so to speak, and thereby making them the basis of vital actions. . . ."

Marxism would do these things, Gramsci argued, first as a "faith," as an "ideological 'aroma' " emanating from a complex world view. But what would mark it off from the religions which it at first would resemble is that Marxism would not

> maintain the "simple souls" [*semplici*] in their primitive, common-sense philosophy, but on the contrary would try to lead them to a high conception of life. One affirms the necessity of an alliance between the intellectuals and the simple people which does not function to limit scientific activity or to maintain a unity at the lower [intellectual] level of the masses, but precisely to construct a moral-intellectual bloc which will make the intellectual progress of the masses politically possible and not restrict that process to a small group of intellectuals.

Clearly, I have appropriated a great deal of Gramsci in my conception of the function of a new integrating consciousness which will arise in the course of political and social struggles. But what has been learned about this process since Gramsci first conceived of it? In a few words: it has become infinitely more problematic, more difficult—but no less necessary.

Gramsci wrote at a time when a Marxist, and socialist, "counter-culture" still existed. The Central European social democracy before World War I, and above all the German Social Democratic Party, had created, not simply a political alternative to bourgeois leaders, but a cultural alternative to bourgeois society. There were Marxist centers for philosophy, art, theater, and even if, just as Gramsci said, their intellectual content was not always of the highest, they did propose a philosophy for the masses. The Italian socialists, and then the Communists after the split in the movement, inherited that tradition, and Gramsci wrote from within it. He was also working within a particularly backward capitalist society which had more than a few feudal elements and allocated an important ideological (and repressive) role to the Catholic Church. Yet he was sensitive to changes in that situation, seeing the Christian Democracy as the functional equivalent of a new religious order. (The Church, in his view, had traditionally dealt with discontent by creating religious orders to absorb it—witness the taming of the Franciscans—and the Christian Democrats were the most recent variant of this hallowed strategy.)

But since Gramsci's death, capitalism, even Italian capitalism, has transformed itself in a way that makes his perspective much more difficult to achieve. Just as the decline of militant, integralist religion has sapped the strength of an atheism which was its *Doppelgänger*, so the "liberalization" of capitalism in the welfare states after World War II undermined, not simply much of the traditional socialist program, but the socialist psychology as well. Semi-affluent societies politically committed to increasing mass consumption remained under the control of even stronger corporate forces than before, but they often sought to co-opt, rather than destroy, the opposition. The people (as Gramsci and Lenin and Karl Kautsky had understood) had always internalized many of the norms and values of those who lorded over them, but mass society now turned this production of a false consciousness into a major industry.

As I write, it is possible that the historic period which began at the end of World War II in the West is now coming to an end. For one of the premises of that "permissive," co-opting strategy was endless growth, and this utopia has been subverted by stagflation in every advanced capitalist society. It could be, in short, that social and political battles over stagnant, or declining, resources will revive old-fashioned class struggles. But even if that happens, the cultural complexities introduced in the years between 1945 and 1970 are likely to persist, even if in somewhat subdued form.

There is no question, then, of hiding the difficulties involved in a "moral and intellectual reform." Indeed, if one were to calculate odds, the chances are that the dominant consciousness of the next historic period will be technocratic, elitist and manipulative. Fortunately, the very immensity of the transformation in progress, and the length of time that it will take, makes any attempt at calculation questionable. There is no alternative to struggling for that reformation, since no one knows how the future will turn out. Who would have predicted the tremendous surge in self-conscious dignity among Southern blacks in the years after World War II? Who could have calculated the impact of Martin Luther King, Jr.? Or the growth of feminist consciousness in the late sixties and the seventies?

But what, precisely, is being advocated here? This chapter has suggested a united front of believers and nonbelievers in defense of the very existence of values. It has summarized the relationship between psychological and spiritual attitudes on the one hand and social and economic structure on the other, suggesting that a socialist analysis of the need for systemic change must lie beneath the attempt to create a social experience of transcendentals which is not necessarily based upon the supernatural. It has said that politics are essential to the kind of reformation described by Antonio Gramsci. But what kind of politics? Should parties now adopt "spiritual platforms"? If they did, wouldn't that simply mean a burgeoning of vague rhetoric which is even less embarrassing than a campaign promise since it cannot be quantified?

I am *not* suggesting that parties take positions on spiritual matters. Indeed, one of the most hopeful developments in European socialism in recent years has been the abandonment of official *Weltanschauungen*. That one need not even be a nominal Marxist to belong to any of the socialist parties in Europe is a positive aspect of the disappearance of socialist counter-faith, for it has opened these movements up to currents, most emphatically including religious currents, which they once excluded on principle. They have, in a very real sense, adopted a consensus model of socialism, an ideological pluralism motivating a unity of action, quite like the one being urged here.

Moreover, the evidence of this book demonstrates anew that man-made religions usually end up arrogating divine power to the founders and thus providing a rationale for authoritarian, or totalitarian, creeds. The state cult of atheism in the Communist countries is the most obvious, and profoundly negative, case in point. Either transcendentals arise out of the common experience of people, or they will not come to exist. What I propose is not a world view which will be imposed upon society by political means but one which will develop spontaneously out of a social process of self-definition.

Does that mean, then, that one sits contemplatively and hopes that the masses will find some new values? Not at all. If political religions are dangerous and contradictory, politics can take into account those economic and social measures which are more likely to create an environment in which individuals and communities can work out their own values. Capitalism was not intended to subvert Judeo-Christian spirituality; indeed, the original hope was that it would fulfill that tradition. But we can now, retrospectively, read the anti-spiritual design that was and is implicit in the capitalist reality. And that permits us to recognize, and actively seek, a new design which will create, not a new spirituality, but the social and economic preconditions that make it possible.

I propose, then, that every social and economic measure which is proposed in our politics be examined, not only in terms of its impact upon Gross National Product and price level, but also in terms of how it hinders or facilitates the values described earlier in this chapter. The promotion of *community* would then be a criterion for the effectiveness of any national economic plan. One would be systematically biased in favor of measures which accomplish functions on the most immediate, intimate level of social life (this is the Catholic principle of "subsidiarity" as well as the libertarian socialist and anarchist principle of decentralization).

Second, the kind of politics I propose would, at every level, encourage the use of *moral incentives* rather than economic incentives. If, I argued in *Decade of Decision*, there were a reduction in the inequality of wealth and income in Western society, if, in Christopher Jencks's phrase, one reduced the "punishments of failure and the rewards of success," it might be possible for people—the young most obviously, but not only the young—to choose careers, not on the basis of anticipated gain, but in terms of social, psychological and even moral values.

Third, the ideal of democratic participation, which has been so profoundly limited by the capitalist economic and social structure, has to be socialized in a double sense. It must be extended to the great mass of the people for whom it hardly exists; it must be made real by tax and other policies which, by transferring economic power, also democratize political power.

And, finally, there is a moral dimension to every national policy: that it must, as far as is possible, be formulated so as to help the most vulnerable members of the human family, whether they live in the Third World or in the third worlds within advanced capitalist societies.

There are endless examples of the practical application of these broad principles. If participation and community are imperative, for instance, then wherever there is planning there must be public funds for anti-planning by the opponents of those in democratic control of the computers and experts. For the allocation of information has now become as central to the exercise of power as the allocation of money. But I have no intention of getting into programmatic detail, not the least because I have already done so at book length (most recently in *Decade of Decision*). My practical point is that men and women of faith and anti-faith should, in the secular realm at least, stop fighting one another and begin to work together to introduce moral dimensions into economic and social debate and decision. That means that the structures of corporate "rationality" will have to be challenged in the name of a human rationality. We are emerging into a much more collective time, in each nation and even when anti-collective conservatives rule; and explicit values are becoming more socially important than they have been for four hundred years.

It is at this precise moment—and the conjunction is not an accident—that the political and social God of the Western tradition is dying. An atheism of fools could rejoice in the emptiness of the heavens he leaves behind; a theism of fools could keep on singing the old hymns. But the real issue is whether the horizon is being wiped away, not how it is defined. No politics can answer that question—and only a politics of all those concerned with the survival of the spirit, whether it is said to be holy or only human, can work to create the social structures in which people are more likely to answer it for themselves.

APPENDIX A

ANY GENERALIZATIONS which contrast the religious cultures of "East" and "West" over several thousand years must obviously suppress an enormous amount of complexity. For instance, Indian religion is famous for its passivity, its adaptation to endless rhythms of birth and rebirth. Yet Eliade points out that the *Bhagavad Gita*, which synthesized a variety of sometimes contradictory Indian attitudes, is quite close to the Jewish conception of God. Vishnu, Eliade argues, creates and rules the world. "Man is no longer the hostage of a cosmos-prison that created itself, since the world is the work of a personal and omnipotent God. What is more: he is a God who did not abandon the world after its creation but continues to be present in it and active on all planes. . . . This brings the God of the *Bhagavad Gita* close to Yahweh, creator of the world and lord of history, as the prophets understood him."

Moreover, as Jürgen Habermas shows in a recent study, the "East" cannot be labeled as "world-denying," since Confucianism, a not unimportant philosophy, affirms the value of the world—but does not seek to master it as the Judeo-Christian tradition does. Still, the distinction between cosmic and creator God made in the text has a rough usefulness. In his monumental studies of religious sociology, Weber understood that the psychology, the attitude toward reality, implicit in a religion is often of greater importance for the economic and political behavior of the believers than the explicit economic and political doctrine. For that matter, as Chapter 6 shows, it is possible for the actual worldly impact of a religion upon the faithful to contradict its explicit social teaching.

That point has been developed by a number of writers. In an essay written in the 1930s, Karl Löwith, one of the most serious scholars in this area, wrote about the difference between cosmic religions and Christianity. Heraclitus, says Löwith, is an exponent of the cosmic view in Western culture. His thirtieth fragment says, "This cosmos, here before us, the same for all, has not been created by one of the gods or by a man. It was always thus, it is and will be." In such a view, Löwith continues, the cosmos is self-sufficient and therefore divine. But when the cosmos is no longer the *summum bonum*, when it is the creation of a God external to it, then the earth is devalued. That, he aruges, had already begun to happen with the Stoics. And it became decisive in the West with Christianity. But this then lays the philosophic basis for an instrumental, scientific and technological manipulation of the world (a critique which is dealt with at greater length in Chapter 2, when we confront the Frankfurt School's attack on the Enlightenment).

Mircea Eliade makes a related point:

> When the sacred made itself known only in the Cosmos, it was easily recognizable; for a pre-Christian religious man it was, on the whole, easy to distinguish a sign that was charged with power—a spiral, a circle or a swastika, etc.—from all those that were not; easy, even, to separate liturgical time from profane time. . . . But in Judaism, and above all, in Christianity, divinity has manifested itself in history. . . . To the Christian, consequently, there was a radical additional difference between different historical events: certain events were theophanies (above all the presence of Christ in history) while others were merely secular events. . . . He has continually to *choose* to try to distinguish, in the tangle of historical events, the event which, *for him*, may be charged with a saving significance.

In another study, Eliade effectively argues that the Marx-Feuerbach critique of religion as the projection of an imaginary realm in the heavens is a parochial generalization of Judeo-Christian doctrine. "Alienation and estrangement of man from earth are unknown, and, moreover, inconceivable in all religions of the cosmic type, primitive as well as oriental," Eliade wrote. "In this case (that is to say in the overwhelming majority of religions known to history), the religious life consists exactly in exalting the solidarity of man with life and nature."

Hegel has a somewhat different view. In his *Lectures on the Philosophy of History*, he not only credits the Greek atomistic philosophers with explaining the development of the world from within the world itself but also insists, in a most Hegelian reading of Aristotle, that the latter had a similar point of view. But for Hegel the Christian break with the naturalistic theories of man's relations with the cosmos, the stress upon a self-conscious divinity, was the basis of the high value placed upon human consciousness, subjectivity and freedom in Western culture. In making this point, Hegel counterposes himself to Löwith (and perhaps to Eliade) and all those who yearn for the earlier cosmic unity, emphasizing, as always, the creative value of the negative.

Several recent studies bear on Hegel's point. The contemporary French historian Pierre Chaunu (a man whose strident anti-feminism undermines his scholarship but who is certainly worth reading) marks the decisive break in religious history, not with the God-man, Christ, but with the creator God of Judaism. Eliade notes that the constant Jewish struggle against the alien Canaanite religion was directed against a cosmic religiosity. "The 'joy of life' that is bound up with every cosmic religion was [for the Hebrew prophets] not only an apostasy, it was illusory, bound to disappear in the imminent national catastrophe."

However one evaluates these various analyses, it is clear that the conception of God as either cosmic-immanent or personal-transcendental is one of the great cultural divides of all time. If, as noted at the outset, it is not a seamless distinction, it is an exceedingly useful one. Indeed, as Franz Borkenau documented in some fascinating essays, the East-West distinction operates *within* Christianity itself. The Byzantine church was much more mystical and contemplative than the activist—Pelagian—church of Rome. It is for this reason that this book does not simply focus on Christianity (and Judaism) as against the non-Christian religions but concentrates on the distinctively Western version of Christianity itself.

APPENDIX B

THESE NOTES are intended to expand and complicate the notion of Kant as a "bourgeois" thinker.

To begin with, it should again be stressed that he lived in a relatively backward society, dependent upon the favor and tolerance of a monarchy and, on at least one occasion—when King Friedrich Wilhelm II decided that Kant's *Religion Within the Limits of Mere Reason* had attacked the Bible—forced to make a fairly humiliating recantation. He assured the king that he should be allowed to speak his mind only because he did so in rather abstruse, scholarly fashion and agreed that those who taught in schools or preached in churches should not be granted the same freedom. And he also avowed that the Bible was the best possible basis for bettering the souls of a nation and should therefore not be subject to rude public criticism. He submitted to this humiliation at a time (1794) when he was still openly defending the French Revolution.

Kant had little personal experience of the capitalist revolution, though he participated in it vicariously in his reading of Enlightenment thinkers like Hume and Montesquieu. The point is, a bourgeois thinker is not necessarily a bourgeois, or even a citizen of a bourgeois society; he is a person who is caught up in the cultural surge accompanying the capitalist revolution. The examples given in the text are obvious cases of the historic limitations imposed upon a great man's thought. The entire Enlightenment, for all of its talk of freedom and reason, was terrified of the "mob" below.

A complex and profound account of the bourgeois nature of Kant's thought is to be found in Georg Lukacs's *History and Class Consciousness*. Lukacs argues that Kant's metaphysics—indeed, the very concept of the *Ding-an-sich*—arises out of the conditions of capitalist society in an intricate way. On the one hand, Kant is a principled defender of rationalism and science who carefully explores, through reason, how the mind is able to comprehend a world of nature. But, on the other, there is the sharp limit on the rational, above all the fact that it cannot achieve a theory of the whole.

Previously, Lukacs argued, the irrational appeared

at that point at which the possibility of the powers of human knowledge ceased, where absolute transcendence, the kingdom of faith, etc., began. Now, however, irrationality appears as the necessary consequence of a known, knowable, rational system of laws. It is a necessity which, as the critical philosophy recognizes in contrast to its dogmatic predecessors, cannot be conceptualized in its ultimate causes and all-embracing totality, but in which each part—of the environment in which men live—is in increasing measure reckoned and anticipated.

This, Lukacs continues, is a refraction of the dual nature of reality within capitalist society: man makes a second nature which is his own creation but in which he is an alien; he is the object of his own genius, not its controlling subject. Thus it is that Schiller, Kant's mentor on this point, looks back to prescientific nature and criticizes the alienation of fabricated nature. Capitalism is the system which is scientific in every detail but irrational in its totality—and so is Kant's system.

I have merely evoked Lukacs's thesis, but at least it suggests how he relates social reality, not simply to social ideas, but to metaphysics itself. As long as one takes such connections with a grain of salt—as insights, illuminations, not as finished theories—I think they are of value.

There is a complication, however. In the late part of the nineteenth and the early twentieth centuries, there were not a few socialists, and even some Marxists like Max Adler, who saw Kant as a pre-socialist thinker. In 1911 Karl Vorlander published a book on Kant and Marx which claimed Kant for the socialist tradition and even quoted some of the material I have cited, to prove Kant a bourgeois thinker, as evidence of the opposite conclusion. There were, and still are, attempts to argue that the neo-Kantian tendency in German socialism was "revisionist" (in other words, conservative, as against the orthodox Marxists), but given the number of Austro-Marxists who were also Kantians, that proposition does not hold. Of course, I am not convinced by the Kantian socialists, either. That Kant, like every other Enlightenment figure, said things which eventually became a part of the socialist heritage is true—but, then, socialism and Marxism are, in my opinion, the culmination, the completion (in Hegel's term, the *Aufhebung*) of the Enlightenment. Still, that does not make him a socialist, particularly since his work is permeated by the unconscious assumptions of the bourgeois cultural revolution. Franz Mehring, a Marxist and Marx's first biographer, understood this point very well. Jean Jaures, interestingly enough, insisted on such limitations yet included Kant (and Fichte and Luther) in his genealogical chart of German socialism, *Les Origines du socialisme allemand*.

APPENDIX C

THERE SEEMS TO BE a glaring contradiction in Lenin's writings on philosophy and religion. On the one hand there is *Materialism and Empirio-Criticism*, written in 1908 and published in 1909. It is fanatically "materialist," arguing that "consciousness is only the reflection of being, best an approximately true (adequate, perfectly exact) reflection of it. From this Marxist philosophy, *which is cast from a single piece of steel*, you cannot eliminate one basic premise, one essential part, without departing from objective truth, without falling a prey to bourgeois-reactionary falsehood" (emphasis added). The social world, then, is as much a sphere of law and causal determination as the chemical and physical world described in nineteenth-century science.

On the other hand, there are the *Philosophical Notebooks*, and particularly Lenin's notes on Hegel's (Greater) *Logic*. They date from September to December 1914, the period immediately after the outbreak of World War I and the effective collapse of the international socialist movement. Rather than focusing upon a rigid, structured world, Lenin enthuses over Hegel's stress on "Movement and 'self-movement' . . . 'change,' 'movement and vitality,' 'the principle of all self-movement,' 'impulse' . . . the opposite to '*dead Being*'— who would believe that this is the core of 'Hegelianism' . . . (ponderous, absurd?) Hegelianism?? This core had to be discovered, understood, *hinüber-tretten* [rescued], laid bare, refined, which is precisely what Marx and Engels did." Such passages are usually cited to show that, at least during the period of enforced philosophic calm when his political hopes seemed ruined, Lenin had gone beyond the mechanistic materialism of his 1909 book.

In *Marxism and Hegel*, Lucio Colletti has another, and most striking, reading: that Lenin (and Engels, Plekhanov and the other founders of "dialectical materialism") unwittingly smuggled Hegel's God into Marx's philosophy, thus committing "an error which by now lies at the basis of almost a century of theoretical Marxism." If this is true—and I think there is substance to Colletti's point—then Lenin's anti-religious point of view was . . . religious.

Let me briefly summarize this complex analysis (relying on Colletti but citing some additional texts from both Hegel and Lenin).

In all of his writings, Hegel was sharply opposed to the notion of a transcendental God "out there." In particular, he was against the "bad infinite," that conception of God which defines him as the basis of the real world, as its ultimate cause. That, he argued, reduced the deity to being "merely the *limit* of the finite . . . a specific, finite infinite." For Hegel, God was *in* the world, not outside it. Moreover, the categories of philosophy and logic were, for him, cognitive statements of the same truths dramatized in images by Christianity. This gives rise to a very real ambiguity, for Hegel's notion of religion can be seen as identical to philosophy, differing only in the form of their presentation. That is why some scholars think Hegel an atheist, others find him a pious, and incredibly ingenious, Christian. Such a dispute need not divert us here, however, since it is clear that Hegel's philosophic discussion is parallel to Christian theology. When Lenin delights in the former he is unwittingly endorsing much of the latter.

For example, Lenin quotes Hegel to the effect that "it is the nature of the finite to pass beyond itself, to negate its negation and to become infinite. . . ." When one looks carefully at Hegel's text it is clear that the reason it is the "nature" of the finite to act in this way is that the infinite (God's purpose, teleology) is at work within it: "The infinite is not a fixed being over against the finite. . . . Insofar as the finite is raised up into the infinite, it is not some foreign power which does this to it but, rather, its own nature. . . ." And that, Hegel makes quite clear in Volume II of the *Logic*, is the working of God within reality, identical with it, developing with it, conferring a meaning upon it.

Why is all the movement and change and instability and contingency of life meaningful and purposive? Hegel has a clear answer: God. Lenin, as Colletti says, takes over Hegel's providential view of the finite—matter is dialectical—but omits Hegel's carefully reasoned argument as to why the finite contains this meaning. Therefore, dialectical materialism, from Engels on, is a kind of religious faith. Again, it should be stressed that Marx—who was, unlike Engels and Lenin, an academically trained philosopher (and a much more profound thinker)—never indulged in such speculation.

All of these complexities took on a practical importance as the twentieth century unfolded. That integral world view—"cast from a single piece of steel"— and that mystic sense of the teleological purposiveness of matter became more and more problematic as the possible lines of historic development became much more ambiguous than was dreamed of in Lenin's philosophy. There was movement enough to satisfy the most ardent Hegelian, but whether it was tending toward a destination, as Hegel and Lenin thought, was a questionable proposition. That was part of the crisis of the religion of atheism.

APPENDIX D

THERE IS A LONG and complex debate over why and when Hegel changed his political-philosophic tack. A scholar like Löwith located the shift in 1800, but Shlomo Avineri, while recognizing that there was a significant transition at that time, stresses that Hegel's "French" loyalties lasted until 1815 or so. This discussion bears very much on the thesis that Hegel idolatrized the state and was therefore at least an agent of Prussianism and perhaps even a proto-Nazi.

In the notes for his doctoral dissertation the young (pre-Marxist) Marx was very critical of the theory that one could explain Hegel's philosophy in terms of an accommodation with the world. For Hegel, he argues, that philosophy was a living, developing process, not the finished system which those who come after him know. On this or that detail, he might even have consciously accommodated himself to external pressures.

> But what he did not know was that this seeming accommodation had its deepest roots in an inadequacy, or an inadequate conception, of his principles. If a philosopher did indeed make such accommodations, then his students must explain it in terms of his inner, and most essential, consciousness. . . . One does not blame the particular conscience of the philosopher but, rather, construes the essential forms of his consciousness, raising it up to the level of a specific *Gestalt* and thereby making it possible to go beyond it.

That a thinker formulates a philosophy of accommodation, Marx is saying, is much more important than whether or not he does so in order to make personal accommodations. That, I think, is quite right.

Georg Lukacs puts Hegel's accommodation with reality into a Marxist framework. "As a German thinker at the turning point of the eighteenth and nineteenth centuries," Lukacs wrote, "Hegel had a choice only between utopian illusions and coming to terms with the miserable reality of Germany at that time." In this view, Hegel's personal behavior is of a piece with the "position taken by the great German humanists vis-à-vis bourgeois society." Yet it is

Lukacs who, as his critic George Lichtheim concedes, assembled the data to show that the philosophic-political transition of 1800 was preceded by a psychological crisis which included hypochondriac symptoms. Lichtheim, however, finds Lukacs's interpretation of the facts "both banal and misleading."

The personal crisis can be glimpsed in letters from the late 1790s, as Lukacs shows. It was specifically alluded to in a letter much later on, in 1810, in which Hegel wrote of having suffered from hypochondria for two years. He then immediately comments: "Every man has such a turning point in life, the gloomy point at which his being contracts and he must push through this narrow space to establish and assure his own security, the security of the customary, daily life, and, if he has already made himself incapable of being filled up by daily life, to achieve the security of an inner, more noble existence." Given that confession, I think Lukacs is quite right to argue that Hegel's generalities on the transition from adolescence to manhood (written in the 1820s, when he was at the height of his influence and power) in the *Encyclopedia of the Philosophic Sciences* refract more than a little of his own personal experience.

The adolescent (*Jungling*), Hegel writes, thinks of himself as true and good and of the world as accidental. To become a man he must realize that it is the world that is substantial and the individual who is accidental. The individual must find his satisfaction within the world, not counterposed to it. In the process of becoming a man, the adolescent learns that the ethical world order is not his work but is there, in fixed form, before him. The ideals about love as counterposed to that world thus give way to a new realism. However, before the process is completed, it sometimes involves . . . hypochondria.

"The later a man enters this period, the more critical are its symptoms." Hegel, not so incidentally, was in his late twenties during his crisis. "In weak natures, those symptoms can last throughout an entire life." The cure? "If a man is not to break down, he must acknowledge the world as independent of him and in its essentials *fixed* [*in Wesentlichen fertige*]." Moreover:

> this unity with the world must be seen, not as a relationship arising out of necessity, but as a relation which derives from reason. The reasonable, the divine, possesses the absolute power to effectuate itself and has done so from time immemorial. It is not so impotent that it must wait for the beginning of its effectuation. The world is this effectuation of divine reason and it is only on its surface that the play of irrational accident rules.

Avineri argues, as we have seen, that Hegel remained something of a radical and idealist—if one can put an identification with Napoleon under such a rubric—for more than a decade *after* the crisis of 1787–1800. That is true and important, particularly when one remembers that, as the young Engels pointed out, the Hegelian system was essentially in place before 1810; in other words, it was the product of a time in which he was sympathetic to the French.

In January 1807, shortly after the Battle of Jena, Hegel wrote an extraordinary letter to a former student, Zellmann. It confirms Avineri's interpretation of him and is worth quoting in its own right.

Nothing is more certain than that culture will triumph over rawness and the spirit [Geist] will be victorious over a spiritless understanding and sophistry. Science is the only theodicy. It guards us against reacting to events with an animal-like amazement or, more sophisticated, by explaining them in terms of the accidents of the moment or the talent of an individual, making the destiny of a kingdom depend on whether one hill is taken or not. And it keeps us from weeping over the victory of injustice and the defeat of right. There are those who think that what is being lost today is what is good and possessed of a divine right, while what is being won is taken with bad conscience. Such notions of right are false. . . .

The French nation has been freed by the bath of its revolution, not only of many institutions which the human spirit leaves behind like baby shoes, institutions which weighed upon France and still weigh upon others, like fetters, but also individuals were freed from the fear of death and the life of custom which because of the change of scene no longer have meaning. This is the source of the great strength they exhibit against others.

Seven years later, in 1814, Hegel's reaction to Napoleon's defeat and exile to Elba was quite sympathetic to the French Emperor: "This is the most consequential event there is. The great mass of the mediocrities, with its absolute, leaden weight, presses ceaselessly and without quarter until it drags the higher down to its own level or even beneath itself." Two years later, in 1816, he wrote to his friend Niethammer, a Protestant educator under Catholic (and reactionary) attack, "I believe that the world spirit has given the command to advance. Such a command will be obeyed." The spirit, he continued, is guided "as by an invisible hand" and the reactionaries who oppose it will actually embrace it, wanting to place their own seal on the hated reality so as to be able to read there, "We made this."

Three months after that letter, Hegel again wrote Niethammer, discussing Napoleon and the French. The recently deposed Emperor, he commented, hated free and independent universities. Such institutions, Hegel went on, were of the very essence of a Protestantism which, lacking the bishops and hierarchical structures of Rome, regarded "the *universal* moral and intellectual education . . . as the holy." But Napoleon, if he did not like them, had, on practical grounds, come to tolerate them. This complex analysis was of a piece with Hegel's general view of Napoleon, which has been well summarized by Franz Rosenzweig: as the man who restored order after the excesses of the Revolution *and* thereby guaranteed that there would be no return to the *ancien régime.*

In recent times, an extremely influential book by Joachim Ritter, *Meta-*

physik und Politik, has argued that Hegel's concern for intellectual freedom shows that "his allegedly absolute state [*Machtstaat*] had precisely the function of defending the freedom of the individuals against the claims of the society." In a lucid reading of sections 238 and 243 of the *Philosophy of Right*, Ritter holds that Hegel saw the totalitarian potential in bourgeois-statism and felt that the "atheism of the moral world" in the nineteenth century could lead to the total domination of man and society by the government. This theological theory of totalitarianism is also discussed in Chapter 5.

In thus showing that Hegel's "liberal" sympathies extended far beyond his youth, I do not, however, want to suggest that he was some kind of secret radical. In the years after he left Jena and before he came to Berlin (from 1807 to 1818) his correspondence is filled with references to economic necessity, the search for a professorship and the like. He spent almost two of those years as the editor of a provincial paper—and as a cultural Protestant in a South Germany dominated by political Catholics—and another four as the rector of a Gymnasium. And once he got to Berlin he admitted that, having reached the age of fifty, he wished that the turbulent times, with all of their fears and hopes, would become more placid. But, he added, things were in fact going to become more difficult. Such passages give one reason to argue that he had made some kind of a psychological accommodation with established power in Berlin.

However, the really critical point is the one made by George Lichtheim, who focuses, as Marx rightly said one should, on the philosophic principles rather than the personal anecdotes. Lichtheim said:

> his seminal work, the *Phenomenology of Mind*, published at a time (1807) when he still looked hopefully to France, already struck the contemplative and conciliatory note dominant in his post-Napoleonic writings: the hidden essence of reality was seen to be in harmony both with itself and with the divinity. In less exalted language, the world was held to be precisely what it ought to be, namely reasonable. It is well to bear in mind that Hegel had evolved this conviction long before, in the 1820s, when he discovered the Prussian state to be a fairly close approximation to the rational state.

That last point—that Hegel idealized the Prussian state—is unfair. But Lichtheim was right on the essential: there was a structural tendency toward reconciliation—and conservatism—in Hegel's philosophy even when he himself was far from reconciled or conservative. That, however, is a much more complex reality than the one conjured up by those—be they Stalinist hacks or serious writers like Sidney Hook—who dismiss Hegel as a creature of the Prussian reaction.

APPENDIX E

HEGEL'S ANALYSIS of the Trinity is an open invitation for people to engage in the propagation of more nonsense about his fascination with threes. It is widely, and erroneously, believed that he saw a universal pattern in human life, a progression from thesis through antithesis to synthesis. In fact, as I documented in *Twilight of Capitalism*, those terms hardly occur in his writing at all (they are much more integral to Fichte) and, more to the point, the notion of an automatic and mechanistic dialectic is totally alien to his mind.

Walter Kaufmann points out that the only place where Hegel uses thesis, antithesis and synthesis together is in the history of philosophy. In this passage, "Hegel roundly reproaches Kant for having 'everywhere posited thesis, antithesis, synthesis.' "

However, the theology of the Trinity does relate to Hegel's philosophy, in that he regards this doctrine as a representational image of a fundamental truth which philosophers (but not ordinary believers) can state in nonrepresentational propositions. Thus Hegel interprets the Biblical statement that God sent his son into the world when the times were fulfilled as meaning: "As spirit had so deepened within itself to understand its own infinity and to conceptualize the substantial (God) in the subjectivity of immediate self-consciousness . . ." That conceptualization, moreover, relates to some of the most basic processes of existence. Let me just mention two.

The concept of "life," which was critical for Hegel in all of his phases, can be understood as an abstraction which extends to all living things and is therefore the most general, and empty, of terms. But, then, it can also be seen in its infinite variety and differentiation, as an endless particularity. And finally that particularity can be reintegrated into the concept of a life which persists even as, in each generation, all of its particulars perish. Roughly, the first abstraction is something like the distant and alien God prior to Christ; that consciousness of individuation can be analogized to the incarnation of God in the particular man, Christ; and the unity of life is the Holy Spirit, which brings the Father and Son together again, but now transformed, triune.

Indeed, the individual human consciousness can be analyzed in a similar fashion. We (as individuals, as a species) are first simply conscious of the external world. We want to appropriate it to satisfy our bodily hunger and we want to dominate others in order to satisfy our spiritual hungers. But then we become conscious of our consciousness; we are self-conscious, two people in one. Socially, we externalize ourselves in institutions and in cultures, and these sometimes become an alien force which looms over those who create them. But, after a long historic process, we recognize ourselves in nature and history, we see that the reason within us is also outside us. We are once again whole, both in our consciousness and in our societal life.

But God himself is under a similar imperative to externalize himself. This is, as Leszek Kolakowski has pointed out, one of the central points of Christian mysticism: the explanation of why God created the world. If he is self-sufficient, what need did he have of creation? For Kolakowski, Hegel's predecessor in answering this question—that God could not become his own perfection without the world, that God needs man as man needs God—was Johannes Scotus Erigena, the ninth-century theologian who defined a divine Logos in all things; Bloch identifies Hegel with the German mystic Meister Eckhart. This highly spiritual conception, moreover, has its analogue in Hegel's *Logic*, where the traditional counterposition of essence and appearance (or accident) is rejected on the grounds that the essence must appear. That proposition points toward twentieth-century existential phenomenology.

APPENDIX F

HELMUT GOLLWITZER HAS a lengthy note on the phrase (or concept) "religion as the opium of the people" in his article on "The Marxist Critique of Religion and Christian Faith." Bruno Bauer, Moses Hess and others used it, or similar words. The British Opium War, between 1839 and 1842, in which a Christian nation imposed the drug on an "inferior" people, may, Gollwitzer suggests, have brought the phenomenon of opium to people's attention. If one shifts to a slightly larger analogy—religion as a narcotic in general—one can include Goethe, Heine and Hegel in the list of those who used the image. Indeed, as early as 1761, Holbach had described religion as a way of intoxicating (*d'en-ivrer*) the people, "to keep them from turning to the evils, including those which come from the government, which torment them down here."

In Volume IV of his *Prison Notebooks*, Gramsci offers a much more speculative account of the term. He describes a story by Balzac (Marx's favorite novelist), "La Rabouilleuse" (1841). In it, Balzac talks of the lottery as "the opium of misery" and as the most "powerful fairy of the world." "What is today the social power which can, for forty sous, make you happy for five days and ideally deliver to you all the happiness of civilization." Gramsci goes on to suggest that it is possible that there is a relationship between the Balzacian notion of the lottery as the "opium of the people," Pascal's famous concept of religious faith as a "wager" (*pari*) and Marx's concept of the opium of the people.

APPENDIX G

I ARGUED IN THE TEXT that Marx unquestionably used anti-Semitic language but was not, in my opinion, an anti-Semite.

Part of the evidence for this is internal to the text. Marx, it will be remembered, used the notion of Judaism as a paradigm of capitalist society. The political discrimination against the Jews and the economic power of the wealthy among them was an illustration of the general condition of an economic social formation in which concealed economic power regularly subverted political equality. So it is that Marx not only describes the Jews as "Jewish" in this sense but also argues that "Christianity is the sublime thought of Judaism, Judaism is the general utilization of Christianity, but this application only first becomes universal when Christianity as the ultimate religion *theoretically* completes the self-alienation of man from himself and from nature." But this makes it clear that, unfortunate though his language is, an analysis which equates Judaism and Christianity as both reprehensible because exemplifications of the capitalist reality is not anti-Semitic.

Second, there is a letter from Marx to Arnold Ruge in March 1843 which throws considerable light on the anti–anti-Semitic intent in Marx's analysis of the Jewish question:

> Just now the leaders of the local Israelites came to me and asked me for a petition for the Jews to the provincial legislature. I will do it. Even though the Israeli faith is repugnant [*widerlich*] to me, I still find Bauer's ideas too abstract. The point is to punch as many holes as possible in the Christian state and to smuggle in the rational as far as we can. That must at least be our aim—and the *bitterness* grows with every petition that is turned down.

Also, it should be noted, as David McClellan has documented, that many of the objectionable points in Marx's essay *On the Jewish Question* were taken almost verbatim from Moses Hess's article "On the Essence of Money." Hess, revered in Israel as a founder of Zionism, could hardly be considered an anti-Semite. The distinguished Israeli scholar Shlomo Avineri makes the same point in *The Making of Modern Zionism*.

That point leads to Hal Draper's excellent discussion of this question in *Karl Marx's Theory of Revolution*. Draper shows how the language Marx used was pervasive at the time among Jews and gentiles alike. One can most certainly argue that German culture was shot through and through with anti-Semitic assumptions and connotations—but that does not justify singling out any one person participating in the general phenomenon as an anti-Semite. It proves only that such a person accepted uncritically and wrongly a language which was and, particularly after Adolf Hitler, is unconscionable.

APPENDIX H

ENGELS'S RELIGIOUS CRISIS is detailed in Chapter 2 of Gustav Mayer's biography. It can also be followed in the letters he wrote to his orthodox Protestant friend, Friedrich Graeber, in 1839. In a sense, Engels went through the stages of development which, he and Marx thought, would be the common experience of the working class and society as a whole. They were, as the text shows, wrong.

Briefly, Engels was born into a religious family in the pious community of Wuppertal. He was sent to Bremen, where he lived with a Protestant pastor and heard the theological debates of his day. The strict and dogmatic Protestants were a presence to be reckoned with; they particularly emphasized the doctrine of original sin and the damnation of the majority of the people of the world. The young Engels was affronted—not because he was an atheist, but because he still very much believed in God and Christianity. He turned to two antagonists to try to find a way to keep his faith. On the one hand, he responded to the concept of religion as a matter of feeling, of subjectivity, put forward by the liberal theologian Schleiermacher (who is discussed at greater length in Chapter 8). On the other hand, he developed a humanist and radical version of the Hegelian interpretation, emphasizing the divinity of man.

Two other thinkers were a major influence on Engels: David Friedrich Strauss, whose mythological reading of the Bible had tremendous impact; and Ludwig Feuerbach, whose materialism became a vogue in this period. By 1842, Engels—now twenty-two years old—had completed the transition to atheism. Gustav Mayer's summary is quite good. When Engels became an atheist, Mayer wrote, "the ideas and feelings which arose from the religious experience remained with him. He was so filled with them that the transition from the cult of God to the cult of man, which Feuerbach caused him to make, was not a sad, but an inspiriting, event. . . . The divinity which now descended from the throne of the world was taken up henceforth in his will."

APPENDIX I

UNLIKE THAT OF HEGEL, Nietzsche's work need not be carefully located in a biographical context before it can be interpreted. There is, I believe, a remarkable continuity from the young Nietzsche to the old, a fact he once symbolized in an image of himself as a snake shedding skins—in other words, remaining consistent through all of his changes. Thus, his discussion of Heraclitus in his study *Philosophy in the Tragic Age of Greece* (1873) not only states themes which will appear in his last years, but also uses an image—the innocent world as the plaything of a (cosmic) child—which will be central to *Zarathustra* (1883–85). In this, Nietzsche is similar to Marx, who also demonstrated constancy of basic vision even as he matured and developed.

This is not, however, to say that there was no change in Nietzsche's intellectual life. Karl Löwith has convincingly divided that life into three periods: the time of his infatuation with Wagner and concern for the reanimation of German culture, a period which includes *The Birth of Tragedy* and *Non-Contemporary Reflections (Unzeitgemässige Betractungen)*; the "free spirit" criticizing everything in *Human, All Too Human, Dawn* and the first four books of *The Gay Science*; and the prophet of the eternal return in *Zarathustra* and *Ecce Homo*. Nietzsche himself followed something like the progress Zarathustra described: the "three transformations" from camel to lion to child. As a camel, the spirit is in the desert and obeys the law of "should." As a lion, it is free and says "I will" rather than "Thou must." And as a child, accepting the purposeless world as a game, the spirit says simply "I am."

There is no need for us to go into these transitions here, since, by and large, Nietzsche's basic views about our subject matter did not change that much. There are, to be sure, obvious differences between, say, *The Anti-Christ/Anti Christian* and *The Genealogy of Morals*, the former being much more polemical than the latter. But, as Arthur Danto has sugested, the "vituperative" volume is "informed in its polemic by a structure of analysis and a theory of morality and religion worked out elsewhere. . . ." The shift in mood (*Genealogy* precedes *Anti-Christ*) could be quite significant in other contexts, but not in ours. I therefore feel free to synthesize Nietzsche's views in this area, using material from different periods of his life. I would not do so if our focus were upon the theory of the "Eternal Return," where Nietzsche's changes in attitude play a much more important role than they do in his political and social analysis of religion.

APPENDIX J

NIETZSCHE'S ATTITUDE toward the Jews was deliberately falsified by his sister, Elizabeth Foster-Nietzsche, an ardent anti-Semite.

There are, to be sure, some passages which seem to contradict his contemptuous rejection of the "fake intellectual humbug" of anti-Semitism. In *Human, All Too Human*, Nietzsche wrote that "the youthful Bourse Jew is perhaps the most disgusting discovery of the human race." But right after that comment, he wrote that every people has tendencies which can become dangerous. Much more to the present point, the same passage argues that anti-Semitism has arisen because nationalists—whom Nietzsche dismisses as "crude"—are jealous of the accomplishments of the Jewish people, who are possessed of a higher capacity for action and a greater intelligence than the nationalists, virtues learned by the Jews in their suffering history. The anti-Semites try to scapegoat the Jews, he continued; in fact, the Christians are responsible for much of Jewish misery and are indebted to the Jews "for the most noble man (Christ), the purest of the wise (Spinoza), the mightiest book and the most effective ethics. . . ."

Nietzsche offers these remarks in the context of welcoming the emergence of a mixed race of Europeans and of calculating the Jewish contribution to it. I do not, as the text makes quite clear, absolve Nietzsche completely of blame for creating the intellectual atmosphere which made people receptive to Nazism. I only say that neither he nor his writings were anti-Semitic.

APPENDIX K

H. JEANMAIRE'S *Dionysius: Histoire du culte de Bacchus* has the merit of grasping the complexity of Nietzsche's analysis. It documents the degree to which the Dionysiac rites were phallic and sees the cult of this god as, in general, a throwback to primitivism in Greek society.

Karl Kerenyi's point of view is somewhat more difficult to define. He attacks Nietzsche for making Dionysus too orgiastic and thus misses the emphasis on the Apollonian aspect of the cult in *The Birth of Tragedy*. But Kerenyi then plays down the orgiastic, thinking that he is contradicting Nietzsche, though actually giving support to the latter's dialectical version of the Dionysiac feasts.

In his *History of Religious Ideas*, Eliade devotes considerable attention to Dionysus. In part, he lends support to Nietzsche's thesis: "More than the other Greek Gods, Dionysus astonishes by the multiplicity and novelty of his epiphanies, by the variety of his transformations. . . . He is certainly the only Greek god who, revealing himself under different aspects, dazzles and attracts both the peasants and intellectual elite, politicians and contemplatives, orgiastics and ascetics." But his actual documentation of the rites of Dionysus stresses the phallic and the orgiastic. So I think that the interpretation of this very erotic deity as Hamlet is, in the light of recent scholarship, the exaggeration of a rather important truth which Nietzsche was the first to define and for which he has received precious little credit.

APPENDIX L

TALCOTT PARSONS HAS SUGGESTED that the debate over the Protestant ethic might itself be a good subject for sociological study. "What accounts for the fact," he wrote, "that the controversy has never been settled?"

For instance, the Swedish economic historian Kurt Samuelson published a book-length attack on Weber in 1957 (it was translated into English in 1961). Samuelson tried to document the propositions that there was no empirical connection between economic innovation and Calvinism, that Catholics are to be found among the early capitalists, that Ben Franklin—a paradigmatic figure for Weber—was not an "ascetic" but almost a Libertine, and so on. "There is no justification," Samuelson wrote, "for isolating, as he did, a single fact in a prolonged intricate pattern of development—no matter how clearly definable or capable of isolation from other factors—and correlating it with a vast aspect of the whole history of Western civilization."

When Samuelson concentrates on the broad methodological critique, as in the sentence just quoted, I think he has a point. Indeed, Franz Borkenau made a similar criticism in *Der Übergang vom feudelen zum burgerlichen Weltbild*. Part of the problem, as Karl Löwith has noted, is that Weber was often overreacting to a vulgar Marxism which placed a uni-causal stress on the "economic" factor, and he might therefore seem to commit the opposite error. In fact, Weber's thesis is quite compatible with a sophisticated, non-vulgar Marxism; it never really addresses itself to the *cause* of the Protestant ethic but concentrates on its effects. Weber, Hans Bosse wrote in a study of him, Marx and Troeltsch, can't even disprove the assertion that Protestantism grew out of the social situation rather than vice versa.

There are several recent surveys of the Protestant-ethic controversy which rescue the issue from the fruitless framework of "idealism" against "materialism." Ephraim Fischoff and Herbert Luthy published contributions along these lines in S. W. Eisenstadt's *The Protestant Ethic and Modernization*. Bruno Biermann's contribution to the 1968 *International Yearbook for the Sociology of Religion (Beitrag zur Religions-soziologischen Forschung)*, edited by Joachim Matthes, is valuable on this count, and also in its summary of the discussion on the existence, or nonexistence, of the Protestant ethic in contemporary Western society.

As I noted in the text, I have seen no need to go into complexities which, though important in their own right, are not relevant to my themes.

APPENDIX M

BORKENAU'S *Der Übergang vom feudelen zum burgerlichen Weltbild* was published in Paris in 1934. The author had been associated for some years with the Frankfurt Institut für Sozialforschung and had gone into exile after the Nazis took power in Germany.

Der Übergang was the subject of an extremely lengthy review in the Institute's *Zeitschrift für Sozialforschung* in 1935. Written by H. Grossmann, it was a rather pedantic critique of Borkenau's book which made minor points instead of dealing with the powerful sweep of the basic thesis. For example, Grossmann took Borkenau severely to task for not recognizing that Leonardo da Vinci had anticipated much of the *"burgerlichen Weltbild"* long, long before the late sixteenth and early seventeenth centuries, which Borkenau considered a turning point. But Grossmann himself had to admit that most of the relevant Leonardo manuscripts were not published in his lifetime—indeed, they did not appear until the late nineteenth century. He then had rather lamely to try to explain why this fact did not invalidate his point against Borkenau.

Richard Lowenthal, who edited the posthumous collection of Borkenau's essays, *End and Beginning*, believes that a good part of *Der Übergang* was written to forestall such "orthodox" Marxist criticism from within the Frankfurt group. Specifically, he argues that the theory of the relationship between ideology and the period of "manufacture" is a bow toward that orthodoxy which was "superficial and only conceived as an afterthought." I disagree. First, Lowenthal assumes a vulgar-Marxist notion of "orthodoxy"—that one must derive intellectual categories from the " 'relations of production' "— which Borkenau most certainly would have rejected along with most of the Frankfurt School (Grossmann's somewhat literal-minded Marxism was not at all typical of Frankfurt). Second, the notion of the complexity and unevenness of both the intellectual and the economic transition from feudalism to capitalism is not an "afterthought" for Borkenau but a central theme of his work. Third, and most to the point, I think subsequent history has demonstrated that Borkenau's "superficial" remarks in this area are profound.

Lowenthal also writes that *Der Übergang* was "much appreciated in Ger-

man scholarly circles" after World War II. Given Lowenthal's personal familiarity with, and involvement in, those circles, this is important testimony.
However, George Lichtheim, who was also part of that milieu (even though
he lived in England), referred to *Der Übergang* as an "unfairly neglected work"
in the course of a review of Lucien Goldmann's *Le Dieu caché*. These matters
are, of course, quite relative: both men could be right.

Der Übergang is mentioned in Martin Jay's history of the Frankfurt School,
The Dialectical Imagination, where it is called "almost completely forgotten."
It is not even mentioned in Pedrag Vranicki's *Geschichte des Marxismus* and
is cited in a brief, and inaccurate, paragraph in Leszek Kolakowski's normally
quite fair *Main Currents of Marxism*. Robert Merton mentions it in his study
of the Puritan contribution to the development of science, but I have not been
able to find any other references to it in the literature.

The book is conceptually quite difficult in itself. Moreover, it is written
in German and quotes generously in untranslated Latin and French, which
places it in a dying scholarly tradition—but no more than, say, Weber. I believe
it deserves to be numbered among the classic Marxist analyses.

APPENDIX N

MARX AND ENGELS ENCOUNTERED anthropology relatively late in their own lives and early in its existence. Lewis Morgan's *Ancient Society*, which had such an impact upon Marx (and even more so on Engels), was only published in 1877, six years before Marx's death. Engels enthusiastically and ingeniously overgeneralized the evidence, most notably in *The Origin of the Family, Private Property and the State* (subtitled *In Conjunction with [im Anschluss an] Lewis H. Morgan's Researches*). He was also characteristically generous in acknowledging the contributions of those with whom he disagreed. Bachofen, who theorized a period of "mother's right" in the dawn of history, was a reactionary (Rousseau's savages, Ernst Bloch has commented, were revolutionaries, Bachofen's mothers were conservatives), yet Engels noted his achievement.

In the period right before his death, Marx very carefully read and annotated works by Morgan, Phear, Maine and Lubbock, in some cases critically. If he was not an expert in this fledgling discipline, he was one of the very first European thinkers to realize its enormous potential.

In some of their writings, however, Marx and Engels did participate in the simplistic evolutionary account of human societies, most notably in Marx's Preface to the *Contribution to the Critique of Political Economy*. In that version of their theory—which has been carved in stone by most vulgar Marxists and all Stalinists—there is an inevitable progression from ancient society through slavery and classical antiquity to feudalism, capitalism and socialism. Each new development (with the exception of socialism) is self-contradictory, and its internal conflicts eventually generate the next, higher, stage of society.

In other writings—and, more significantly, in the main thrust of Marx's masterpiece, *Das Kapital*—Marx and Engels were much more sophisticated. They understood, as Anthony Giddens has stressed, that most of human history could not be fitted into a progression which had some limited use in explaining European development. In the *Grundrisse* (which was written *before* the Preface) Marx's cryptic comments on the "forms" of pre-capitalist society are much more complex, and accurate, than the sweeping simplifications of his

244

grand theory. Moreover, the anthropological studies Engels undertook after Marx's death convinced him that preliterate societies could not be understood on the "base-superstructure" model, because kinship relations were more important than production relations (indeed, *were* production relations). The keepers of the "Marxist" religion in the Soviet Union regard this shrewd insight as a deviation on Engels's part.

Finally, Marx and Engels, again following Morgan, sometimes suggested that the communism they advocated would reintroduce relations of solidarity and cooperation which had existed in the first human communities. In this they inverted the colonialist prejudice, taking preliterate society as the model of the future rather than as a dead superstition.

APPENDIX O

IN THE EARLIEST TIMES, Freud argued in *Totem and Taboo*, men and women huddled together in hordes under the domination of a father. The sons, however, resented the father's sexual monopoly over the women of the horde and killed and ate him in order to challenge it. That left them with an enormous sense of guilt. They therefore created totems as a substitute for the murdered father, made taboos of the killing of the totem animal and sexual relations with the women they had liberated. On holidays, though, the totemic animal was ceremoniously eaten in a communion ritual, which revealed the continuing ambivalence toward the father figure, the attempt to kill and eat him as well as to placate him. These events, Freud concluded, were at the origins of religion and the incest taboo.

Freud took his anthropological data mainly from the work of Robertson Smith, generalizing them in a daring fashion. Indeed, Freud himself told in a letter of how extraordinarily unscientific his method was. "The *Totem* work is a beastly business. I am reading thick books without being really interested in them since I already know the results: my instinct tells me that." Most anthropologists at the time *Totem* appeared were aware of how thin the factual data were, which Freud himself recognized at the end of his life. After admitting that he had been severely criticized for his anthropological assumptions and stating that he was not convinced by the attacks, he remarked: "Above all, however, I am not an ethnologist, but a psychoanalyst. It was my good right to select from ethnological data what would serve me for my analytic work."

Herbert Marcuse provided, I think, the shrewdest assessment of the way in which Freud's soaring, and unproved, generalizations can be usefully understood. Marcuse wrote in *Eros and Civilization*:

If Freud's hypothesis is not corroborated by any anthropological evidence, it would have to be discarded altogether except for the fact that it telescopes, in a sequence of catastrophic events, the historical dialectic of domination and thereby elucidates aspects of civilization hitherto unex-

246

plained. We use Freud's anthropological speculation only in this sense: for its *symbolic* value. The archaic events that the hypothesis stipulates may forever be beyond the realm of anthropological verification; the alleged consequences of these events are historic facts, and their interpretation in the light of Freud's hypothesis lends them a neglected significance which points to the historical future. If the hypothesis defies common sense, it claims, in its defiance, a truth which common sense has been trained to forget.

Marcuse is making, it seems to me, a "Kantian" reading of *Totem and Taboo*. Just as Kant reasoned from the fact of experience to a hypothesis about the structure of the human mind which makes that experience possible, so, Marcuse argues, Freud started from the fact of religious guilt and alienation and proceeded to a hypothesis about its origins. The literal truth of Freud's prehistory is most questionable (as I documented in the discussion of Durkheim, contemporary scholars like Lévi-Strauss and Eliade deny that there was a universal, or even a general, totemic stage). But is that prehistory a useful fiction which leads to truth? If it is understood with all the necessary qualifications, Marcuse says, yes.

When men and women "humanize" nature in religion, interpreting reality, as Judeo-Christian culture does, in terms of a relation to God the Father, then one can look in religion for many of the tensions and anxieties which one knows exist in father-mother-sibling relations. The latter exhibit hostility as well as love, guilt along with gratitude, hatred and respect. If Freud's theory of a universal Oedipus complex is less secure than it once was, it is nevertheless true—and known to be true because of Freud—that there are feelings between sons, fathers and mothers which do not fit into idyllic pictures of family life. To echo Marx, is what is true of the earthly family also valid for the heavenly family? Are there anger, sadism and masochism, lust and murder at work even in seemingly serene faiths? It seems to me that the actual history of religion is better understood if one recognizes that this is indeed the case.

Also valuable is Erich Fromm's use of this Freudian framework to provide a psychoanalytic account of the Protestant ethic. Originally, Fromm argued, Christianity had been the religion in which man became God, thus overthrowing the father. But then, as the Church turned into the established faith of an empire, that radical doctrine was reinterpreted. Now it was God who, in his benevolence, became man, not man in his potential divinity who became God. In the new interpretation of Christ, Fromm continued, the people were in a passive, dependent—infantile—relation to God. "Catholicism," Fromm concluded, "signified the disguised return to the religion of the Great Mother which had been defeated by Yahweh. Only Protestantism turned back to the father-god. It stands at the beginning of a social epoch that permits an active attitude on the part of the masses in contrast to the passively infantile attitude of the Middle Ages."

Theodor Reik's *Der eigene und der fremde Gott* is particularly interesting in the discussion of the role of female divinity in Judeo-Christianity. The Hebrews, Reik argued, had, like all the other Semitic peoples, love- and mother-goddesses (of the order of Ishtar, Astarte, Cybele, etc.). This cult was, however, repressed and replaced by the passive—Reik would say "homosexual-feminine"—relation of the faithful to the father God, Yahweh. This repression, however, is constantly challenged by a heterosexual drive within culture. Mary, Reik holds, was a manifestation of this latter tendency.

APPENDIX P

So MUCH OF MY THINKING has been influenced by, and is in response to, Jürgen Habermas's analyses that I feel bound to undertake the very difficult task of summarizing some of his exceedingly complex ideas. I have relied primarily on three sources: a 1974 speech which was based on an essay reprinted in *Zur Rekonstrucktion des historischen Materialismus*; Habermas's two-volume work of 1981, *Theorie des kommunikativen Handelns*; and a translation of a 1981 interview with him which appeared in the journal *Telos*.

Habermas bases himself on Durkheim and Mead. Durkheim had seen morality—and society itself—resting upon a sense of the sacred which was the mystical expression of that solidarity which made human interaction possible. In the earliest stages of history, that solidarity was "mechanical" or "segmentary." That is, every individual, every social unit, was like every other individual and social unit. "Society" was the arithmetical addition of these almost identical segments. But then, with social evolution, came "organic" solidarity, which arose out of an increasingly complex division of labor. The structures of "mechanical" solidarity had clearly been based upon norms and world views; indeed, the norms and world views permeated every aspect of life, and every wrong was therefore, *ipso facto*, a sacrilege.

But what about modern, "organic" solidarity? Did it require norms? One influential bourgeois tradition said no. The market system, impersonal and value-free, automatically created a harmony among those who worked within it. That, Durkheim said, was not true. Markets simply did not produce anything like rules for society. Therefore, progressive differentiation had to be accompanied by the emergence of a new morality. Habermas held that this was, and is, not the case. He therefore sought to reread ("decode") Durkheim using the concept of "communicative rationality."

That concept owes much to George Herbert Mead. For Mead, signals are found not just during the evolutionary transition to the human but in the animal world as a whole. There are cries, calls, alarms. At the beginning of human evolution, these signals are merely gestures. But then the gesture becomes a symbol: it is no longer restricted to the immediate situation or to physical representation. This requires that individuals internalize what had been external and agree on a common meaning, that each must "take the attitude of the other." Speech, which is one of the primary factors differentiating humans from animals, thus demands a certain sense of community. Consequently the analysis of society cannot be carried out by examining individual behavior but only from the perspective of the social whole.

Mead's philosophic anthropology leads Habermas to his notion of "communicative action" (or "communicative rationality"). When people act together on the basis of communication there is a "cooperative interpretative process in which the participants relate to the objective, social and subjective worlds *at the same time. . . .*" They try to determine the objective truth about the situation in which they will act together; they proceed on the basis of norms of action which are social; and they respond to one another as expressive beings communicating feelings as well as propositions. These three spheres, which are a basic component of Habermas's analysis, not so incidentally correspond to the subject matter of Kant's three critiques (pure reason, practical reason, judgment—or cognition, morality, art).

Thus for Habermas there is a consensual and rational element in the very constitution of the human. It is expressed within the framework of a "life-world" (*Lebens-Welt*, a notion taken from the late work of both Husserl and Wittgenstein). The life-world is what the speakers in a communicative situation assume (it is very much like that "horizon," that framework of meaning, which Nietzsche said was necessary if there were to be values). It is unquestioned—or, rather, beyond questioning—based upon a social *a priori*, and, over long periods of time, it is unchanging. There are always new situations within the same life-world; there are only rarely fundamental changes of a life-world.

Mead was the first to discover that "the structure of interaction mediated by norms expressed through speech is the very basis of the social-cultural evolution" of humans. There is, Habermas writes, a *"Versprachligung des Sakralen,"* a phrase which is extremely difficult to translate. *Versprachligung* means a turning-into-speech, and the "sacral" is understood as a sphere in which symbols are dominant. The earliest interpretations of the world were symbolic and sacral, but human evolution is made possible precisely by a process of moving from the community of kinship integrated by mythic symbols to the rational community of speech. The "verbalization of what was once sacred" (which is how I would render *"Versprachligung des Sakralen"*) is one of the first steps in that long process of social and cultural differentiation which leads to the modern.

Indeed, Habermas continues, the communitarian basis of human speech can be given a utopian reading, which is what Mead did. Speech establishes a "universe of discourse" which allows people to resolve conflicts by changing, and even transforming, values. It is rational, and "man cannot act as a rational member of society except as he constitutes himself a member of the wider commonwealth of rational beings." The Kantian categoric imperative—that each act as if his/her conduct were a universal law, binding on all—is thus embedded in the very fact of speech and in the progress of humanity. History is, among other things, a learning process.

It is not, Habermas clearly understands, quite that simple. Class struggle, war and political power hardly obey the imperatives of "communicative rationality." Indeed, one can use that concept to understand what is wrong and pathological in the modern world, i.e., for a most un-utopian purpose. Capitalism, Habermas argues, has been enormously successful. That triumph of functional differentiation has vastly expanded the possibilities of the human. It has created new institutions—the market economy, the bourgeois state— and even if this has subverted the traditional life-world, it marked an advance in freedom. The contemporary situation, however, is characterized by an ominous turn. Economic and political power are not simply differentiating themselves from the life-world; they are now infiltrating it, quantifying everything in money and administrative rules. (The French socialist economist Jacques Atali, now an adviser to President Mitterrand, presented a very similar analysis, on the basis of quite different premises, in *La Nouvelle Economie française* in 1978.)

Indeed, it is precisely because the life-world is menaced that people become aware of its very existence. Here Habermas makes an important analogy to Marx's analysis. Labor, Marx held, had obviously been present from the very beginning of human time. Since it was ubiquitous, it was simply taken for granted; it did not become a concept in its own right. Aristotle might come fairly close to the labor theory of value but, as a privileged member of a slave society, he could not admit that work, the activity of slaves, was a central determinant of value. It was only when capitalism wrenched labor from its natural context, the production of useful goods and services, and rendered it "abstract" in the "units" of factory labor devoted to making, not useful things, but money, that one looked back and realized that labor had been the basis of human life all along.

So with the life-world. Only when it was assaulted by economic and political power did one realize that it had been there since the dawn of the human. And the question today for Habermas is, can the pathologies of rationalization, the deforming and manipulation of the life-world, which are the consequence, not of differentiation *per se*, but of differentiation carried out by elites, be avoided? They cannot be avoided by "de-differentiation," as the romantic radicals propose, not by new myths, for our consciousness is too thoroughly demythologized. But where, then, are we to find norms in a modern society?

In communicative rationality. Habermas, it seems to me, was more positive about this possibility in his 1974 speech and essay than in his 1981 book. If it is possible for everyone in a society to participate—not necessarily through party politics, but in a much more molecular and basic process—in the communication process by means of which society learns to confront its new complexities, that could provide the basis for new identities in complex societies. Though Habermas has distanced himself from party politics in recent years—and is something more of a "Green" than a "Red"—I see this as the restatement of the same socialist possibility which I urge in this book.

BIBLIOGRAPHY

Acquaviva, S. S. *The Decline of the Sacred in Industrial Society*. New York: Harper & Row, 1939.

Adorno, T. W. *Prismen*. Frankfurt-am-Main: Suhrkamp, 1955.

Ahlstron, Sidney E. *Religious History of the American People*. New Haven: Yale University Press, 1972.

Altizer, Thomas, and Hamilton, William. *Radical Theology and the Death of God*. Indianapolis, New York, Kansas City: Bobbs-Merrill, 1966.

Arendt, Hannah. *The Origins of Totalitarianism*. Rev. ed. Cleveland: Meridian, 1958.

Atali, Jacques. *La Nouvelle Economie française*. Paris: Flammarion, 1978.

Aulard, A. *Histoire politique de la révolution française*. Paris: Colin, 1905.

Avineri, Shlomo. *Hegel's Theory of the Modern State*. Cambridge: Cambridge University Press, 1972.

——. *The Making of Modern Zionism*. New York: Basic Books, 1982.

Ayer, A. J. "Religion and the Intellectuals." *Partisan Review* (March 1950).

Bailyn, Bernard. *Ideological Origins of the American Revolution*. Cambridge, Mass.: Belknap, 1971.

Balthasar, Hans Urs von. *The Theology of Karl Barth*. New York: Anchor, 1972.

Banton, Michael, ed. *Anthropological Approaches to the Study of Religion*. London: Tavistock, 1969.

Barth, Karl. *Ad Limina Apostolorum*. Richmond, Va.: John Knox, 1968.

——. *Epistle to the Romans*. Translated by Edwyn C. Hofkyns. Oxford: Oxford University Press, 1968 (1933).

——. *Protestant Theology in the Nineteenth Century*. Valley Forge, Pa.: Judson, 1973.

——. *Der Romerbriefe*. Bern: G. A. Baschlin, 1919.

Bebel, August. *Politik als Theorie und Praxis*. Cologne: Hegner Bücherei, 1967.

Bell, Daniel. *The Cultural Contradictions of Capitalism*. New York: Basic Books, 1976.

Bellah, Robert. *Beyond Belief*. New York: Harper & Row, 1970.

——. "Civil Religion in America." In *Religion's Influence in Contemporary Society*, edited by Joseph E. Faulkner. Columbus: Bobbs-Merrill, 1972.

253

————. "Power and Religion in America Today." *Commonweal* (December 3, 1982).

Bentley, James. *Between Mary and Christ*. London: Verso, 1982.

Berger, Peter. *The Heretical Imperative*. New York: Anchor, 1980.

Berlin, Isaiah. *Against the Current: Essays in the History of Ideas*. Baltimore: Penguin, 1982.

————. *Vico and Herder: Two Studies in the History of Ideas*. London: Hogarth, 1976.

Berman, Marshall. *All That Is Solid Melts into Air*. New York: Simon and Schuster, 1982.

Bielschowsky, Albert. *Life of Goethe*. New York: Putnam, 1908.

Billington, James. *Fire in the Minds of Men*. New York: Basic Books, 1980.

Bloch, Ernst. *Avicenna und die Aristotelische Linke*. Frankfurt-am-Main: Suhrkamp, 1963.

————. *Naturrecht und menschliche Würde*. Frankfurt-am-Main: Suhrkamp, 1977.

————. *Das Prinzip Hoffnung*. Frankfurt-am-Main: Suhrkamp, 1959.

————. *Subjekt-Objekt*. Berlin: Aufbau, 1949.

Bonhoeffer, Dietrich. *Letters and Papers from Prison*. New York: Macmillan, 1967.

Borkenau, Franz. *Der Übergang vom feudelen zum burgerlichen Weltbild*. Paris: Félix Alcan, 1934.

————. *End and Beginning*. Edited by Richard Lowenthal. New York: Columbia University Press, 1981.

Bosse, Hans. *Marx, Weber, Troeltsch*. Munich: Kaiser-Grünwald, 1970.

Braudel, Fernand. *Capitalism and Material Life*. New York: Harper Torchbooks, 1979.

————. *The Structure of Everyday Life*. New York: Harper & Row, 1981.

Braunthal, Julius. *Geschichte der Internationale*. Hanover: Dietz, 1961.

Brecht, Bertolt. *Stücke*. Frankfurt-am-Main: Suhrkamp, 1955.

Bruce-Briggs, B., ed. *The New Class*. New Brunswick, N.J.: Transaction, 1979.

Bultmann, Rudolph. *Kerygma and Myth*. New York: Harper Torchbooks, 1981 (1953).

Burke, Kenneth. *The Rhetoric of Religion*. Berkeley and Los Angeles: University of California Press, 1970.

Burnham, Walter Dean. "Social Stress and Political Response: Religion and the 1980 Election." In *The Hidden Election*, edited by Thomas Ferguson and Joel Rogers. New York: Pantheon, 1981.

Burtt, E. A. *The Metaphysical Foundations of Modern Science*. New York: Anchor, 1954.

Calvez, Jean-Yves. *La Pensée de Karl Marx*. Paris: Seuil, 1956.

Camus, Albert. *L'Homme révolté*. Paris: Gallimard, 1951.

Caporale, R., and Grumelli, A., eds. *The Culture of Unbelief*. Berkeley and Los Angeles: University of California Press, 1971.

Cassirer, Ernst. *Individuum und Kosmos in der Philosophie der Renaissance* Darmstadt: Wissenschaftliche Buch Gesellschaft, 1963 (1927).

──── . *Kant's Life and Thought*. New Haven: Yale University Press, 1981 (1914).

──── . *Myth of the State*. New Haven: Yale University Press, 1946.

──── . *The Question of Jean-Jacques Rousseau*. Bloomington, Ind.: Indiana University Press, 1963.

────. *Rousseau, Kant, Goethe*. Princeton, N.J.: Princeton University Press, 1945.

Chaunu, Pierre. *Histoire et décadence*. Paris: Perrin, 1981.

Christ, Carol P., and Plaskow, Judith, eds. *Womanspirit Rising*. San Francisco: Harper & Row, 1979.

Cipolla, Carlo. *Economic History of World Population*. 6th ed. Baltimore: Penguin, 1974.

Cliff, Tony. *Lenin*. London: Pluto, 1975.

Cole, G. D. H. *History of Socialist Thought*. New York: St. Martin's, 1961.

Colletti, Lucio. *Marxism and Hegel*. London: New Left Books, 1973.

Commentary editors. *The Condition of Jewish Belief*. New York: Macmillan, 1966.

Connecticut Mutual. *The Impact of Belief*. Hartford: Connecticut Mutual, 1981.

Cornu, Auguste. *Karl Marx und Friedrich Engels*. Berlin: Aufbau, 1954.

Cragg, Gerald. *The Church and the Age of Reason*. Baltimore: Penguin, 1970.

Cuddihy, John Murray. *The Ordeal of Civility*. New York: Basic Books, 1974.

Daley, Gabriel, O.S.A. *Transcendence and Immanence*. Oxford: Clarendon, 1980.

Danto, Arthur. *Nietzsche as Philosopher*. New York: Columbia University Press, 1980.

Die deutsche Arbeiterbewegung, 1848–1919, in augenzeugen Berichten. Munich, DTV, n.d.

Deutscher, Isaac. *The Non-Jewish Jew and Other Essays*. Boston: Alyson, 1982.

Dilthey, Wilhelm. *Gesammelte Schriften*. Stuttgart: Teuberner, 1963.

Douglas, Mary. "The Effect of Modernization on Religious Change." *Daedalus* (Winter 1982).

────. *Implicit Meanings*. London: Routledge and Kegan Paul, 1975.

Draper, Hal. *Karl Marx's Theory of Revolution*. New York: Monthly Review, 1977.

Durkheim, Emile. *The Division of Labor in Society*. New York: Macmillan, 1933.

────. *The Elementary Forms of the Religious Life*. New York: Free Press, 1965 (1915).

Eder, Klaus. *Die Entstehung staatlich organisierten Gesellschaften*. Frankfurt-am-Main: Suhrkamp, 1976.

────, ed: *Seminar: Die Enstehung von Klassen-Gesellschaften*. Frankfurt-am-Main: Suhrkamp, 1973.

Eisenstadt, S. W. *The Protestant Ethic and Modernization*. New York: Basic Books, 1968.

Eliade, Mircea. *A History of Religious Ideas*. Vol. 1, *From the Stone Age to the Eleusinian Mysteries*. Vol. 2, *From Guatama Buddha to the Triumph of Christianity*. Chicago: University of Chicago Press, 1978, 1982.

———. *Myths, Dreams and Mysteries*. New York: Harper Torchbooks, 1963.

———. *The Quest: History and Meaning in Religion*. Chicago: University of Chicago Press, 1969.

Emerson, Ralph Waldo. *Collected Works*. Edited by Alfred K. Ferguson. Cambridge, Mass.: Belknap, 1971.

Erikson, Erik. *Young Man Luther*. New York: Norton, 1962 (1958).

Fanfani, Amintore. *Protestantism and Catholicism*. New York: Sheed and Ward, 1938.

Faulkner, Joseph E., ed. *Religion's Influence in Contemporary Society*. Columbus: Bobbs-Merrill, 1972.

Feuerbach, Ludwig. *The Essence of Christianity*. New York: Harper Torchbooks, 1957.

Fetscher, Iring, ed. *Marxismus Studien*. Tübingen: J. C. B. Mohr, 1962.

Fichte, Johann G. *Schriften zur Revolution*. Edited by Benjamin Will. Frankfurt-am-Main: Suhrkamp, 1967.

———. *Werke*. Edited by Fritz Medicus. Leipzig: Felix Meiner, n.d.

Fleischmann, Eugène. "De Weber à Nietzsche." *Archives Européennes de Sociologie* 5, no. 2 (1964).

———. "Metamorphoses Wéberiennes." *Archives Européennes de Sociologie* 5, no. 1 (1964).

Flew, Anthony, and MacIntyre, Alasdair, eds. *New Essays in Politics and Theology*. London: Macmillan, 1955.

Freud, Sigmund. *Civilization and Its Discontents*. London: Hogarth, 1953 (1930).

———. *The Future of an Illusion*. New York: Anchor, 1964 (1927).

———. *Moses and Monotheism*. New York: Vintage, 1967 (1939).

———. *Totem and Taboo*. New York: Vintage, n.d. (1913).

Fromm, Erich. *The Dogma of Christ*. New York: Holt, Rinehart and Winston, 1963.

Gallup, George, Jr., and Poling, David. *The Search for America's Faith*. Nashville: Abingdon, 1980.

Garaudy, Roger. *Gott ist tot*. Vienna: Europäische Verlagsanstalt, 1965 (1962).

Gay, Peter. *The Enlightenment*. New York: Norton, 1977 (1969).

———. *Weimar Culture*. New York: Harper Torchbooks, 1970 (1968).

Gibbon, Edward. *Decline and Fall of the Roman Empire*. New York: Washington Square, 1962.

Giddens, Anthony. *Capitalism and Modern Social Theory*. Cambridge: Cambridge University Press, 1972.

———. *A Contemporary Critique of Historical Materialism*. Berkeley and Los Angeles: University of California Press, 1981.

Gilder, George. *Wealth and Poverty*. New York: Basic Books, 1981.

———. "The Moral Sources of Capitalism." *Society* 18, no. 6 (September–October 1981).

Glasner, Peter. *Sociology of Secularization.* London: Routledge and Kegan Paul, 1977.

Glazer, Nathan. "Toward a New Concordat." *This World* (Summer 1982).

Glock, Charles. "On the Study of Religious Commitment." In *Religion's Influence in Contemporary Society.* Edited by Joseph E. Faulkner. Columbus: Bobbs-Merrill, 1972.

Goethe, J. W. *Faust.* Basel: Birkhauser, 1944.

———. *Gespräche.* Edited by Wolfgang Herwid. Zurich and Stuttgart: Artemis, 1972.

Goldmann, Lucien. *Le Dieu caché.* Paris: Gallimard, 1955.

———. *Immanuel Kant.* London: New Left Books, 1971.

Gollwitzer, Helmut. "Marxistische Religionskritik und christlicher Glaube." No. 7 in *Marxismus Studien,* edited by Iring Fetscher. Tübingen: J. C. B. Mohr, 1962.

Gouldner, Alvin W. *The Coming Crisis of Western Sociology.* New York: Basic Books, 1970.

Gramsci, Antonio, *Quaderni del carcere.* Turin: Einaudi, 1966.

Greeley, Andrew, et al. *Catholic Schools in a Declining Church.* Kansas City: Sheed and Ward, 1976.

Groethuysen, Bernard. *Origine de l'esprit bourgeois en France.* Paris: Gallimard, 1971 (1927).

Grossmann, H. "Die gesellschaftlichen Grundlagen der mechanistischen Philosophie und die Manufactur." *Zeitschrift für Sozialforschung*, no. 2 (1935).

Habermas, Jürgen. "Dialectics of Rationalization: An Interview." *Telos* 49 (Fall 1981).

———. *Legitimationsprobleme in Spät-Kapitalismus.* Frankfurt-am-Main: Suhrkamp, 1975.

———. *Technik und Wissenschaft als "Ideologie."* Frankfurt-am-Main: Suhrkamp, 1981.

———*Theorie des kommunikativen Handelns.* Frankfurt-am-Main; Suhrkamp, 1981.

———. *Zur Rekonstruktion des historische Materialismus.* Frankfurt-am-Main: Suhrkamp, 1976.

Habermas, Jürgen, and Luhmann, Niklas. *Theorie der Gesellschaft oder Sozialtechnologie.* Frankfurt-am-Main: Suhrkamp, 1974.

Hales, E. Y. *Pio Nono.* New York: P. J. Kennedy, 1954.

Harrington, Michael. *The Accidental Century.* New York: Macmillan, 1965.

———. *Socialism.* New York: Saturday Review, 1972.

———. *Twilight of Capitalism.* New York: Simon and Schuster, 1976.

Harris, Marvin. *Cultural Materialism.* New York: Vintage, 1980.

———. *The Rise of Anthropological Theory.* New York: Crowell, 1968.

Hegel, G. W. F. *Briefe von und an Hegel.* Edited by Johannes Hoffmeister. Hamburg: Felix Meiner, 1969.

———. *Hegel's sämtliche Werke.* Edited by Hermann Glockner. Stuttgart: Fromann, 1927–1930.

———. *Jenaer Realphilosophie.* Hamburg: Felix Meiner, 1969.

———. *Theologische Jugendschriften.* Edited by Hermann Nohl. Tübingen: J. C. B. Mohr. 1907.

———. *Werke in zwanzig Bänden.* Frankfurt-am-Main: Suhrkamp, 1969.

Heilbroner, Robert. *Business Civilization in Decline.* New York: Norton, 1976.

Heine, Heinrich. *Selected Works.* Edited by Helen M. Mustard. New York: Vintage, 1973.

Herberg, Will. *Protestant, Catholic, Jew.* Rev. ed. New York: Anchor, 1960.

Hess, Moses. *Judische Schriften.* Edited by Theodor Zlocisti. New York: Arno, 1980.

Hill, Christopher. *Change and Continuity in Seventeenth Century England.* London: Weidenfeld and Nicolson, 1974.

———. *The World Turned Upside Down.* New York: Viking, 1972.

Himmelstein, Jerome L. "God, Gilder and Capitalism." *Society* (September–October 1981).

Hippolyte, Jean. *Genèse et structure de la phénomenologie.* Paris: Aubier Montaigne, 1946.

Hirsch, Fred. *Social Limits to Growth.* Cambridge: Cambridge University Press, 1976.

Hobsbawm, Eric. *Labouring Men.* New York: Basic Books, 1964.

———. *Pre-Capitalist Economic Formations.* New York: International Publishers, 1969.

———. "Religion and the Rise of Socialism." *Marxist Perspectives* 1, no. 1 (Spring 1978).

Hofstadter, Richard. *The Age of Reform.* New York: Vintage, 1955.

———. *The Paranoid Style in American Politics.* New York: Alfred A. Knopf, 1965.

Horkheimer, Max, and Adorno, Theodor. *Dialektik der Aufklärung.* Amsterdam: Querido, 1947.

Horvat, Branko. *The Political Economy of Socialism.* Armonk, N.Y.: M. E. Sharpe. 1982.

Howe, Irving. *Decline of the New.* New York: Harcourt Brace Jovanovich, 1970.

Hughes, H. Stuart. *Consciousness and Society.* New York: Vintage, 1960.

Huizinga, J. *The Waning of the Middle Ages.* New York: Anchor, 1954 (1924).

Hume, David. *David Hume on Religion.* New York: Meridian, 1963.

Huntington, Samuel P. *American Politics: The Promise of Disharmony.* Cambridge, Mass.: Belknap, 1981.

Institute for Educational Affairs–Roper Center. "Theology Faculty Survey." *This World* (Summer 1982).

James, William. *The Varieties of Religious Experience.* New Hyde Park, N.Y.: University Books, 1963.

Jaquet, Constant H. *Yearbook of American and Canadian Churches, 1981.* Nashville: Abingdon, 1981.

Jaspers, Karl. *Nietzsche.* Berlin: Walter de Gruyter, 1950.

———. *Der philosophische Glaube.* Zurich: Artemis, 1948.

Jaures, Jean. *Les Origines du socialisme allemand*. Paris: Maspéro, 1960.

Jay, Martin, *The Dialectical Imagination*. Boston: Little, Brown, 1972.

Jeanmaire, H. *Dionysius: Histoire du culte de Bacchus*. Paris: Payot, 1978.

Jencks, Christopher. *Inequality*. New York: Basic Books, 1972.

Jones, Ernest. *The Life and Work of Sigmund Freud*. Edited and abridged by L. Trilling and S. Marcus. New York: Anchor, 1963.

Jung, C. G. *Collected Works*. Princeton, N.J.: Princeton University Press, 1969.

Kaempfert, Manfred. *Säkularization und neue Heiligkeit*. Berlin: Erich Schmidt, 1971.

Kander, Johannes. "Garantien der Harmonie und Freiheit." *Die neue Gesellschaft* (January 1981).

Kant, Immanuel. *Gesammelte Schriften*. Prussian Academy edition. Berlin: George Reimer, 1911.

Kaufmann, Walter. *Hegel: A Reinterpretation*. New York: Anchor, 1965.

———. *Nietzsche*. 4th ed. Princeton, N.J.: Princeton University Press, 1974.

———, ed. *Hegel's Political Philosophy*. New York: Atherton, 1970.

Kautsky, Karl. *Foundations of Christianity*. New York: Augustus Kelly, 1958.

Kelley, Dean. *Why the Conservative Churches Are Growing*. New York: Harper & Row, 1972.

Kerenyi, Karl. *Dionysos: Archetypical Image of Indestructible Life*. Princeton, N.J.: Princeton University Press, 1976.

Kierkegaard, Søren. *Attack upon "Christendom."* Edited by Walter Lowrie. Princeton, N.J.: Princeton University Press, 1968.

Kolakowski, Leszek. *Main Currents of Marxism*. Oxford: Clarendon Press, 1978.

———. "The Priest and the Jester." *Dissent* (Summer 1962).

———. *Religion*. Oxford: Oxford University Press, 1982.

———. *Toward a Marxist Humanism*. New York: Grove, 1968.

Kosik, Karel. *Dialektik des Konkreten*. Frankfurt-am-Main: Suhrkamp, 1976.

Krieger, Leonard. *The German Idea of Freedom*. Chicago: University of Chicago Press, 1957.

Kristol, Irving. "About Equality." *Commentary* (November 1972).

Küng, Hans. *Does God Exist?* New York: Doubleday, 1980.

Lamennais, H.-F. *Paroles d'un croyant*. Paris: Garnier Frères, n.d.

Le Bras, Gabriel. *Etudes de sociologie religieuse*. Paris: PUF, 1955.

Lederer, Emil. *State of the Masses*. New York: Norton, 1940.

Lenin, V. I. *Collected Works*. Moscow: Progress Publishers, 1966.

Lenski, Gerhard. *The Religious Factor*. New York: Anchor, 1963.

Leser, Norbert. *Zwischen Reformismus und Bolschewismus*. Vienna: Europa, 1968.

Lévi-Strauss, Claude. *Anthropologie structurelle deux*. Paris: Plon, 1973.

———. *La Pensée sauvage*. Paris: Plon, 1962.

Lewy, Guenter. *Religion and Revolution*. Oxford: Oxford University Press, 1974.

Lichtheim, George. *The Concept of Ideology*. New York: Vintage, 1967.

——. *From Marx to Hegel*. New York: Seabury Press, 1974.

——. *Marxism*. New York: Praeger, 1961.

——. *Origins of Socialism*. New York: Praeger, 1969.

——. *A Short Hisotry of Socialism*. New York: Praeger, 1970.

Linesch, Michael. "Uncivil Religion: The Ideological Origins of the Religious Right." Unpublished paper. New England Political Science Association, November 13, 1981.

Lipsett, Seymour Martin. *The First New Nation*. New York: Anchor, 1967.

Lipsett, Seymour Martin, and Raab, Earl. *The Politics of Unreason*. 2nd ed. Chicago: University of Chicago Press, 1978.

Lobkowicz, Nicholas. *Theory and Practice: History of a Concept from Aristotle to Marx*. Notre Dame, Ind.: University of Notre Dame Press, 1967.

Löwith, Karl. *From Hegel to Nietzsche*. New York: Anchor, 1967.

——. *Gesammelte Abhandlungen: Zur Kritik der geschichtlichen Existenz*. Stuttgart: Kohlhammer, 1960.

——. *Nietzsches Philosophie der ewigen Wiederkehr des Gleichen*. Stuttgart: Kohlhammer, 1956.

——, ed. *Die Hegelsche Linke*. Stuttgart: Fromann, 1962.

Lubac, Henri de. *Le Drame de l'humanisme athée*. Paris: Spes, 1944.

——. *Proudhon et le christianisme*. Paris: Seuil, 1945.

Luckmann, Thomas. *The Invisible Religion*. New York; Macmillan, 1967.

——. "Verfall, Fortesbestand, oder Verwandlung des Religiosen in der modernen Gesellschaft?" In *Hat Religion Zukunft?*, ed. by Oskar Schatz. Styria, Graz, Vienna, Cologne, 1971.

Luhmann, Niklas. *Funktion der Religion*. Frankfurt-am-Main: Suhrkamp, 1977.

——. "Die Weltgesellschaft." In *Archiv für Recht und sozial Philosophie (ARSP) 1971*.

Lukacs, Georg. *Geschichte und Klassenbewusstsein*. Berlin: Malik, 1923.

——. *Goethe und seine Zeit*. Berlin: Aufbau, 1955.

——. *Der junge Hegel*. Berlin: Aufbau, 1954.

——. *Die Zerstörung der Vernunft*. Neuwied: Luchterhand,1961.

Machiavelli, Niccolò. *The Prince and Selected Discourses*. New York: Bantam, 1971.

MacIntyre, Alasdair. *Against the Self Image of the Age*. Notre Dame, Ind.: University of Notre Dame Press, 1978.

MacIntyre, Alasdair, and Ricoeur, Paul. *The Religious Significance of Atheism*. New York: Columbia University Press, 1969.

McClellan, David. *Karl Marx*. New York: Harper & Row, 1973.

McPherson, C. B. *Political Theory of Possessive Individualism*. Oxford: Oxford University Press, 1962.

Malraux, André. *Antimémoires*. Paris: Gallimard, 1967.

——. *The Voices of Silence*. Translated by Stuart Gilbert. New York: Doubleday, 1953.

Manuel, Frank. *The New World of Henri Saint-Simon*. Cambridge, Mass.: Harvard University Press, 1956.

Marcuse, Herbert. *Eros and Civilization.* New York: Vintage, 1962.
———. *One Dimensional Man.* Boston: Beacon, 1964.
———. *Soviet Marxism.* New York: Columbia University Press, 1958.
Maritain, Jacques. *The Social and Philosophical Thought of Jacques Maritain.* Edited by Joseph W. Evans and Leo Ward. Garden City, N.Y.: Doubleday, 1955.
Marsden, George M. *Fundamentalism and American Culture.* Oxford: Oxford University Press, 1980.
Martin, David. *A General Theory of Secularization.* New York: Harper & Row, 1978.
———. "Revived Dogma and New Cult." *Daedalus* (Winter 1982).
Marty, Martin. *A Nation of Behavers.* Chicago: University of Chicago Press, 1976.
———. "Religion in America Since Mid-Century." *Daedalus* (Winter 1982).
Marx, Karl. *Die Ethnologische Exzerpthefte.* Edited by Lawrence Krader. Frankfurt-am-Main: Suhrkamp, 1976.
———. *Grundrisse der Kritik der politischen Oekonomie.* Berlin: Dietz, 1953.
Marx, Karl, and Engels, Friedrich. *Werke.* Berlin: Dietz, 1960– .
Mathiez, Albert. *Les Origines des cultes révolutionnaires.* Paris: Société Nouvelle de Librairie et d'Edition, 1904.
Matthes, Joachim. *Beitrag zur Religions-soziologischen Forschung.* Verlag Koln und Opladen, 1968.
Mayer, Gustav. *Friedrich Engels.* The Hague: Martinus Nijoff, 1934.
Mead, George Herbert. *Works.* Vol. 1, *Mind, Self and Society.* Chicago: University of Chicago Press, 1972 (1934).
Mehring, Franz. *Geschichte der deutschen sozial Demokratie.* Berlin: Dietz, 1960.
Mehta, Ved. *The New Theologians.* New York: Harper & Row, 1965.
Merleau-Ponty, Maurice. *Les Aventures de la dialectique.* Paris: Gallimard, 1955.
Merton, Robert, *Social Theory and Social Structure.* Rev. ed. New York: Free Press, 1968.
Metz, Johann Baptist. *Faith in History and Society.* New York: Seabury, 1980.
Miranda, José. *Marx and the Bible.* Maryknoll, N.Y.: Orbis, 1971.
Moltmann, Jürgen. *The Crucified God.* New York: Harper & Row, 1974.
———. *Religion, Revolution and the Future.* New York: Scribner's, 1969.
Moore, Barrington. *Injustice: The Social Bases of Obedience and Revolt.* Boston: Beacon, 1979.
———. *Social Origins of Democracy and Dictatorship.* Boston: Beacon, 1966.
Mote, Frederick. *Intellectual Foundations of China.* New York: Alfred A. Knopf, 1971.
Murchland, Bernard, ed. *The Meaning of the Death of God.* New York: Random House, 1967.

Niebuhr, H. Richard. *The Social Sources of Denominationalism.* Cleveland: Meridian, 1964 (1929).

262 · BIBLIOGRAPHY

Nietzsche, Friedrich. *Werke.* Edited by Giorgio Colli and Mazzino Montinari. Berlin: Walter de Gruyter, 1981.
———. *Werke in drei Bänden.* Edited by Karl Schlechta. Munich: Karl Hansen, 1966.

Ortega y Gasset, José. *La deshumanización del arte.* Madrid: El Arquero, 1976.
Otto, Rudolf. *The Idea of the Holy.* Oxford: Oxford University Press, 1970 (1923).

Parsons, Talcott. *Action Theory and the Human Condition.* New York: Free Press, 1978.
———. "Belief, Unbelief and Disbelief." In *The Culture of Unbelief,* edited by R. Caporale and A. Grumelli. Berkeley and Los Angeles: University of California Press, 1971.
———. "The Church in an Urban Environment." In *Religion's Influence in Contemporary Society.* Columbus: Bobbs-Merrill, 1972.
Pascal, Blaise. *Pensées.* Paris: Livres de Poche, 1972.
Paz, Octavio. *El laberinto de la soledád.* 8th ed. Mexico City: Fonda de Cultura Economica, 1980.
Phillips, Kevin. *Post-Conservative America.* New York: Random House, 1982.
Plant, Raymond. *Hegel.* Bloomington: University of Indiana Press, 1973.
———. "Hegel's Social Theory." *New Left Reviews.* Nos. 103 and 104 (1977).
Plato. *Laws.* Translated by Trevor Sanders. Baltimore: Penguin, 1975.
Plongeron, Bernard. *Conscience religieuse en révolution.* Paris: A and J Picard, 1969.
Poggioli, Renato. *The Theory of the Avant Garde.* Cambridge, Mass.: Belknap, 1968.
Portelli, Hughes. *Gramsci et la question religieuse.* Paris: Anthropos, 1974.

Rahner, Karl. *Foundations of the Christian Faith.* Seabury, N.Y.: Crossroads, 1978.
Reich, Wilhelm. *The Mass Psychology of Fascism.* New York: Farrar, Straus & Giroux, 1970.
———. *Sex-Pol: Essays 1929–1934.* Edited by Lee Baxandal. New York: Vintage, 1972.
Reik, Theodor. *Der eigene und der fremde Gott.* Frankfurt-am-Main: Suhrkamp, 1975 (1923).
Ricoeur, Paul. *The Symbolism of Evil.* Boston: Beacon, 1967.
Ritter, Joachim. *Metaphysik und Politik.* Frankfurt-am-Main: Suhrkamp, 1969.
Rosenzweig, Franz. *Hegel und der Staat.* Munich and Berlin: Oldenbourg, 1920.
Rosten, Leo, ed. *Religions in America.* New York: Simon and Schuster, 1975.
Roszak, Theodore. *The Making of a Counter Culture.* New York: Anchor, 1969.
Rousseau, Jean-Jacques. *The Essential Rousseau.* Translated by Lowell Blair. New York: NAL, 1974.
———. *Social Contract.* New York: NAL, 1974.

Saboul, Albert. *Paysans, sans-culottes et Jacobins.* Paris: Librairie Clavreuil, 1966.

Sahlins, Marshall. *Stone Age Economics.* New York: Aldine, 1979 (1972).

Saint-Simon, Claude-Henri. *Doctrine de Saint-Simon.* Edited by Bougle and Halévy. Paris: Marcel Rivière, 1924.

————. *Oeuvres.* Paris: Anthropos, 1966.

————. *Selected Writings.* Translated by Keith Taylor. London: Croom Helm, 1975.

Sammons, Jeffrey. *Heinrich Heine: A Modern Biography.* Princeton, N.J.: Princeton University Press, 1979.

Samuelson, Kurt. *Religion and Economic Action: A Critique of Max Weber.* New York: Harper Torchbooks, 1961.

Sandkuhler, Hans, ed. *Marxismus und Ethik.* Frankfurt-am-Main: Suhrkamp, 1974.

Saner, Hans. *Kant's Political Thought.* Chicago: University of Chicago Press, 1973.

Schapiro, Leonard. *The Communist Party of the Soviet Union.* New York: Random House, 1960.

Schatz, Oskar, ed. *Hat Religion Zukunft?* Graz, Vienna, and Cologne: Styria, 1971.

Schillebeeckx, Edward. *Jesus.* New York: Vintage, 1981.

Schiller, J. C. F. *Werke.* Leipzig: Bibliographische Institut, n.d.

Schleiermacher, Friedrich. *On Religion.* Richmond: John Knox, 1969 (1806; notes, 1821).

Schopenhauer, Arthur. *Die Welt als Wille und Vorstellung.* Leipzig: Brockhaus, 1859.

Schumpeter, Joseph. *Capitalism, Socialism and Democracy.* Rev. ed. New York: Harper & Row, 1950.

Simmel, Georg. *Sociology of Religion.* New York: Philosophic Library, 1959.

Sölle, Dorothee. *Atheistisch an Gott glauben.* Walter Verlag Olten und Freiburg im Breisgau, 1968.

————. *Christ the Representative.* Philadelphia: Fortress, 1967.

————. *Politische Theologie.* Stuttgart: Kreuz, 1982.

Sorokin, Pitirim. *Social and Cultural Dynamics.* Boston: Porter Sargeant, 1957.

Southern, R. W. *Western Society and the Church in the Middle Ages.* Baltimore: Penguin, 1977.

Spengler, Oswald. *Prussianism and Socialism.* Chicago: Regnery, 1968 (1918).

————. *Der Untergang des Abendlandes.* Abridged ed. Munich: C. H. Beck, 1959.

Stalin, Joseph. *History of the Communist Party of the Soviet Union (Bolsheviks).* New York: International Publishers, 1939.

Stern, Fritz. *The Politics of Cultural Despair.* Berkeley and Los Angeles: University of California Press, 1961.

Strong, Tracy. *Friedrich Nietzsche and the Politics of Transformation.* Berkeley and Los Angeles: University of California Press, 1975.

Strout, Cushing. *The New Heavens and New Earth.* New York: Harper & Row, 1973.

Taylor, Charles. *Hegel*. Oxford: Oxford University Press, 1975.
Thompson, E. P. *The Making of the English Working Class*. Baltimore: Penguin, 1963.
———. *The Poverty of Theory*. New York: Monthly Review, 1978.
Tillich, Paul. *The Socialist Decision*. New York: Harper & Row, 1977.
———. *Theology of Culture*. Oxford: Oxford University Press, 1959.
Titmus, Richard. *The Gift Relation*. New York: Pantheon, 1971.
Toynbee, Arnold J. *Civilization on Trial*. New York: Oxford University Press, 1948.
Trilling, Lionel. *The Opposing Self*. New York: Harcourt Brace Jovanovich, 1979.
Troeltsch, Ernst. *The Social Teachings of the Christian Churches*. Glencoe: Free Press, 1949.
Tuchman, Barbara. *A Distant Mirror*. New York: Ballantine, 1978.

U.S. Department of Commerce. *Social Indicators, 1976*. Washington, D.C.: GPO, 1976.

Vidler, Alec. *The Church in an Age of Revolution*. Rev. ed. Baltimore: Penguin, 1974.
Voltaire. *Essais sur les moeurs et l'esprit des nations*. Paris: Garnier Frères, 1963.
Vorlander, Karl. *Kant und Marx*. Rev. ed. Tübingen: J. C. B. Mohr, 1926.
Vranicki, Pedrag. *Geschichte des Marxismus*. Frankfurt-am-Main: Suhrkamp, 1972.

Wallerstein, Emmanuel. *The Capitalist World Economy*. Cambridge: Cambridge University Press, 1979.
———. *The Modern World System*. New York: Academic Press, 1974.
Weber, Max. *Economy and Society*. Edited by Guenther Roth and Claus Wittich. Berkeley and Los Angeles: University of California Press, 1979.
———. *Gesammelte Aufsätze zur Religions-Soziologie*. Tübingen: J. C. B. Mohr, 1972 (1920).
Wedgewood, C. V. *The Thirty Years War*. New York: Methuen, 1982.
Weidenholzer, Josef. *Auf dem Weg zum "neuen Menschen."* Vienna: Europa, 1981.
Wetter, Gustav. *Der dialektische Materialismus*. Vienna: Herder, 1958.
Whitehead, Alfred North. *Science and the Modern World*. New York: Free Press, 1967.
Wuthnow, Robert. "The Moral Crisis in American Capitalism." *Harvard Business Review* (March-April 1982).

NOTES

Full bibliographic information can be found in the Bibliography.

PAGE   **1: A BOOK CRYING WOLF**

1 ". . . the discovery of infinite geometric space . . .": Lucien Gold-mann, *Le Dieu caché*, p. 45.

1n Theodor Reik . . . Rosemary Ruether: Theodor Reik, *Der eigene und der fremde Gott*, pp. 63–64; Carol P. Christ and Judith Plaskow, eds., *Womanspirit Rising*, p. 49.

2 Napoleon asked an astronomer: Hans Küng, *Does God Exist?*, p. 82.

2 For Hegel on Pascal, see his *Werke in zwanzig Bänden*, II, p. 11.

2 The Enlightenment . . . had replaced: Ibid., III, p. 423.

2 The mature Hegel: Ibid., XVII, p. 343

2 "Do you hear . . .": Heinrich Heine, *Selected Works*, p. 365.

3 "the central question of politics . . .": Isaiah Berlin quoted in Richard Titmus, *The Gift Relation*, p. 237.

3 Presbyterian Church: Alec Vidler, *The Church in an Age of Revolution*, p. 237.

3 "famine of the churches . . .": Ralph Waldo Emerson, *Collected Works*, I, pp. 85, 88.

3 "unshakeable faith . . .": J. Huizinga, *The Waning of the Middle Ages*, pp. 160–62.

3 For Nietzsche on God's shadow, see his *The Gay Science*, Book III, paragraph 105. (For a bibliographic comment on Nietzsche see the note to page 84 on page 275.)

4 "*is an element in the structure . . .*": Mircea Eliade, *The Quest: History and Meaning in Religion*, Preface (not numbered).

4 religion is . . . "relocating": Martin Marty, "Religion in America Since Mid-Century," p. 154.

4 "retreat to the private world . . .": Daniel Bell quoted in Mary Douglas, "The Effect of Modernization on Religious Change," p. 13.

5 For Rome and China, see Küng, *Does God Exist?*, p. 588ff.

5 "have regarded the cosmos and man . . .": Frederick Mote, *Intellectual Foundations of China*, pp. 18, 27.

6 "institutional specialization": Thomas Luckmann, *The Invisible Religion*, p. 68.

6 "a medieval cathedral . . . further destiny": Karel Kosik, *Dialektik des Konkreten*, pp. 123, 136–37.

10 "a sensation of 'eternity' . . .": Sigmund Freud, *Civilization and Its Discontents*, p. 8.

10 "religious nature without religion": Georg Simmel, *Sociology of Religion*, p. 84.

11 the contemporary Catholic theologian: Jürgen Moltmann, *The Crucified God*, p. 224.

PAGE   **2: THE CRISIS OF FAITH AND REASON**

12–13 The population of the world: Carlo Cipolla, *Economic History of World Population*, pp. 33, 52–53; see also Pierre Chaunu, *Histoire et décadence*, pp. 140, 203.

13 In 1500, Europe knew less: Alfred North Whitehead, *Science and the Modern World*, pp. 9, 40.

13 Aristarchus of Samos: Chaunu, *Histoire et décadence*, pp. 94–97.

13 China made steady, gradual progress: Fernand Braudel, *Capitalism and Material Life*, p. 277.

13 " 'holy alliance between science . . .' ": Robert Merton, *Social Theory and Social Structure*, p. 653.

14 "to the Glory . . .": Ibid., p. 630.

14 "Previously one assumed . . .": Immanuel Kant, *Gesammelte Schriften*, III, p. 12.

14 For Fichte on "I," see his *Werke*, I, p. 411.

14 For Fichte on politics, see ibid., pp. 472, 483–88, and see his *Schriften zur Revolution*, p. 118.

15 "The history of Kant's life . . .": Heinrich Heine, *Selected Works*, p. 368.

15 "There can scarcely be . . .": Leszek Kolakowski, *Main Currents of Marxism*, I, pp. 47–48.

15 On Newton's God, see E. A. Burtt, *The Metaphysical Foundations of Modern Science*, pp. 297–99.

15–16 For Kant on experience, see his *Gesammelte Schriften*, IV, p. 108ff.

17 For Kant on God, see ibid., III, p. 403ff.

17–18 "This book is the sword . . .": Heine, *Selected Works*, p. 379ff.

18 Kantian terms: Dietrich Bonhoeffer, *Letters and Papers from Prison*, p. 140.

19   For Kant on history, see his *Gesammelte Schriften*, VIII, pp. 17, 20, 22–23, 27. For contrasting interpretations, see Hans Saner, *Kant's Political Thought*, p. 169, and Leonard Krieger, *The German Idea of Freedom*, p. 95.

19–20   Why does evil exist: Leszek Kolakowski, *Religion*, Chapter 1.

20   ". . . new subject of responsibility . . .": Ernst Cassirer, *The Question of Jean-Jacques Rousseau*, p. 75.

20   "we are *structured* . . .": E. P. Thompson, *The Poverty of Theory*, p. 153.

20   On Kant and freedom, see Kant, *Gesammelte Schriften*, IV, pp. 454, 462–63.

21   ". . . *limiting condition* . . .": Ibid., pp. 430–31.

21   ". . . such an assumption . . .": Hans Küng, *Does God Exist?*, p. 545.

21   "civilized custom": Fred Hirsch, *Social Limits to Growth*, p. 117.

21   "an event of our age . . .": Kant, *Gesammelte Schriften*, VII, p. 85.

22   a Foreword which capitulated: Ibid., p. 7ff.

22   against the overthrow: Ibid., V, 375n.

22   from the "generic" to the "genetic": Ernst Cassirer, *Rousseau, Kant, Goethe*, p. 69.

23   "even if they do not make men . . .": Kant, *Gesammelte Schriften*, V, p. 432ff.

23   most utopian of his writings: Ibid., VI, pp. 115ff.

23   Kant as . . . John the Baptist: Lucien Goldmann, *Immanuel Kant*, p. 205.

23   great Protestant: Karl Barth, *Protestant Theology in the Nineteenth Century*, p. 291ff.

24   "a great Lord . . .": Kant, *Gesammelte Schriften*, VI, pp. 121–22.

24   "The veiled goddess . . .": Ernst Cassirer, *Kant's Life and Thought*, pp. 382–86.

24   "the starry skies . . .": Kant, *Gesammelte Schriften*, V, p. 161ff.

25   "This mystery is not . . .": Napoleon Bonaparte quoted in Alex Vidler, *The Church in an Age of Revolution*, p. 19.

25   difficult question in history: Barrington Moore, *Injustice: The Social Bases of Obedience and Revolt*, p. 49.

25–26   "the first thing these people say . . .": Plato, *Laws*, pp. 417, 442–43.

26   ". . . city without temples . . .": Plutarch quoted in Antonio Gramsci, *Quaderni del carcere*, VI, p. 292.

26   "It is convenient . . .": Ovid quoted in Peter Gay, *The Enlightenment*, I, p. 154.

26   ". . . religion for the state . . .": Montesquieu quoted in ibid., p. 155.

26   ". . . modes of worship . . .": Edward Gibbon, *Decline and Fall of the Roman Empire*, I, pp. 14, 17.

26   "no theology . . .": Gay, *The Enlightenment*, I, p. 166.

26   David Hume thought: Ibid., pp. 167, 169.

26 "Roman Christianity": Jean-Jacques Rousseau, *The Essential Rousseau*, p. 109ff.

27 Voltaire . . . wrote . . . to Diderot: Gay, *The Enlightenment*, II, p. 521.

27 "In a future age . . .": David Hume, *David Hume on Religion*, p. 15.

28 anecdote about Voltaire: Gay, *The Enlightenment*, I, p. 526.

28 Gibbon talked: Ibid., p. 395.

28 " 'I believe! . . . ' ": Ibid., p. 122.

28 ". . . Voltaire found his readers . . .": Gabriel Le Bras, *Etudes de sociologie religieuse*, II, p. 406.

29 "socializes the bourgeois mind . . .": Joseph Schumpeter, *Capitalism, Socialism and Democracy*, pp. 145, 153–54, 157, 331.

29 motivated both by a hypocritical desire: Irving Kristol, "About Equality," p. 37.

29 ". . . capitalism is an edifice . . .": George Gilder, *Wealth and Poverty*, p. 7.

30 "take back" Kant: Max Horkheimer and Theodor Adorno, *Dialektik der Aufklärung*, pp. 105–05, 138.

31 Lukacs joined together . . . Marx and . . . Weber: Jürgen Habermas, *Theorie des kommunikativen Handelns*, II, pp. 489–90.

31 "Bio-technology becomes . . .": London *Economist*, June 13, 1981.

31 ". . . far exceeding human ability": *Business Week*, July 6, 1981.

32 The myth of Eden: Horkheimer and Adorno, *Dialektik*, p. 212.

32 "Where religion . . .": Herbert Marcuse, *Eros and Civilization*, p. 66.

34 "But should these . . . ethical powers . . .": Kant, *Gesammelte Schriften*, VI, p. 449.

PAGE   **3: "TO KILL GOD AND BUILD A CHURCH"**

35 "A rain of Gods . . .": Leszek Kolakowski, "The Priest and the Jester," p. 234.

35 "To kill God . . .": Albert Camus, *L'Homme révolté*, p. 131.

36 "From the simple fact . . .": Jean-Jacques Rousseau, *Social Contract*, pp. 6, 9.

36 "without temples . . .": Ibid., p. 109.

36 "religion within . . . reason": Leonard Krieger, *The German Idea of Freedom*, p. 87

36 "Aside from that . . . the positive law": Rousseau, *Social Contract*, p. 113.

37 "Maximilien Robespierre . . .": Heinrich Heine, *Selected Works*, p.368. For a contemporary scholar making much the same point, see A. Aulard, *Histoire politique de la révolution française*, p.422.

37   sacred things: Emile Durkheim, *The Elementary Forms of the Religious Life*, p. 245; see also Albert Mathiez, *Les Origines des cultes révolutionnaires*, passim.

37   "de-Christianization": Bernard Plongeron, *Conscience religieuse en révolution*, p. 118.

37   "ideologues": George Lichtheim, *The Concept of Ideology*, pp. 4–5, 10, 27.

37–38   For Napoleon on the ideologues, see Lichtheim, ibid., p. 5 and n. 5.

38   spontaneous cults of the masses: Albert Saboul, *Paysans, sansculottes et Jacobins*, p. 189.

38   For Plongeron on the same phenomenon, see his *Conscience religieuse*, p. 149.

38   In Mexico: Octavio Paz, *El laberinto de la soledád*, p. 76.

38   "the myth of origin": Paul Tillich, *The Socialist Decision*, p. 5.

38   ". . . political revolution . . .": James Billington, *Fire in the Minds of Men*, p. 9.

39   "that the industrial working class . . .": Alasdair MacIntyre and Paul Ricoeur, *The Religious Significance of Atheism*, p. 43.

39   "the French communists . . .": Karl Marx and Friedrich Engels, *Werke*, I, p. 487.

39   ". . . thresholds of . . . modern disbelief": Gabriel Le Bras, *Etudes de sociologie religieuse*, I, p. 208.

39   religious geography: Ibid., II, p. 740.

40   Saint-Simon was . . . seminal: George Lichtheim, *A Short History of Socialism*, pp. 43–44.

40   "masters and slaves . . .": Claude-Henri Saint-Simon, *Doctrine de Saint-Simon*.

40   For Saint-Simon on the Middle Ages, see G. D. H. Cole, *History of Socialist Thought*, I, p. 41.

40   "Council of Newton": Claude-Henri Saint-Simon, *Oeuvres*, I, pp. 49–52.

40–41   Saint-Simon found support: Lichtheim, *Short History of Socialism*, p. 44; Frank Manuel, *The New World of Henri Saint-Simon*, p. 340.

41   "The Catholic system . . .": Claude-Henri Saint-Simon, *Selected Writings*, p. 224.

41   new "Christianity": Ibid., p. 289.

41   de Maistre and Bonald: Jeffrey Sammons, *Heinrich Heine: A Modern Biography*, p. 164.

41–42   "The originality . . .": George Lichtheim, *Origins of Socialism*, pp. 44–45.

42   Goethe was deeply influenced: Albert Bielschowsky, *Life of Goethe*, p. 192; Marshall Berman, *All That Is Solid Melts into Air*, p. 72.

42   "the human race . . .": J. W. Goethe, *Gespräche*, III-2, p. 640.

43   utopia leaves the sky: Ernst Bloch, *Das Prinzip Hoffnung*, II, p. 1194.

43 as Marshall Berman argued: Berman, *All That Is Solid*, p. 73.
43 workers made their own interpretation: Saint-Simon, *Doctrine*, p. 203 nn. 238, 239.
43 "productively misunderstood": Bloch, *Das Prinzip Hoffnung*, I, p. 566.
43–44 Lamennais began: Hans Küng, *Does God Exist?*, p. 71; Cole, *History of Socialist Thought*, IV, p. 194.
44 a passionate book: H. F. Lamennais, *Paroles d'un croyant*, pp. 31, 167.
44 "instead of trying to exorcise . . .": Alec Vidler, *The Church in an Age of Revolution*, p. 69.
44 "court Jews": Hannah Arendt, *The Origins of Totalitarianism*, pp. 12, 17.
44 Between 1815 and 1914: Shlomo Avineri, *The Making of Modern Zionism*, p. 5.
44 Moses Hess's family: Isaiah Berlin, *Against the Current*, p. 214, see also ibid., 214–15; Auguste Cornu, *Karl Marx und Friedrich Engels*, p. 214; Avineri, *The Making of Modern Zionism*, Chapter 3.
45 "vague and mystical": Marx and Engels, *Werke*, III, pp. 478–89.
45 In the 1850s: Moses Hess, *Judische Schriften*, pp. 53, 107, 120; Berlin, *Against the Current*, p. 213ff.
45 "non-Jewish Jews": Isaac Deutscher, *The Non-Jewish Jew and Other Essays*, Chapter 1.
45 Jewish masses of Eastern Europe: Billington, *Fire in the Minds*, pp. 445–46, 650 n. 117.
45 all churchly rituals be eliminated: Eric Hobsbawm, "Religion and the Rise of Socialism," p. 22.
45 *L'Atelier*: Lichtheim, *Origins of Socialism*, p. 75.
45 "Communism probably . . .": Billington, *Fire in the Minds*, p. 255.
46 Methodism . . . was a major factor: Eric Hobsbawm, *Labouring Men*, p. 33.
46 "were forever professing their submission . . .": E. P. Thompson, *The Making of the English Working Class*, p. 30; see also Gerald Cragg, *The Church and the Age of Reason*, p. 148.
46 "Pindar of the automatic factory": Marx and Engels, *Werke*, XXIII, p. 441.
46 "a vast population . . .": Andrew Ure quote in Thompson, *English Working Class*, p. 316ff.
46 Chartist hymns: Ibid., p. 399.
46 "idleness and drunkenness": Robert Owen quoted in ibid., p. 781.
46–47 "kindly Papa of Socialism . . .": Cole, *History of Socialist Thought*, I, p. 124.
47 "celibacy . . . crime against nature": Thompson, *English Working Class*, p. 788.
47 Hostility to religion: Marx and Engels, *Werke*, XXVII, p. 426.
47–48 ". . . religious practice declined . . .": Hobsbawm, "Religion," p. 17.

48 "The Communist Manifesto . . .": Küng, *Does God Exist?*, p. 254.

48 present-day theologian: Helmut Gollwitzer, "Marxistische Religionskritik und christlicher Glaube," in Iring Fetscher, ed., no. 7 in *Marxismus Studien*, p. 74.

48 Marx became furious: Marx and Engels, *Werke*, IV, p. 12.

48 "We do not assert . . . ": Ibid., I, p. 352.

48 ". . . atheism is not . . .": Gollwitzer, "Marxistische Religionskritik," p. 29.

48 For Marx on Bakunin, see Marx and Engels, *Werke*, XXXIII, p. 329.

48 ". . . not only God is almighty . . .": Ibid., p. 669.

48–49 "Critique of the Gotha Program": Ibid., XIX, p. 30.

49 "who cannot wait . . .": Ibid., XX, p. 295.

49 religion to be a "private matter": Franz Mehring, *Geschichte der Deutschen Sozial Demokratie*, p. 486ff.

49 "Religion will not be 'abolished' . . .": August Bebel, *Politik als Theorie und Praxis*, pp. 227, 229.

49 In the Ruhr: Barrington Moore, *Injustice: The Social Bases of Obedience and Revolt*, pp. 230, 247, p. 182 table 3.

50 "simple and coherent . . .": A. J. Ayer, "Religion and the Intellectuals," p. 18.

50 On Engels and dialectical materialism, see Michael Harrington, *Twilight of Capitalism*, Chapter 2.

50 *Moses or Darwin*: Hobsbawm, "Religion," p. 24.

50 "At two o'clock . . .": Julius Braunthal, *Geschichte der Internationale*, I, pp. 349–50.

51 "The Catholic priest . . .": V. I. Lenin, *Collected Works*, XXXV, p. 122.

52 "private matter . . . different case for it": Ibid., XV, p. 411.

52 "completely irrelevant . . .": Leonard Schapiro, *The Communist Party of the Soviet Union*, p. 109.

53 "God-seekers" . . . "God-builders": Gustav Wetter, *Der dialektische Materialismus*, pp. 105–06; Tony Cliff, *Lenin*, I, p. 75.

53 secondhand Feuerbach: Leszek Kolakowski, *Main Currents of Marxism*, II, p. 457.

53 "is cast from a single piece . . .": Lenin, *Works*, XIV, p. 326.

53 "history seen as a relation . . .": Maurice Merleau-Ponty, *Les Aventures de la dialectique*, p. 89.

53–54 On Lenin's last days, see Michael Harrington, *Socialism*, pp. 166–69.

54 In 1931: Wetter, *Der dialektische Materialismus*, p. 207.

54 the *History* did not find: Branko Horvat, *The Political Economy of Socialism*, p. 30.

54 "Dialectical and Historical Materialism . . .": Joseph Stalin, *History of the Communist Party of the Soviet Union (Bolsheviks)*, p. 103.

54 "guided by the laws . . .": Ibid., p. 115.

55 *wissenschaftlicher Sozialismus*: Marx and Engels, *Werke*, XVIII, pp. 635–36.

55 "every new ritual . . .": Leszek Kolakowski, *Toward a Marxist Humanism*, pp. 99–100.

55 compared this totalitarian faith: Herbert Marcuse, *Soviet Marxism*, p. 88.

55 "semi-religious environment . . .": Horvat, *Political Economy*, pp. 42–43.

55–56 "The individual has . . .": Bertolt Brecht, *Stücke*, IV, p. 298.

56 "the organization of . . .": Karl Kautsky, *Foundations of Christianity*, p. 388.

56 "Dean of the Theology Faculty . . .": Talcott Parsons, "Belief, Unbelief and Disbelief," in *The Culture of Unbelief*, edited by R. Caporale and A. Grumelli, p. 243 n. 25.

57 "conventional and comfortable . . .": David Martin, "Revived Dogma and New Cult," p. 67.

57 "to proclaim a new heaven . . .": Theodore Roszak, *The Making of a Counter Culture*, pp. xii–xiii, 68, 240.

57 "tête-à-tête . . .": Billington, *Fire in the Minds*, p. 50.

57 Carbonari . . . woodwinds: Ibid., pp. 126–27, 555 n. 1.

PAGE · 4: THE INVERTED WORLD

58 "External insecurity . . .": Karl Marx and Friedrich Engels, *Werke*, IV, pp. 464–65.

58 "inverted world . . .": G. W. F. Hegel, *Werke in zwanzig Bänden*, III, pp. 386–87.

60 "sketched a scheme . . .": George Lichtheim, *Marxism*, p. 36.

60 "I believe . . .": G. W. F. Hegel, *Briefe von und an Hegel*, I, p. 24.

60 Hegel clearly moved away: G. W. F. Hegel, *Theologische Jugendschriften*, pp. 77, 89, 91.

60 ". . . what is must be . . .": Hegel, *Werke*, I, p. 463 (the German Constitution).

60 For Hegel's French bias, see Shlomo Avineri, *The Making of Modern Zionism*, p. 63.

60 "the world soul . . .": Hegel, *Werke*, III, p. 493.

60 In 1818: Ibid., X, p. 400.

61 Religion . . . is philosophy: Ibid., XVI, p. 141.

61 "The popular feasts . . .": Ibid., I, p. 41.

61 "Religion is the place . . .": Ibid., XII, p. 70.

61 For Hegel on China, India and Greece, see ibid., XII, pp. 32, 311; XVI, pp. 322, 347.

61–62 "The spirit of a people . . .": Ibid., I, p. 142.

62 Montesquieu's "immortal work": Ibid., II, p. 524.

62 "peaceful domination": Ibid., III, p. 401.

62 "A religion that brought . . .": Marx and Engels, *Werke*, XIX, pp. 297–98.

62 isn't religion only valid: Hegel, *Werke*, III, pp. 497–98.

63 "in the vigorous youth of spiritual life": Ibid., p. 28.
63 "the inner bonds . . . talents in humanity": J. C. F. Schiller, *Werke*, IX, p. 166ff.
63–64 "free republican . . .": Hegel, *Werke*, I, pp. 99–100, 205.
64 "*Sittlichkeit* . . .": Ibid., III, pp. 513, 525.
64–65 The original Greek gods: Ibid., XVII, pp. 9, 103, 104, 109, 132, 128.
65 "Fortunate wars . . .": Ibid., I, pp. 206–07.
65–66 "spiritless community . . . lord of the world": Ibid., XII, p. 311.
66 "Trust in the eternal . . .": Ibid., III, p. 547.
66 explicitly attacks political anti-Semitism: Ibid., VII, p. 421 and n. (paragraph 270).
66 Hegel saw the Jews: Ibid., XVI, pp. 222, 229, 233.
66 the Flood: Ibid., I, pp. 274–75.
67 "the eternal myth . . .": Ibid., XII, p. 389.
67 "The snake's head . . .": Ibid.
67 the deity first appears: Ibid., XII, p. 241; XVII, pp. 50, 53.
67 "the highest worth of man . . .": Ibid., XVII, p. 254.
67 "The Jewish people . . .": Jean Hippolyte, *Genèse et structure de la phénomenologie*, p. 185.
67 In the Psalms: Hegel, *Werke*, XII, pp. 388–89.
67 servility in Jewish life: Ibid., XVII, p. 80ff.
67–68 an enormous advance: Ibid., pp. 72, 83.
68 Israel was subjected: Ibid., I, p. 106.
68 purified and spiritualized: Ibid., XII, pp. 390–91.
68 "against the background . . .": Guenter Lewy, *Religion and Revolution*, p. 34.
68 "quiet, secret revolution . . .": Hegel, *Werke*, I, p. 203.
69 "men no longer found . . . unbelief everywhere": Ibid., XIX, p. 417.
69 "only out of this feeling . . . slavery of men": Ibid., III, p. 355; XII, p. 339.
69 discredits the "objective" gods: Ibid., XIX, p. 405.
69 salvation from an individual: Ibid., I, p. 100.
69–70 "In the womb . . .": Ibid., p. 209.
70 doctrine of the Trinity: Ibid., XVI, pp. 432–33; XVII, pp. 236–37.
70 "Faith": Ibid., XVII, pp. 349, 236.
70 Philo: Ibid., XIX, p. 403ff.
70 "a world-shattering marriage . . .": Peter Berger, *The Heretical Imperative*, p. 143.
71 fatherhood and sonhood: Hegel, *Werke*, XII, p. 392.
71 the Christian sect: Ibid., I, pp. 144–45, 187–88, 219–20.
71 the Middle Ages: Ibid., XIX, pp. 537, 587, 596.
71 For the young Hegel on Luther, see ibid., I, pp. 63–64.
72 dramatic shift: Georg Lukacs, *Der junge Hegel*, p. 521ff.
72 "a magnificent sunrise": Hegel, *Werke*, XII, p. 529.
72 "the world was not yet ripe . . .": Ibid., p. 499.
72 the Enlightenment was another: Ibid., III, pp. 403, 413.
72 "when all prejudices . . .": Ibid., p. 431ff.

72   influence of Sir James Steuart: Raymond Plant, *Hegel*, p. 65ff.

72–73   repeated in the *Philosophy of Right*: Hegel, *Werke*, VII, pp. 243–45, 389–90.

73   "shining forth of the divine life . . .": Ibid., XVI, pp. 111–12.

73   state is based on reason: Ibid., XII, pp. 56–57.

73   " 'educated' . . . whose skepticism . . .": Karl Löwith, *From Hegel to Nietzsche*, p. 216.

73   at least an authoritarian: Sidney Hook in Walter Kaufmann, ed., *Hegel's Political Philosophy*; see also Shlomo Avineri in ibid.; Charles Taylor, *Hegel*, p. 367.

73–74   the editor himself: Hegel, *Werke*, VII, p. 403.

74   "the Hegelian system . . .": Kaufmann introduction in Kaufmann, *Hegel's Political Philosophy*.

74   opposed to the French Revolution: Raymond Plant, "Hegel's Social Theory," No. 104, p. 110.

74   His analysis . . . parallels Marx's: Lucio Colletti, *Marxism and Hegel*, Chapter 12.

74   economics is the basis: Hegel, *Werke*, VII, p. 346.

74   the glory of Protestantism: Ibid., X, pp. 358–59.

75   ". . . opium of the people": Marx and Engels, *Werke*, I, p. 378.

75   regularly misread: Hans Küng, *Does God Exist?*, p. 239.

75–76   ". . . *inverted world* . . .": Marx and Engels, *Werke*, I, p. 229.

76   "religion is not simply . . .": Hans Küng, *Does God Exist?*, p. 229.

76   not an invention of Marx's: Henri de Lubac: *Proudhon et le christianisme*, p. 214.

76   "Theses on Feuerbach": Marx and Engels, *Werke*, III, p. 6.

76–77   "false positivism . . . true human life": Ibid., Suppl. Vol. I, pp. 573, 581.

77   atheism will no longer make any sense: Ibid., p. 546.

77   a practical atheist: Jean-Yves Calvez, *La Pensée de Karl Marx*, p. 551.

78   "The contradiction between . . .": Marx and Engels, *Werke*, I, p. 374.

78   capitalist state . . . is really Christian: Ibid., XXIII, p. 93.

78–79   Julius von Stahl's official theology: Calvez, *La Pensée*, p. 59.

79   Beaumont: Marx and Engels, *Werke*, I, p. 352ff.

79   "atheistic Christians": Moses Hess in Karl Löwith, ed., *Die Hegelsche Linke*, pp. 48–50.

79   "naturalism . . .": Marx and Engels, *Werke*, Suppl. Vol. I, p. 536.

80   "cosmic pessimist . . .": Gustav Mayer, *Friedrich Engels*, II, p. 324.

80   "Millions of years . . .": Marx and Engels, *Werke*, XX, p. 324.

80   a Marxist "wager": Lucien Goldmann, *Le Dieu caché*, p. 99.

81   "Copernican man . . .": Antonio Banfi quoted in Pedrag Vranicki, *Geschichte des Marxismus*, II, p. 952.

82   "Is religion . . .": Labriola quoted in Leszek Kolakowski, *Main Currents of Marxism*, II, pp. 185–86.

82   On the Austro-Marxists, see Josef Widenholzer, *Auf dem Weg zum "Neuen Menschen"*, p. 41; Norbert Leser, *Zwischen Reformismus und Bolschewismus*, p. 523ff.

5: CATASTROPHIC ATHEISM
84 "shatterings, earthquakes . . . *great politics*": Friedrich Nietzsche, *Ecce Homo*, "Why I Am a Destiny," paragraph 1. The text of Nietzsche's work is found in many editions and there are still scholarly disputes over the ordering of the posthumous manuscripts (which were arranged for her own purposes by Nietzsche's anti-Semitic sister). For all of his works except the posthumous aphorisms I will not cite specific editions but book, section and paragraph numbers, which should permit the reader to find the reference in any edition (including the translations). In the case of the posthumous material, the citations are to *Nietzsches Werke* edited by Gerhard Stenzel. This two-volume collection abridges various books and essays and does not contain all of the posthumous works. It was, however, the edition in which I first read Nietzsche and annotated my own interpretation. In other contexts, I would have carefully retraced that reading and used a more scholarly (unabridged) edition. But this did not seem necessary here, since everything alluded to is to be found in the scholarly editions as well as in Stenzel's *Werke*. I cross-checked the references—and, where the abridged edition omitted certain material, made original identifications—in two recent editions: Karl Schlecta's extremely useful *Werke in drei Bänden* and the complete critical editon of Nietzsche's *Werke* edited by Giorgio Colli and Mazzino Montinari. The translations are my own.

84–85 "I know my fate . . . happened on earth": *Ecce Homo*, "Why I Am a Destiny," paragraph 1.

85 "Have you not heard . . .": *The Gay Science*, Book III, paragraph 125.

86 Religion . . . begins: *Human, All Too Human*, Book I, section 3, paragraph 3.

86 "the deepest and most sublime . . .": *The Genealogy of Morals*, first essay, paragraphs 7, 8.

86 "fake intellectual humbug": Ibid., third essay, paragraph 26.

87 The Jews . . . were the only nation: Paul Tillich, *Theology of Culture*, p. 35.

87 "morality is no longer . . .": *The Genealogy of Morals*, third essay, paragraph 26.

87 "God on the cross . . .": *Beyond Good and Evil*, third essay, paragraph 46.

87 "The slave wants the unconditional . . .": Ibid.

87–88 "the lowest strata . . .": *The Anti-Christ*, paragraph 31.

88 "Platonism . . .": *Beyond Good and Evil*, foreword.

88 Plato is seen: "History of an Error" in *The Twilight of the Idols*.

88 guilt in this world: *The Genealogy of Morals*, second essay, paragraph 20.

89 Nietzsche's open admiration for Christ: *The Anti-Christ*, paragraph 39.

90   On Dionysus and the Greeks, see *The Birth of Tragedy from the Spirit of Music*, paragraph 2.

90–91   On Dionysus and Hamlet, see ibid., paragraph 7.

91–92   "these ascetic priests . . .": *The Genealogy of Morals*, third essay, paragraphs 11–14.

92   "Life . . . is not possible . . .": *Thus Spake Zarathustra*, Book I, "A Thousand and One Goals."

92–93   "certain powers . . .": *Schopenhauer as Educator*, section 4.

93   ". . . war of the spirits": *Ecce Homo*, "Why I Am a Destiny," paragraph 1.

93   "spiritualized": *The Twilight of the Idols*, "Morality as Against Nature," section 3.

93   "social wars" . . . "philosophic principles": *Werke*, I, p. 1010.

93   functions of religion: *Human, All Too Human*, Book I, section 8, paragraph 472.

93   ". . . self-belittling of men . . .": *The Genealogy of Morals*, third essay, paragraph 25.

93   "Since Copernicus . . .": *Werke*, I, p. 909.

94   the lightning and its light: Ibid., p. 699.

94   "The *disclosing* . . .": *Ecce Homo*, "Why I Am a Destiny," paragraph 8.

94   "the last *anti-political* German": Ibid., "Why I Am So Wise," paragraph 2.

95   "Life . . . is a fountain of delight . . .": *Thus Spake Zarathustra*, Book II, "Of the Rabble" ("Vom Gesindel").

95   "The peasants eaten up . . .": *Werke*, Stenzel ed., I, p. 875.

95–96   "One complains . . . higher type of men": Ibid., pp. 891, 895, 902.

96   "The merchant spirit . . .": Ibid., p. 992.

96   "There is an Indian-like primitiveness . . .": *The Gay Science*, Book IV, paragraph 329.

97   "inverse cripples": Nietzsche quoted in Tracy Strong, *Friedrich Nietzsche and the Politics of Transformation*, p. 222.

97   "The press . . .": Nietzsche quoted in Karl Jaspers, *Nietzsche*, p. 246.

97   "latent Christianity . . .": *Werke*, I, p. 682.

97   "a sickness . . .": *Human, All Too Human*, "The Wanderer and His Shadow," Book II, paragraph 292.

97   "*demonstratio ad absurdum* . . .": *Werke*, Stenzel ed., I, p. 751.

98   For socialism leading to terrorism, see ibid., eighth essay, paragraph 473.

98   "Air travel . . .": Nietzsche quoted in Jaspers, *Nietzsche*, p. 271.

98–99   "*powers* in excess . . . in his sphere": *Werke*, Stenzel ed., I, pp. 1094–95.

99   "We good Europeans . . .": Ibid., p. 1014.

100   "We children of the future . . . a faith!": *The Gay Science*, Book V, paragraph 377.

100   the last Pope: *Thus Spake Zarathustra*, Book IV, "At Liberty" ("Ausser Deinst").

100 Kaempfert has documented: Manfred Kaempfert, *Säkularization und neue Heiligkeit*, p. 146.

101 *"Doppelgänger"*: *Ecce Homo*, "Why I Am So Wise," paragraph 2.

101 "superior races . . .": *The Genealogy of Morals*, first essay, paragraph 11.

101 the most sensible interpretation: Arthur Danto, *Nietzsche as Philosopher*, pp. 169–70.

101–02 "Nietzsche is perhaps best known . . .": Walter Kaufmann, *Nietzsche*, pp. 412–13.

102 Lukacs fundamentally misrepresents: Georg Lukacs, *Die Zerstörung der Vernunft*.

102 the German cult of feelings: *Dawn*, Book III, paragraph 197.

103 ". . . fin de siècle attitude . . .": George Lichtheim, *From Marx to Hegel*, p. 111.

103 "a particularly brilliant representative . . .": Michael Harrington, *The Accidental Century*, p. 45.

103 "in a lovely, modern hotel . . .": Georg Lukacs, *Die Zerstörung der Vernunft*, p. 219.

103 Oswald Spengler: H. Stuart Hughes, *Consciousness and Society*, p. 378.

104 Fritz Stern argues: Fritz Stern, *The Politics of Cultural Despair*, p. 196.

104 anticipated Dr. Goebbels: T. W. Adorno, *Prismen*, p. 58.

104 "The word triumphs . . .": Oswald Spengler, *Der Üntergang des Abendlandes*, pp. 398–99.

105 "Behind the Spenglerian proclamation . . .": Adorno, *Prismen*, p. 67.

105 "hunger for wholeness . . . the city": Peter Gay, *Weimar Culture*, p. 96.

105 Nietzsche's anticipation: Stern, *Politics*, p. 292.

105–06 "the revolutionary break . . .": Karl Löwith, *From Hegel to Nietzsche*, pp. 285, 307, 385.

106 The rootless people of mass society: Emil Lederer, *State of the Masses*, passim; Hannah Arendt, *The Origins of Totalitarianism*, passim.

107 ". . . cannot deal with Chaos": Quoted in Michael Banton, ed., *Anthropological Approaches to the Study of Religion*, p. 14.

PAGE   **6: THE AGNOSTIC ECONOMY**

109 "Agreed that Weber exaggerated . . .": Kurt Samuelson, *Religion and Economic Action: A Critique of Max Weber*, pp. 24–25.

109 "As God created the world . . .": Thomas Aquinas quoted in Ernst Bloch, *Naturrecht und menschliche Würde*, p. 57.

109 Niklas Luhmann: Niklas Luhmann, *Funktion der Religion*, p. 55 and n. 79.

110 Under feudalism work: C. B. McPherson, *Political Theory of Pos sessive Individualism*, p. 49.

110   idealization of the high Middle Ages: Franz Borkenau, *Der Übergang vom feudelen zum burgerlichen Weltbild*, p. 24; see also p. xi.

110   times of retrogression: Emmanuel Wallerstein, *The Modern World System*, passim, and *The Capitalist World Economy*, passim.

110   times of . . . pessimism: Barbara Tuchman, *A Distant Mirror*, passim; J. Huizinga, *The Waning of the Middle Ages*, passim.

110   In the Renaissance: Borkenau, *Übergang*, pp. 54, 78, 46–47.

110   Cusa was . . . the first modern man: Ernst Cassirer, *Individuum und Kosmos in der Renaissance*, pp. 10, 26–27, 56, 64.

110   in Machiavelli: Borkenau, *Übergang*, p. 104.

110   "The sharp knife . . .": Ernst Cassirer, *Myth of the State*, p. 140.

111   why capitalism had failed in Italy: Antonio Gramsci, *Quaderni del carcere*, I, p. 224ff.

111   a private sphere: Borkenau, *Übergang*, p. 109.

112   living standard . . . declined: Fernand Braudel, *The Structure of Everyday Life*, p. 194.

112   work as a "calling": Jürgen Habermas, *Theorie des kommunikativen Handelns*, I, pp. 310–11.

112   "senseless inversion . . . the individual": Max Weber, *Gesammelte Aufsätze zur Religions-Soziologie*, I, pp. 35–36.

112   "the glorification of God . . .": Ernst Troeltsch, *The Social Teachings of the Christian Churches*, II, pp. 588, 607.

112   ". . . release and relief . . .": Christopher Hill, *Change and Continuity in Seventeenth Century England*, p. 90.

112   limited, but real democracy: C. V. Wedgewood, *The Thirty Years War*, p. 20.

112–13   "Protestant preachers . . .": Christopher Hill, *The World Turned Upside Down*, pp. 260–61, Appendix 1.

113   "Each ego . . .": Blaise Pascal, *Pensées*, fragments 454, 451, 294, 308.

113–14   For Borkenau on Hobbes and Pascal, see Borkenau, *Übergang*, pp. 486–89; Lucien Goldmann, *Le Dieu caché*, passim.

114   On Jansenism, see Hans Küng, *Does God Exist?*, p. 75ff.; Barrington Moore, *Social Origins of Democracy and Dictatorship*, p. 59.

115   earliest forms of religion: Max Weber, *Economy and Society*, II, p. 399ff.

115   Hebrew monotheism: Weber, *Gesammelte Aufsätze*, I, pp. 94–96.

115–16   "The Elector Palatine . . .": Wedgewood, *Thirty Years War*, p. 42.

116   difference between East and West: Weber, *Gesammelte Aufsätze*, I, pp. 108, 257–58; Habermas, *Theorie*, I, p. 282.

116   ironic anticipations: Weber, *Gesammelte Aufsätze*, I, p. 545.

116   Cistercian monks: R. W. Southern, *Western Society and the Church in the Middle Ages*, p. 250ff.

116–17   the Confucians and the Taoists: Weber, *Gesammelte Aufsätze*, II, pp. 435–36.

117 all that remained of the Protestant ethic: Ibid., I, p. 203.

117 "The rational organization . . .": Karl Löwith, *Gesammelte Abhandlungen: Zur Kritik der geschichtlichen Existenz*, p. 26.

117–18 For Weber's relation to Nietzsche, see Eugène Fleischmann, "De Weber à Nietzsche," p. 218.

118 "The old gods. . .": Habermas, *Theorie*, I, pp. 355–56.

118 more than a few scholars: Anthony Giddens, *Capitalism and Modern Social Theory*, p. 29ff.

118–19 "The Puritans . . . stage of humanity": Weber, *Gesammelte Aufsätze*, I, pp. 203–04.

119 fatalism and despair: Fleischmann, "De Weber à Nietzsche," p. 218.

119–20 Under feudalism: Karl Marx and Friedrich Engels, *Werke*, I, pp. 368–69.

120 the state becomes agnostic: Ibid., p. 353.

120 capitalist rent in the land: Ibid., XXV, p. 790ff.

121 basic theological dualism: Ibid., I, p. 354ff.

121 ". . . Middle Ages . . . nor Greece . . .": Ibid., XXIII, p. 96 n. 23; see also Habermas, *Theorie*, II, p. 252.

122–23 "The well-ordered life . . . institute a new order": Bernard Groethuysen, *Origine de l'esprit bourgeois en France*, pp. 172, 287–88.

123 sublimated into the erotic: Weber, *Gesammelte Aufsätze*, I, p. 544ff.

123–24 "property marriage . . .": Hill, *World Turned Upside Down*, pp. 247–48.

124 bohemian life style: Habermas, *Theorie*, I, pp. 230–31.

124 "the 'new capitalism' . . .": Daniel Bell, *The Cultural Contradictions of Capitalism*, p. 78 and passim.

125–27 Society . . . is becoming more complex: Fred Hirsch, *Social Limits to Growth*, pp. 3, 118, 120, 132.

127 reduced the rewards of success: Christopher Jencks, *Inequality*, p. 8.

127–28 On the left: Robert Heilbroner, *Business Civilization in Decline*, passim.

128 "an edifice . . .": George Gilder, *Wealth and Poverty*, pp. 7, 258ff.

128 God and Mammon: Jerome L. Himmelstein, "God, Gilder and Capitalism," p. 81.

128 an article in 1982: Robert Wuthnow, "The Moral Crisis in American Capitalism."

PAGE   **7: DOES THE DEVIL EXIST?**

129 "Primitive civilizations . . .": Emile Durkheim, *The Elementary Forms of the Religious Life*, pp. 18–20.

129 simplicity of those early societies: Claude Lévi-Strauss: *Anthropologie structurelle deux*, pp. 60–61.

129 one tends to lose sight: Robert Merton, *Social Theory and Social Structure*, p. 83.

130 "Anthropologists . . .": Barrington Moore, *Injustice: The Social Bases of Obedience and Revolt*, p. 3.

130 "an attempt to suppress . . .": Lévi-Strauss, *Anthropologie*, pp. 43, 80, 386–87.

130 before the nineteenth century: Isaiah Berlin, *Vico and Herder: Two Studies in the History of Ideas*, passim.

131 *Golden Bough* . . . Lévy-Bruhl: Marvin Harris, *The Rise of Anthropological Theory*, p. 205; Ernst Cassirer, *Myth of the State*, p. 12.

131 Marx and Engels . . . not . . . anthropological scholars: Eric Hobsbawm, *Pre-Capitalist Economic Formations*, p. 24ff.

131 history of that discipline: Harris, *Anthropological Theory*, p. 228ff.

131 *the* error of bourgeois thought: Karl Marx and Friedrich Engels, *Werke*, XXIII, pp. 95–96.

131–32 ". . . no childish peoples . . .": Lévi-Strauss, *Anthropologie*, p. 391.

132 "a relatively condensed . . .": Robert Bellah, *Beyond Belief*, p. 11.

132 small-scale society: Georg Simmel, *Sociology of Religion*, p. 41.

132 "*humanize natural laws* . . .": Claude Lévi-Strauss, *La Pensée sauvage*, pp. 62, 292–93, 21, 46.

133 ". . . most important distinction . . .": Pierre Chaunu, *Histoire et décadence*, p. 37.

133 "Over its career . . .": Clifford Geertz in Michael Banton, ed., *Anthropological Approaches to the Study of Religion*, p. 18.

133 the "profane" and the "sacred": Durkheim, *Elementary Forms*, p. 52.

133 "real, innermost core . . .": Rudolf Otto, *The Idea of the Holy*, pp. 6, 109–10.

133–34 "not merely the numinous . . .": Ibid., p. 84.

134 ". . . grandeur of its superpower . . .": Simmel, *Sociology of Religion*, pp. 2, 23, 25, 26.

134 "The sacred . . .": Mary Douglas, *Implicit Meanings*, pp. xiii, iv.

135 ". . . essential postulate of sociology . . .": Durkheim, *Elementary Forms*, p. 14.

135 Durkheim "socialized" Kant: Harris, *Anthropological Theory*, p. 472.

135 "If men did not agree . . .": Durkheim, *Elementary Forms*, p. 30.

135–36 For Durkheim on totems, see his *Elementary Forms*, pp. 221ff., 236–37. But for a contemporary critique of Durkheim's data, see Mircea Eliade, *The Quest: History and Meaning in Religion*, p. 20; Lévi-Strauss, *Pensée sauvage*, p. 299.

136 precursors of twentieth-century: Jürgen Habermas, *Theorie des kommunikativen Handelns*, II, p. 80.

136 "the great things . . .": Durkheim, *Elementary Forms*, p. 476.

136 "if primitive man . . .": Douglas, *Implicit Meanings*, pp. 25–26.

137 cause and effect: Klaus Eder, *Die Entstehung staatlich organisierten Gesellschaften*, pp. 50–72.

137 "gives each perceptible element . . .": Jürgen Habermas, *Zur Rekonstruktion des historische Materialismus*, p. 30.

137 "domestic mode of production . . .": Marshall Sahlins, *Stone Age Economics*, pp. 176, 198.

138 Eder emphasizes: Klaus Eder, ed., *Seminar: Die Entstehung von Klassen-Gesellschaften*, pp. 290–91.

138 first millennium: Bellah, *Beyond Belief*, p. 22.

138 Poverty . . . comes into existence: Sahlins, *Stone Age Economics*, p. 37.

138 "As soon as the organization . . .": Habermas, *Theorie*, II, pp. 280–81. See also Marvin Harris, *Cultural Materialism*, pp. 108–10.

139 mysterious and teleological providence: Eder, *Staatlich organisierten Gesellschaften*, p. 68; Peter Glasner, *Sociology of Secularization*, p. 31.

139 possibility of a conflict: Habermas, *Zur Rekonstruktion*, p. 100.

140 art and religion were one: G. W. F. Hegel, *Werke in zwanzig Bänden*, XIII, pp. 409–10; XIV, p. 234.

140 "turn *against* . . .": Ibid., XIV, p. 234.

141 "In the beginning . . .": Ibid., XIII, p. 142.

141 "end of the art period": Georg Lukacs, *Goethe und seine Zeit*, p. 235ff.

141–42 "Up until now . . .": José Ortega y Gasset, *La deshumanización del arte*, p. 172.

142 "the twilight of the absolute . . .": André Malraux, *The Voices of Silence*, p. 624.

142 "In civilizations . . .": Ibid., p. 516.

142 "a great Egyptian work . . .": Ibid., p. 20.

142 ". . . negroid sculpture . . .": Renato Poggioli, *The Theory of the Avant Garde*, p. 55.

142–43 For Malraux on bourgeois art, see his *Voices of Silence*, pp. 492, 296, 558.

143 Georges Rouault: Poggioli, *Avant Garde*, p. 128.

143 aesthetic faith was short-lived: Irving Howe, *Decline of the New*, p. 16.

144 "Many of our representations . . .": Malraux, *Voices of Silence*, pp. 540–41.

144 "plenitude of sophistication . . .": Howe, *Decline of the New*, pp. 24–25.

145 wanted to free society: Sigmund Freud, *The Future of an Illusion*, p. 72.

146 "God's kindness . . .": Ibid., pp. 61–62.

146 "but it does not rest . . .": Ibid., p. 87.

146 "Our God Logos . . .": Ibid., pp. 88–89.

147 "nothing once formed . . .": Sigmund Freud, *Civilization and Its Discontents*, p. 15.

147 "We must conclude . . .": Sigmund Freud, *Moses and Monotheism*, pp. 170, 66, 67.

147 "an inborn tendency . . .": Freud, *Civilization*, p. 6; see also pp. 56, 80–81, 102, 121.

147 Wilhelm Reich: Ernest Jones, *The Life and Work of Sigmund Freud*, p. 447.

147 For Reich's synthesis of psychoanalysis and Marxism, see his *The Mass Psychology of Fascism; Sex-Pol: Essays 1929–1934* (Baxandal, ed.).

147 "basic" repression: Herbert Marcuse, *Eros and Civilization*, p. 32.

147–48 Marx's distinction: Marx and Engels, *Werke*, XXIII, p. 350.

148 "collective unconscious . . .": C. G. Jung, *Collected Works*, XI, pp. 345–50.

149 "During the past . . .": Ibid., XI, pp. 334–36.

PAGE   **8: GOD'S CHRISTIAN BURIAL**

150–51 anecdote about Friedrich Schleiermacher: Alec Vidler, *The Church in an Age of Revolution*, p. 27.

151 ". . . man is learning . . .": Friedrich Schleiermacher, *On Religion*, pp. 111, 42, 161, 143, 141.

151–52 "speak a magic word . . .": Ibid., pp. 240–41.

152 "a dog is the best Christian": G. W. F. Hegel, *Werke in zwanzig Bänden*, XI, p. 58.

152 The Reformation: Ibid., III, pp. 389–92.

152 "pure yearning . . .": Ibid., p. 423.

152 For Feuerbach on Schleiermacher, see Karl Löwith, *From Hegel to Nietzsche*, pp. 332–33.

152 Engels's voyage to disbelief: Karl Marx and Friedrich Engels, *Werke*, Suppl. Vol. II, p. 408.

152 David Friedrich Strauss: Löwith, *Hegel to Nietzsche*, p. 330ff.

153 "millions of Christians . . .": Søren Kierkegaard, *Attack upon "Christendom,"* pp. 32, 46–47, 115, 158.

153 "a world determined . . .": Löwith, *Hegel to Nietzsche*, p. 160.

154 "the Puritan passion . . .": H. Richard Niebuhr, *The Social Sources of Denominationalism*, p. 105.

154 "the moral sentiment . . .": Ralph Waldo Emerson, *Collected Works*, I, p. 77.

154 "*the feelings . . .*": William James, *The Varieties of Religious Experience*, p. 31.

154 On Schleiermacher and the American Evangelicals, see George M. Marsden, *Fundamentalism and American Culture*, pp. 20–21.

155 keeper of the world view: Antonio Gramsci, *Quaderni del carcere*, IV, p. 268.

155 "In modern times . . .": Hans Küng, *Does God Exist?*, p. 510.

155 "beliefs are dead . . .": Mazzini quoted in E. Y. Hales, *Pio Nono*, p. 66.

156 "Warm of heart . . .": Metternich quoted in ibid., p. 67.

156 "domino" theory: Ibid., p. 271.

156 Syllabus of Errors: Ibid., p. 258.

156 "only the dangers . . .": Küng, *Does God Exist?*, p. 240.

156 emphasis on Thomism: Gabriel Daley, O.S.A., *Transcendence and Immanence*, pp. 18–19.

156–57 "modern" tendency: Gramsci, *Quaderni*, p. 225; see also Hughes Portelli, *Gramsci et la question religieuse*, Part III.

157 Religion . . . "cannot be imposed . . .": Daley, *Transcendence*, p. 192.

157 anti-Modernist oath: Küng, *Does God Exist?*, p. 514.

157 "step by step . . .": Leszek Kolakowski, *Religion*, p. 134.

157 ". . . the aging and women": Gramsci, *Quaderni*, p. 237.

158 *Christian Herald*: Marsden, *Fundamentalism*, pp. 84–85.

158 "Baconians" . . . "common sense": Ibid., pp. 55, 14–15.

158 "attacking freedom of thought . . .": Richard Hofstadter, *The Age of Reform*, pp. 288–89.

158 Why this dramatic shift: Seymour Martin Lipsett and Earl Raab, *The Politics of Unreason*, p. 114ff.

159 Catholic and Protestant . . . alliance: Richard Hofstadter, *The Paranoid Style in American Politics*, p. 80.

159 "men would never . . .": Vidler, *Church in an Age*, p. 214.

159 "the church father . . .": Karl Barth, *Protestant Theology in the Nineteenth Century*, p. 425.

160 essay on Feuerbach: Ibid., p. 537.

160 On Barth and Catholicism, see Küng, *Does God Exist?*, p. 515.

160 "For all faith . . .": Barth quoted in Vidler, *Church in an Age*, p. 216.

160 Baudelaire, Nietzsche and Rilke: Hans Urs von Balthasar, *The Theology of Karl Barth*, p. 32.

160 praised his social liberalism: Barth, *Protestant Theology*, pp. 432–33, 463, 460.

160 Schleiermacher had tried: Balthasar, *Theology of Karl Barth*, p. 160.

161 "Religion, so far from being . . .": Karl Barth, *Epistle to the Romans*, p. 258.

161 ". . . innate capacity of men . . .": Peter Berger, *The Heretical Imperative*, p. 69.

161 "loves the deus absconditus . . .": Barth, *Epistle*, pp. 42, 369, 30.

161 "the hardcore center . . .": Balthasar, *Theology of Karl Barth*, p. 56.

161 "if God is indeed . . .": Edward Schillebeeckx, *Jesus*, p. 627.

162 "social democratic . . .": Barth, *Epistle*, p. 390.

162 On Barth's politics, see Küng, *Does God Exist?*, p. 515.

163 Barth's vision: Ernst Bloch, *Das Prinzip Hoffnung*, II, pp. 1405–06

163 "idiotic . . .": Karl Barth, *Ad Limina Apostolorum*, p. 9.

163 "All of this . . .": Rudolph Bultmann, *Kerygma and Myth*, pp. 3, 4, 13, 197.

164 Barth once refused: Anthony Flew and Alasdair MacIntyre, eds., *New Essays in Politics and Theology*, p. 1 n. 2.

164 "a sort of empiricist objectivism . . .": Schillebeeckx, *Jesus*, pp. 644–45, 75.

164 ". . . few theologians . . .": Niebuhr quoted in Ved Mehta, *The New Theologians*, p. 39.

164 "It does not mean . . .": Karl Rahner, *Foundations of the Christian Faith*, p. 436.

165 "theistic existentialism . . ": Alasdair MacIntyre, *Against the Self Image of the Age*, pp. 16–17.

165 On Heidegger and the question of God, see Küng, *Does God Exist?*, p. 497.

165 1981 survey: Institute for Educational Affairs–Roper Center, "Theology Faculty Survey," pp. 50–51.

165 "For contemporary . . .": John Warrick Montgomery in Bernard Murchland, ed., *The Meaning of the Death of God*, p. 54.

166 "*problem of freedom . . .*": Paul Tillich, *The Socialist Decision*, p. 49.

166 "the meaning-giving substance . . .": Paul Tillich, *Theology of Culture*, p. 42.

166–67 "as man's relation . . . ultimate concern": Ibid., pp. 4–5, 17, 25, 35, 40, 7–8.

167 "immunization strategies . . .": Albert quoted in Küng, *Does God Exist?*, p. 334.

167 ". . . all his life . . .": Jerald Bauer quoted in Mehta, *New Theologians*, p. 43.

167 "among other sensations . . .": Max Weber, *Gesammelte Aufsätze zur Religions-Soziologie*, I, p. 253.

167 "working hypothesis": Dietrich Bonhoeffer, *Letters and Papers from Prison*, p. 168.

167–68 " '. . . religious *a priori* . . .' ": Ibid., p. 140.

168 ". . . religionless Christians . . .": Ibid.

168 "a precondition for faith": Ibid., p. 172.

168 secular salvations: Ibid., p. 169.

168 For Gramsci on Pius XI, see his *Quaderni*, IV, p. 266ff.

169 meaningless for modern man: Küng, *Does God Exist?*, pp. 181, 185, 187, 588ff.

169–70 Schillebeeckx still insisted: Edward Schillebeeckx, *Jesus*, pp. 59–61, 587.

170 "translates the transcendent Beyond . . .": Thomas Altizer and William Hamilton, eds., *Racial Theology and the Death of God*, pp. 106–07, 15.

171 "the new experience . . .": Dorothee Sölle, *Christ the Representative*, pp. 11, 99.

171 "believe in God atheistically . . .": Dorothee Sölle, *Atheistisch an Gott glauben*, pp. 79, 53.

171–72 "... one had asserted ...": Max Horkheimer in Oscar Schatz, ed., *Hat Religion Zukunft?*, p. 113.

172 Medieval Catholicism: Ernst Troeltsch, *The Social Teachings of the Christian Churches*, II, pp. 1011–12.

172 "Today ...": Ernst Troeltsch quoted in Hans Bosse, *Marx, Weber, Troeltsch*, pp. 37–38.

PAGE **9: THE RISEN GOD OF SOCIOLOGY**

175 "The creed of the Englishman ...": Alasdair MacIntyre, *Against the Self Image of the Age*, p. 26.

175 surveys of a London borough: Ibid., p. 21.

175 five dimensions: Charles Glock, "On the Study of Religious Commitment," in Joseph E. Faulkner, ed., *Religion's Influence in Contemporary Society*, p. 38ff.

175 empirical study: Joseph Faulkner and Gordon De Jong, "Religiosity in Five D," in ibid., passim and p. 65.

176 "... significant tendencies ...": "Religion and the Intellectuals," *Partisan Review*, February 1950, p. 103.

176 "God is dead ...": Friedrich Nietzsche, *The Gay Science*, Book III, paragraph 108. (For a bibliographical comment on Nietzsche see the note to page 84 on page 275.)

176 "very marginal ...": Samuel P. Huntington, *American Politics: The Promise of Disharmony*, p. 229.

176 "... the dissidence of dissent ...": Edmund Burke quoted in Huntington, *American Politics*, p. 46.

176 The frontier: H. Richard Niebuhr, *The Social Sources of Denominationalism*, p. 145.

177 "America is unique ...": Huntington, *American Politics*, p. 155.

177 This exuberant pluralism: Niebuhr, *Social Sources*, p. 201.

177 Biblical literalism: George M. Marsden, *Fundamentalism and American Culture*, p. 224.

177 the United States and Canada: Walter Dean Burnham, "Social Stress and Political Response: Religion and the 1980 Election," p. 133.

177 Tocqueville: Cushing Strout, *The New Heavens and New Earth*, p. 331.

177 theocratic dream: Sidney E. Ahlstron, *Religious History of the American People*, pp. 131–36, 154. For a somewhat different view see Strout, *The New Heavens*, p. 4.

177 Even in Virginia: Bernard Bailyn, *Ideological Origins of the American Revolution*, pp. 248–49, 253; see also Ahlstron, *Religious History*, p. 265.

177 On the awakenings, see Ahlstron, *Religious History*, pp. 416, 435; Seymour Martin Lipsett, *The First New Nation*, pp. 181, 160–61.

178 secularism was powerful: Seymour Martin Lipsett and Earl Raab, *The Politics of Unreason*, p. 40.

178 "the fervour of each . . .": Alexis de Tocqueville quoted in Lipsett, *First New Nation*, p. 175.

178 Church membership: Max Weber, *Gesammelte Aufsätze zur Religions-Soziologie*, I, pp. 209–10.

178 That trend: Lipsett, *First New Nation*, p. 191.

178 empirical study: Gerhard Lenski, *The Religious Factor*, p. 9.

179 "America . . . seems to be . . .": Will Herberg, *Protestant, Catholic, Jew*, pp. 3, 39, 61.

179 On Catholic church attendance, see Andrew Greeley *et al.*, *Catholic Schools in a Declining Church*, pp. 29, 145.

179 "new" religions: Martin Marty, *A Nation of Behavers*, p. 108.

179 "civil millenarianism": Michael Linesch, "Uncivil Religion: The Ideological Origins of the Religious Right," p. 33

180 Kennedy and Johnson administrations: Robert Bellah, "Civil Religion in America," in Faulkner, ed., *Religion's Influence*, p. 350ff.

180 "our government . . .": Dwight Eisenhower quoted in Robert Bellah, *Beyond Belief*, p. 170

180 The God of civil religion: Marty, *Nation of Behavers*, p. 187.

180–81 American numbers: Leo Rosten, ed., *Religions in America*, p. 342; U.S. Department of Commerce, *Social Indicators, 1976*, p. 55.

181 "the impact of religious belief . . .": Connecticut Mutual, *The Impact of Belief*, p. 6.

181 other studies: Kenneth Briggs, "Religion Is Found a Strong Force," *The New York Times*, December 25, 1981; George Gallup, Jr., and David Poling, *The Search for America's Faith*.

181–82 eight questions: Connecticut Mutual, *Impact*, p. 43.

182–84 For results of questionnaire, see ibid., p. 49.

184–85 On moral issues: Ibid., p. 89.

185 one-to-one relationship: Everett Ladd, in B. Bruce-Briggs, ed., *The New Class*, p. 108 table 8–4.

185 women who work: Thomas Luckmann, *The Invisible Religion*, p. 30.

185 "countercultural" religions: David Martin, "Revived Dogma and New Cult," p. 67.

185 "Fourth Great Awakening": Kevin Phillips, *Post-Conservative America*, pp. 81, 91.

186 On fundamentalists and class, see Richard Hofstadter, *The Paranoid Style in American Politics*, p. 75; *Psychology Today*, September 1976; Lipsett and Raab, *Politics of Unreason*, p. 392.

187 ". . . ascetic Protestantism . . .": Hofstadter, *Paranoid Style*, pp. 79.

187 "more secularized . . .": Marsden, *Fundamentalism*, p. 228; see also Nathan Glazer, "Toward a New Concordat," passim.

187 underlying theme: Peter Glasner, *Sociology of Secularization*, passim.

187–88 "The rise . . .": Robert Bellah in R. Caporale and A. Grumelli, eds., *The Culture of Unbelief*, p. 41.

188 Bellah's definition of religion: Ibid., pp. 50–51.

188 "the real metaphysical questions . . .": Ernst Bloch, *Naturrecht und menschliche Würde*, p. 311.

188 For Weber on intellectuals, see his *Gesammelte Aufsätze*, I, pp. 252–54.

188 ". . . intense and adverse imagination . . .": Lionel Trilling, *The Opposing Self*, Preface (not numbered).

189 "being deliberately paradoxical . . .": Talcott Parsons, *Action Theory and the Human Condition*, p. 241 n. 11.

189 two forms of social solidarity: Emile Durkheim, *The Division of Labor in Society*, pp. 127, 133, 177.

189 *differentiation*: Talcott Parsons, "The Church in an Urban Environment," in Faulkner, ed., *Religion's Influence*, pp. 431–35.

189–90 In medieval Christendom: Parsons, *Action Theory*, p. 190; Parsons, "Urban Environment," pp. 442, 438.

190 The Protestant Reformation: Parsons, *Action Theory*, pp. 222–32 nn. 218–19.

190 twentieth-century America: Parsons, "Urban Environment," pp. 456–59; Talcott Parsons, "Belief, Unbelief and Disbelief," in Caporale and Grunmelli, eds., *Culture of Unbelief*, pp. 230–31.

190 ". . . *civil religion*": Parsons, *Action Theory*, p. 240.

191 "many young people . . .": Gallup and Poling, *Search for America's Faith*, p. 19.

191 "decisions about the higher good . . .": Philip Hammond in Faulkner, ed., *Religion's Influence*, p. 283.

192 "The Parsonian 'sacred' . . .": Alvin W. Gouldner, *The Coming Crisis of Western Sociology*, pp. 259–60.

192 fall in the birth rate: Pierre Chaunu, *Histoire et Décadence*, pp. 341–42; see also S. S. Acquaviva, *The Decline of the Sacred in Industrial Society*, p. 136.

192 ". . . part-time norms": Luckmann, *Invisible Religion*, p. 39.

192 George Herbert Mead: George Herbert Mead, *Mind, Self and Society*, p. 47.

192 "the moral unity . . .": Luckmann, *Invisible Religion*, pp. 48, 49.

192 realm of religion: Ibid., pp. 56–61; see also "Verfall" in Oskar Schatz, ed., *Hat Religion Zukunft?*, p. 77.

193 had the Enlightenment occurred: Bellah, *Beyond Belief*, p. 238.

193 Sorokin: Pitirim Sorokin, *Social and Cultural Dynamics*.

193 Toynbee: Arnold J. Toynbee, *Civilization on Trial*.

193 more pessimistic thinker: Niklas Luhmann, "Die Weltgesellschaft," pp. 17–18, 12, 11, 14.

194 "the *social-structural* relevance . . .": Niklas Luhmann, *Funktion der Religion*, pp. 232, 116–17.

194–95 Bellah has recognized: Robert Bellah, "Power and Religion in America Today," p. 655 and passim.

195–96 "It is doubtful . . .": Sigmund Freud, *The Future of an Illusion*, p. 61.

196 surviving the decline of religion: Acquaviva, *Decline of the Sacred*, p. 48.

PAGE **10: PROLEGOMENA TO A POLITICAL MORALITY**

198 ". . . immediacy of belief": Paul Ricoeur, *Symbolism of Evil*, p. 351.

198 social void: Ernst Troeltsch, *The Social Teachings of the Christian Churches*, I, p. 381.

200 "Transcendence . . . never complete": Roger Garaudy quoted in James Bentley, *Between Marx and Christ*, p. 111.

201 "A change to a new type . . .": Plato, *Republic*, Book IV, 424–C.

202 "I believe that . . .": André Malraux, *Antimemoires*, pp. 334–35.

202–03 For Marcuse on *de facto* atheism, see his *One Dimensional Man*, passim.

203 "It is not modern thought . . .": *Commentary* editors, *The Condition of Jewish Belief*, p. 30.

203–04 For Maritain on "*Babelism*," see Jacques Maritain, *The Social and Philosophical Thought of Jacques Maritain* (Evans and Ward, eds.), pp. 132, 138, 133.

206 "that theology is going . . .": Dorothee Sölle, *Politische Theologie*, pp. 66–67.

207 bourgeois norm: Johann Baptist Metz, *Faith in History and Society*, Chapter 3.

207 "deep schism": Jürgen Moltmann, *Religion, Revolution, and the Future*, pp. 200, 219.

212–13 "moral and intellectual reform": Antonio Gramsci, *Quaderni del carcere*, I, p. 86.

213 "where Luther appears . . .": Ibid., pp. 24–25.

213 ". . . analogous to the Reformation . . .": Ibid., pp. 3–16.

214 Marxism had to fight: Ibid., p. 84.

214 "To create a new culture . . .": Ibid., p. 5.

214 "faith" . . . "ideological 'aroma' ": Ibid., pp. 13, 16.

214 "maintain the 'simple souls' . . .": Ibid., p. 11.

217 "punishment of failure . . .": Christopher Jencks, *Inequality*, pp. 8–9.

PAGE **APPENDIX A**

219 "Man is no longer . . .": Mircea Eliade, *From Guatama Buddha to the Triumph of Christianity*, p. 246.

219 "East" cannot be labeled as "world-denying": Jürgen Habermas, *Theorie des kommunikativen Handelns*, I, p. 293.

219–20 essay written in the 1930s: Karl Löwith, "Wert und Menschenwelt," in *Gesammelte Abhandlungen: Zur Kritik der geschichtlichen Existenz*.

220 "When the sacred . . .": Mircea Eliade, *Myths, Dreams and Mysteries*, p. 153.

220 "Alienation and estrangement . . .": Mircea Eliade, *The Quest: History and Meaning in Religion*, p. 64 n. 7.

220 somewhat different view: G. W. F. Hegel, *Werke in zwanzig Bänden*, XVIII, p. 361; XIX, pp. 158–59, 174, 494.

220 decisive break: Pierre Chaunu, *Histoire et décadence*, p. 248.

220–21 "The 'joy of life' . . .": Mircea Eliade, *From the Stone Age to the Eleusinian Mysteries*, pp. 354–55.

221 as Franz Borkenau documented: Franz Borkenau, *End and Beginning*, pp. 304, 324, 336, 395, 405.

PAGE **APPENDIX B**

222 For Kant on censorship, see Immanuel Kant, *Gesammelte Schriften*, V, p. 115ff.

222–23 complex and profound account: Georg Lukacs, *Geschichte und Klassenbewusstsein*, pp. 12, 149, 150.

223 book on Kant and Marx: Karl Vorlander, *Kant und Marx*, Chapter 1, parts I and II.

223 On Neo-Kantians as revisionists, see Hans Sandkuhler, "Kant, neukantianischer Sozialismus, Revisionismus," in Hans Sandkuhler, ed., *Marxismus und Ethik*.

223 genealogical chart: Jean Jaures, *Les Origines du socialisme allemand*, passim.

PAGE **APPENDIX C**

224 "consciousness is only . . .": V. I. Lenin, *Collected Works*, XIV, p. 326.

224 "Movement and 'self-movement' . . .": Ibid., XXXVIII, p. 141.

224 "an error . . .": Lucio Colletti, *Marxism and Hegel*, p. 27.

225 the "bad infinite": G. W. F. Hegel, *Werke in zwanzig Bänden*, V, p. 152.

225 "merely the *limit* . . .": Ibid., pp. 138–39, 1249–50.

225 "it is the nature . . .": Ibid., VI, pp. 79–80.

PAGE **APPENDIX D**

226 "But what he did not know . . .": Karl Marx and Friedrich Engels, *Werke*, Suppl. Vol. I, p. 327.

226 "As a German thinker . . .": Georg Lukacs, *Der junge Hegel*, p. 135.

227 "both banal and misleading": George Lichtheim, *Marxism*, p. 10 n.

227 "The later a man . . . accident rules": G. W. F. Hegel, *Werke in zwanzig Bänden*, X, pp. 78, 396.

227 the young Engels pointed out: Marx and Engels, *Werke*, Suppl. Vol. II, p. 176.

228 "Nothing is more certain . . .": G. W. F. Hegel, *Briefe von und an Hegel*, I, p. 137ff.

228 ". . . the most consequential event . . .": Ibid., II, p. 28.

228 "I believe . . .": Ibid., II, p. 85.

228 "the *universal* . . .": Ibid., II, p. 141.

228 Hegel's general view of Napoleon: Franz Rosenzweig, *Hegel und der Staat*, II, p. 24.

229 "his allegedly absolute state . . .": Joachim Ritter, *Metaphysik und Politik*, pp. 255, 231–33.

229 "his seminal work . . .": Lichtheim, *From Marx to Hegel*, pp. 74, 7–8.

230 "Hegel roundly reproaches . . .": Walter Kaufmann, *Hegel: A Reinterpretation*, p. 154 n. 37.

230 theology of the Trinity: G. W. F. Hegel, *Werke in zwanzig Bänden*, XVII, p. 310; III, p. 140.

231 Johannes Scotus Erigena: Leszek Kolakowski, *Main Currents of Marxism*, I, p. 23ff.

231 Meister Eckhart: Ernst Bloch, *Subjekt-Objekt*, p. 303.

232 lengthy note: Helmut Gollwitzer, "Marxistische Religionskritik und christlicher Glaube," in Iring Fetscher, ed., no. 7 in *Marxismus Studien*, p. 14ff.

232 more speculative account: Antonio Gramsci, *Quaderni del carcere*, IV, pp. 288–89.

233 "Christianity is the sublime . . .": Karl Marx and Friedrich Engels, *Werke*, I, p. 376.

233 ". . . leaders of the local Israelites . . .": Ibid., XXVII, p. 418.

233 taken almost verbatim: David McClellan, *Karl Marx*, p. 86.

233 Shlomo Avineri: Shlomo Avineri, *The Making of Modern Zionism*, p. 41.

234 excellent discussion: Hal Draper, *Karl Marx's Theory of Revolution*, I-2, p. 591ff.

PAGE   **APPENDIX H**

235   letters . . . to . . . Friedrich Graeber: Karl Marx and Friedrich Engels, *Werke*, Suppl. Vol. II, p. 39ff.

235   "the ideas and feelings . . .": Gustav Mayer, *Friedrich Engels*, I, p. 80.

PAGE   **APPENDIX I**

236   discussion of Heraclitus: Friedrich Nietzsche, *Werke*, II, Stenzel ed., p. 1099.

236   three periods: Karl Löwith, *Nietzsches Philosophie der ewigen Wiederkehr des Gleichen*, p. 25.

236   "three transformations": Friedrich Nietzsche, *Thus Spake Zarathustra*, Book I, first speech.

236   "vituperative . . .": Arthur Danto, *Nietzsche as Philosopher*, p. 182.

PAGE   **APPENDIX J**

238   Elisabeth Foster-Nietzsche: Arthur Danto, *Nietzsche as Philosopher*, pp. 26–27.

238   "the youthful Bourse Jew . . .": Friedrich Nietzsche, *Human, All Too Human*, Book I, paragraph 475.

PAGE   **APPENDIX K**

239   H. Jeanmarie's *Dionysius: Dionysius: Histoire du culte de Bacchus*, pp. 87, 42–43, passim.

239   Karl Kerenyi's point of view: Karl Kerenyi, *Dionysos: Archetypical Image of Indestructible Life*, pp. 138–39.

239   "More than the other Greek gods . . .": Mircea Eliade, *From the Stone Age to the Eleusinian Mysteries*, p. 375.

239   actual documentation: Ibid., pp. 365, 367, 369; Mircea Eliade, *From Guatama Buddha to the Triumph of Christianity*, pp. 281–83.

PAGE   **APPENDIX L**

240   "What accounts for the fact . . .": Talcott Parsons, *Action Theory and the Human Condition*, p. 168 n.

240   "There is no justification . . .": Kurt Samuelson, *Religion and Economic Action: A Critique of Max Weber*, pp. 57, 150.

240   a similar criticism: Franz Borkenau, *Der Übergang vom feudelen zum burgerlichen Weltbild*, pp. 158–59.

240   Weber was often overreacting: Karl Löwith, *Gesammelte Abhandlungen: Zur Kritik der geschichtlichen Existenz*, pp. 37, 62.

240 Weber . . . can't even disprove: Hans Bosse, *Marx, Weber, Troeltsch,* p. 63.

PAGE   **APPENDIX M**

242 took Borkenau severely to task: H. Grossmann, "Die gesellschaft-lichen Grundlagen der mechanistischen Philosophie und die Man-ufactur," pp. 161ff., 166–67.

242 Richard Lowenthal: Franz Borkenau, *End and Beginning,* ed. Rich-ard Lowenthal, pp. 6–7.

243 "unfairly neglected work": George Lichtheim, *The Concept of Ide-ology,* pp. 279, 281.

243 "almost completely forgotten": Martin Jay, *The Dialectical Imag-ination,* p. 16.

243 normally quite fair: Leszek Kolakowski, *Main Currents of Marx-ism,* II, p. 344.

243 study of the Puritan contribution: Robert Merton, *Social Theory and Social Structure,* pp. 552, 663.

PAGE   **APPENDIX N**

244 Engels enthusiastically: Karl Marx and Friedrich Engels, *Werke,* XXI, p. 27ff.

244 Rousseau's savages: Ernst Bloch, *Naturrecht und menschliche Würde,* pp. 116–17.

244 Marx very carefully read: Karl Marx, *Die Ethnologische Exzer-phthefte,* passim.

244 most of human history: Anthony Giddens, *A Contemporary Critique of Historical Materialism,* p. 76ff.

PAGE   **APPENDIX O**

246 In the earliest times: Sigmund Freud, *Totem and Taboo,* pp. 43–44, 182–88 and passim.

246 "The *Totem* work . . .": Sigmund Freud quoted in Ernest Jones, *The Life and Work of Sigmund Freud,* p. 280.

246 For anthropologists on Freud, see Marvin Harris, *The Rise of An-thropological Theory,* p. 425ff.

246 "Above all . . .": Sigmund Freud, *Moses and Monotheism,* p. 169.

246 "If Freud's hypothesis . . .": Herbert Marcuse, *Eros and Civili-zation,* p. 54.

247 Christianity had been the religion: Erich Fromm, *The Dogma of Christ,* pp. 62–63, 90–91.

248 role of female divinity: Theodor Reik, *Der eigene und der fremde Gott,* pp. 32–33, 20.

APPENDIX P

249 Habermas held: Jürgen Habermas, *Theorie des kommunikativen Handelns*, II, p. 178.

249 "decode": Jürgen Habermas, "Dialectics of Rationalization: An Interview," p. 13.

250 his notion of "communicative action . . .": Habermas, *Theorie*, II, p. 184.

250 "the structure of interaction . . .": Ibid., pp. 217, 163, 145.

251 Class struggle, war and political power: Ibid., p. 169.

251 infiltrating it: Habermas, "Dialectics," p. 18ff.

251–52 more positive: Jürgen Habermas, *Zur Rekonstrucktion des historishe Materialismus*, p. 115ff.

INDEX